600 Days in Hiding

Based on the True Story of a Jewish Family in Nazi-Occupied Thessaloniki, Greece

Andreas Algava

A Survivor of the Greek Holocaust

For Passion Publishing Company, LLC
Bellingham, WA

FOR-PASSION
PUBLISHING

For Passion Publishing Company, LLC

Copyright © 2018 Andreas A. Algava

Published by For Passion Publishing Company, LLC
PO Box 28312
Bellingham, WA 98228
www.ForPassionPublishing.com
First Edition.
ISBN 978-1983462542
Printed in the United States of America.

Disclaimer

In writing this book the author has relied on the facts recorded in the interview transcripts of the author's parents, Henri and Allegra Algava, and has also made every effort to achieve historical accuracy and assure authenticity. To make these events more palpable, the author has created linking scenes and legitimately recreated events to engage the reader in the telling of this remarkable story of character and courage. In some instances, names and identifying details have been changed to protect the privacy of individuals.

Best efforts have underscored the writing of this book, and neither the author nor For Passion Publishing Company, LLC, make representations or warranties of any kind and assume no liabilities of any kind with respect to the accuracy or completeness of the contents, and specifically disclaim any implied warranties of use for any particular purpose. Neither the author nor For Passion Publishing Company, LLC, shall be held liable or responsible to any person or entity with respect to any loss or incidental or consequential damages caused, or alleged to have been caused, directly or indirectly, by the information contained in this book, or disruption caused by errors or omissions, whether such errors or omissions result from negligence, accident, or any other cause.

Dedication

This book is dedicated to the heroes of Thessaloniki who risked their lives and the lives of their families to hide us from the Nazis...

Marcos Hombitis
Nicos Efcarpides
Marika Karakitsou
Stefanos and Sultana Chrissafis
Costas and Evghenia Papapavlou

along with the other courageous Greeks
who embodied the best of humanity

...and to my parents, Henri and Allegra Algava, whose story follows.

About the Author

Andreas Algava was born in Thessaloniki, Greece in 1939, the only son of Henri Algava and Allegra Carasso-Algava. When Andreas was 16 months old, Hitler's forces invaded the country of his birth. Having to decide whether to believe the Nazi propaganda about a safe haven for Jews in Poland or go into hiding and risk execution, Andreas's parents chose the latter, relying on the courage and character of their Christian friends. This book is about their story of survival in the Greek Holocaust.

After the war, the Algava family moved to New York City and became U.S. citizens. Andreas attended college at Cornell University where he earned an engineering degree. This was followed by military service in the U. S. Army including a tour of duty in France. After his military service, Andreas worked with his father in the family export business in the United States and Argentina.

Soon after, Andreas joined IBM and worked on assignment in Germany where he lived with his wife, Priscilla, and where his two daughters, Alisa and Carin, were born. Andreas now lives in Providence, RI to be close to his daughters Alisa, Carin, her husband Michael, and his grandchildren Drew and Sabria.

Now a man of 78, Andreas regards this book, the telling of his family's story, as his declaration to speak out for people to live in peace and harmony. Today's emotional and political climate feels like what he experienced as a child of the Holocaust. Just as his family was persecuted and saved from death by people who risked their lives, so now we are faced with hardship, heartache, and survival, and we need the courage and commitment of heroes with the moral capacity to take action.

This book is the first in a series of publications to provide Andreas with the means to make a strong impression that will enroll people to join, to align, and to act for a just world.

If you would like to meet Andreas or book him for a speaking engagement, please contact him through his website at 600DaysInHiding.com.

Acknowledgements

I wish to personally thank the following people for helping me attain a lifelong dream, and a dream long-desired by my parents, Henri and Allegra Algava. They are the source for my life, for our survival, and for this story being told. I am so grateful.

Dr. Daniel Levine, my co-author, publisher and editor; your insights, support, personal dedication and friendship made this project fun and exciting. You are my wish fulfilled.

Maurice, Daisy, and Maky Carasso, my cousins and lifelong friends; I am grateful for your companionship and love all these years. Maurice, we share a similar history and your on-the-ground research and feedback on the text were invaluable. Daisy and Maky, your logistical and moral support made a true difference.

Aunt Eva Carasso, beautiful wife of Pepo; I am grateful for the love and endless hospitality of your heart, and for your courage, strength and will to live.

Alisa and Carin Algava, my extraordinary daughters; in the final months of this lifelong endeavor, your highly-tuned organizational skills, generosity of self, and boundless vision of possibility got us to the finish line.

Carin Algava and Michael Gow, for nourishing me with food and grandchildren, support and patience every step of the way.

Priscilla Algava and Martin Silverman, for ongoing reviews and valuable feedback, and for your generous gifts of care and spirit.

Virginia (Lee) Forbes, my personal assistant; your good humor and ability to keep me on task through the vicissitudes of this project got us here! Thank you for your patience and steady guidance.

Yolanda O'Neill, assistant and advisor; you asked all the right questions and provided insights that enhanced the telling of this tale.

Mayor Yiannis Boutaris and Anna Konstantinou, for your dedication to recognizing the heroes of Thessaloniki and ensuring their place in its history and future. Your support of me in the production of this book is just one small example of your vision and impact.

Andreas Assael, historian, friend and photography contributor; your expert knowledge of this time period has been invaluable, and I appreciate your many corrections that made this book accurate and true.

Erika Perahia, for your cooperation in making available to us the resources of The Jewish Museum of Thessaloniki. Thank you.

Joel Hedlund and Anika Klix, associate editors; your careful reflections and unique backgrounds in style, history, redrafting, and professional acuity have immensely improved the quality of this book.

Lindsay Packer and Alisa Algava, for cover design brilliance.

Wenty Hill, for your support and guidance in enhancing my spiritual awareness, especially in its applications to this story.

Alexander Zing Levine, for technical assistance with book layout and early cover design; your cheerful attitude and dedication to diligent work is laudable and highly valued.

Karl Dominey, for your keen eye and for capturing in your photos me and my family living in the moment.

Charles Barrett, my publicist, and Paula Johnson, my web designer; thank you for helping me tell my family's story to the world so we can raise people's awareness of how far we have strayed from being heartful human beings.

I am also deeply grateful to Mazal Korabelnik, Maya and Assa Drori, Beatrice Benforado, Barry and Fran Ivker, and Dan Fauci for your help with advancing the production of this book.

And, I'd like to express my endless dedication and love to my family, Alisa, Carin, Michael, Drew, Sabria, Priscilla, and Martin, and to the Carasso and Attias families across the ocean. I wake up in the morning and go to sleep at night in gratitude for you. I love you all beyond measure.

Editor's Notes

Andreas Algava was a child during the Greek Holocaust in Thessaloniki. His family was one of three that miraculously survived by hiding from the Nazis during and after the deportation of 56,000 Jews to Auschwitz and other concentration camps. This true story is compelling with its twists and turns, near discoveries, frightening moments, and constantly uncertain outcome.

Andreas regards this book as a first step in speaking out for human rights. Just as his family was persecuted and saved from death by people who risked their lives, so now others are facing hardship, heartache, and survival.

It's time to let go of the old hatreds, time to let go of an eye for an eye, it's time to stop holding on to our darkness and fear. As the heroes in this story, we must now join together and act, we must create a space for understanding and accepting each other, for living grander, more honorable and more charitable lives, lives that are valued by the degree of kindness and compassion we give.

This is the first in a series of publications intended to provide Andreas with the visibility needed to make a strong impression and define a pathway for justice, and for the kindness and compassion each of us can give to improve the human condition and brighten the Light within.

What is the choice that you will make?

What will you choose?

Dr. Daniel Levine
Co-Author, Editor and Publisher
For Passion Publishing, LLC
Bellingham, WA U.S.A.

Foreword

Yiannis Boutaris, Mayor of Thessaloniki

This is more than a remarkable tale of survival against overwhelming odds. This is the story of courage, compassion, and character.

The story you're about to read describes events in the lives of a single Jewish family who hid from Nazi persecution and escaped deportation on the trains to Auschwitz, defying the fate of about 56,000 Thessalonikan Jews.

The theme of man's inhumanity to man runs throughout this book, and sadly we notice it in our lives today, even coming to accept it. In a sense, many of us have built resistance, an immunity, to taking action and serving those in need.

However, there are also many historic exceptions which exhibit honor and portray humanity's higher values, and one of them is this story of heroism, personal risk, and sacrifice in our city during the Nazi occupation. These Greek heroes risked their lives and the lives of their children to protect this desperate family.

In addition to those in this story, many citizens in Thessaloniki saw what was happening and became Greek heroes, but not by choice. Acts of heroism are not born from deliberate, conscious thought but rather from the essence of a person's character. Heroes become heroes because it is in their nature. In reality, the heroes you will see on these pages had no choice because they could do no other.

There was no choice between commitment and betrayal, no choice between character and barbarism, no choice between courage and cowardice. There was no choice, even, between life and death.

These great men and women of Thessaloniki are examples of the capacity for greatness in every one of us, living up to the best attributes of our humanity. Today we have similar opportunities to be moved by the suffering of others, to take action with courage and compassion and relieve their fear and torment.

As the mayor of Thessaloniki, I am proud of the many citizens who, in the past and again today, step forward to guide us through difficult times toward an uncertain future. Like the heroes in this story, we now have the opportunity to live courageously, to express kindness and embrace compassion.

I offer you this message with my best wishes to all of you to take to heart the lessons in this story.

Γιάννης Μπουτάρης
Yiannis Boutaris
Mayor, Thessaloniki, Greece

Introduction

Alisa and Carin Algava

Visiting our grandparents as children, we always knew they were Greek *and* Jewish. And they spoke Ladino and Greek. And Spanish, French and English. We knew they talked about having more than one birth-day. We ate Greek food and Sephardic food. And we heard them tell their stories of the years in hiding. That's what we called them. The years in hiding. Which was pretty close to the unimaginable truth. In 1943, they left the ghetto for the certainty of an uncertain future. For 600 days our grandparents, Allegra and Henri (Yaya and Papou to us), their young son Andreas (who would eventually be our father), and Papou's parents Avram and Myriam took on Greek Christian identities and hid in the homes of courageous Greek Christian families. And the day Greece was liberated on October 30, 1944 was like another day of birth to them. We also knew that of the almost 56,000 Jews in Thessaloniki before the Nazi occupation, only 1,900 returned from the concentration camps or from hiding and fighting in the mountains. Only three families had remained in the city for the duration and survived. And the Algavas were one. An entire community eradicated. And they were still there.

From the time our dad was in college, he wanted to record our grandparents' story. As we were growing up in the 1980s, he would sit at one of the early IBM home computers wearing headphones and transcribing their recorded words and memories. As young adults in 1996, just over 50 years after the liberation from the Nazis, we felt privileged to travel with our Yaya and Papou for a month in Greece. We saw Thessaloniki with our own eyes. The stories we always had heard now had different meaning. We visited the synagogue where they were married in 1935, Plateia Elefthereias (Liberty Square) where they stood on the balcony watching historic events unfold, and 7 Tsimiski Street where our grandfather worked with men who would alter his destiny—and ours. We drove by the orchards on the edge of the city where our family had spent a day in terror. We saw the building where our Papou had spent anxious hours hiding under a bed. We visited our Yaya's family's dye factory that they had barely managed to reclaim when the war ended. We climbed the stone stairs inside the White Tower at the edge of the Aegean Sea where our father attended scout meetings after the war, before further political upheaval pushed them across the seas and the ocean to the city of New York. These are the stories we heard and internalized and can consciously retell; some of them even shifted over time and retelling, as stories tend to do. And then there are all the stories and details of events, places and people we never knew and now have learned from reading our dad's book.

Moments of miracle in time and space are embedded in the fabric of our memories and our understanding of who we are. The stories they shared with us throughout our childhoods and young adulthoods brought home to us our grandparents' strength, our family's luck, and the courage of the Greek Christian families who risked their own lives to save ours. Recent research about epigenetics and children of Holocaust survivors informs us of the countless other stories wired in our unconscious. It was only recently that we realized how these powerful tapestries of miracle have been forever interwoven and patched together with trauma.

Yaya was always less talkative about those years in hiding. She would sit next to Papou on the sofa and listen, sometimes nodding, sometimes watching, and once in a while offering her own memory into the narrative. Papou's version of their story was always accompanied by tears of love. We all knew it was because of Yaya—her intuition and force of will—that we even exist. Yaya was the eldest of seven sisters and brothers. Of everyone in the Carasso family, everyone including her parents and siblings, grandparents and even a niece or nephew, only one brother returned. And yet, for all the years of our lives with her, she only saw the good in people, she only spoke kindly of others. What did it take for our Yaya to step into each day with appreciation anew, to integrate or perhaps ignore the irrevocable pain of loss? We wish we could ask her now. Without words, though, she showed us how to be generous and forgiving, stubborn and caregiving.

What does it mean to survive? Against all odds, a small part of our family survived; less than one-hundredth of one percent chance. And we survived.

Our dad talks and lives in gratitude. He is grateful to his parents and his family, to his daughters and our mom, to the Greek families who saved us all. His gratitude is inseparable from the pain and fear of loss. For him, to survive means to serve, or as he puts it: "To manifest compassion, kindness, generosity and forgiveness for myself and others in order to relieve the suffering in the world." And one powerful way our dad serves is by realizing his dream of telling of his parents' story. While this experience of miracle and trauma may seem quite extraordinary, it hopefully will resonate for all of us whose moments of seemingly ordinary survival are also quite extraordinary. Each of us has our own stories of trauma, humanity and inhumanity to integrate, share, learn from, live with.

Our family's story is the prism through which we understand ourselves and our world. We both have pursued paths as educators because we know that everyone has the capacity to learn to stand up, to care for, to speak or write or fight for what is just. And we see the conditions of inequity that constrain and restrain, the structures and the individual actions that not only permit but promote a banality of evil in 1492 and 1942 and 2018, too. We must ask ourselves: Would I take a stand? Would I harbor you? Would you harbor me?*

On small and large scales, what can each one of us do? Our families, communities, and societies transform us

_____

With appreciation for Hannah Arendt's writings about the banality of evil and Sweet Honey in the Rock's vision of moral courage and harboring the so-called "other"—their words deeply resonate today.

as individuals, but we also must work courageously to transform them. Our grandparents taught us that storytelling—purposeful, loving, liberatory storytelling—can be transformational, helping us move through and beyond trauma, beyond a relived past or an imagined future. Stories ground us in the present by connecting us to each other. With strength and courage, stubbornness and luck, our Yaya and Papou and our dad have shown us what it means to be more fully human.

Prologue

The Immigration of Sephardic Jews to Greece

Anti-Semitism was common in 15th century Spain with many massacres, restricted freedoms, and forced conversions culminating with the Edict of Expulsion, also known as the Alhambra Decree, promoted by Torquemada, the Grand Inquisitor.

King Ferdinand and Queen Isabella issued the order that all Jews either convert to Catholicism or leave the Spanish kingdom by the end of July 1492. Jews were allowed to take their property, except they were required to leave behind their gold, silver, and money. The number of Jews leaving the Spanish kingdom is estimated at 40,000. These Jews were Sephardic, meaning they lived on the Iberian Peninsula.

Most Sephardic Jews immigrated to the Ottoman Empire, particularly the Balkans and North Africa. Some traveled farther to areas in the Middle East. Many Portuguese Jews migrated to Holland, establishing and expanding the diamond industry there.

It was Sultan Bayezid II who granted the Sephardic Jews permission to settle in the Ottoman Empire, sending his Navy to evacuate them safely. He also gave a decree to his provincial governors that the new refugees were to be well-treated. The Sultan was so pleased with the arrival of the Jews that he is quoted as saying to his courtiers,

"You venture to call Ferdinand a wise ruler, he who has impoverished his own country and enriched mine!"

Entrepreneurship flourished, and many new intellectual ideas and cultural developments in science, astronomy, and the arts were introduced.

A Brief History of Thessaloniki, Greece

Also known as Thessalonica and Salonica, Sephardic Jews arrived here soon after their expulsion from Spain in 1492. Thessaloniki was nicknamed *"la madre de Israel,"* the mother of Israel. Jews were allowed to practice their religion without interference, and Jews, Christians, and Muslims lived together in harmony, each respecting the other's culture and religion.

The Jews of Thessaloniki spoke Ladino, a medieval Spanish language, also called Judeo-Spanish. Jews who spoke Greek were easily recognized because of the language's almost lyrical accent. Very few people speak Ladino today; once the spirited expression of a thriving cultural community, it is now a dying language.

The commercial interests of Thessaloniki's Jews, and trade with other cities and countries, became extensive. Jews were active in all economic areas, and lived in all levels of society, from laborers to landowners. Because of the city's location, as the Ottoman Empire declined, so did the fortunes of the Jews, and many migrated to Palestine, and also to Constantinople, and Izmir in Turkey.

At the end of the First Balkan War in 1912, Thessaloniki came under the control of Greece. The Jewish population was accepted, and Jews were allowed to observe the Sabbath and work on Sundays. In 1917, the Great Thessaloniki Fire left over 50,000 Jews homeless, and some decided to migrate to Palestine.

With the end of the Greco-Turkish war in 1922, Thessaloniki's ethnic composition was significantly altered with a population exchange between Greece and Turkey, reducing the Jewish population percentage from a majority to a minority of about 40 percent. Many Greeks living in the Ottoman Empire moved to Thessaloniki while many Muslims moved from Thessaloniki to Turkey. The native Greeks of Thessaloniki continued their friendly association with their Greek Jewish neighbors, but the new Greek Orthodox population had little empathy, and the bonds that had once integrated the two communities, nurtured over centuries, were severed.

Laws were changed, and working on Sundays was prohibited in 1922; this meant that Jews had to work on the Sabbath or lose income. In 1931 there was an anti-Semitic riot in a Jewish neighborhood called Camp Campbell; the entire community was burned down and about 500 Jewish families were homeless. Many more Jews decided to move to Palestine.

Events Leading Up to the Invasion of Greece

The Greek general and dictator Ioannis Metaxas seized power in 1936 and served as the Prime Minister of Greece until his death in 1941. Metaxas was known to favor Germany because he had studied there, and because Germany was Greece's largest trading partner.

Metaxas wanted to keep Greece out of World War II and sought a neutral path between the United Kingdom and Germany. This intention was thwarted by the designs of Mussolini who wanted to prove to Hitler that he was a capable military commander deserving the *Fuhrer's* respect and admiration. Without Hitler's approval, Mussolini sent his ambassador, Emanuele Grazzi, to demand that Metaxas allow Italian military units to occupy all strategic Greek sites.

Our story begins at 3:00 a.m. on October 28, 1940.

Chapter 1
*"Ochi!"**

October 28, 1940

The Prime Minister of Greece was awakened by the startling sound of his phone ringing in the middle of the night. It was exactly 3:00 a.m. on Monday morning, October 28, 1940.

Ioannis Metaxas got out of bed, put on his dressing robe, and walked rapidly to the insistent phone in the next room.

"Hello?"

It was Travlos, his head of security, at the front gate.

"Prime Minister, I'm sorry to disturb you. French Ambassador Maugras is here and requests a meeting with you immediately."

"Yes, of course. Send him in," Metaxas told his aide. "What does he want?" thought Metaxas. "I just saw him a few hours ago at the reception..."

The word for "No" in Greek is *"Ochi."* This single word spoken by the Prime Minister became the rallying cry of the Greek resistance to the Italian invasion, and inspired a patriotic holiday known as Ochi Day, celebrated every October 28.

Metaxas returned to his bedroom. Lela, his wife, was awake. "What is it, Ioannis? You look disturbed."

"The French ambassador is here. It's three o'clock in the morning!"

"Do you know why?" asked Lela, stifling a yawn.

"I have no idea," her husband replied grumpily. "What's up with Maugras? What indiscretion and how inconsiderate at this ungodly hour..."

Metaxas straightened his tousled hair and went to greet the French ambassador. Opening the door, he was surprised to see not Maugras, but the Italian ambassador, Emanuele Grazzi. The chill night air caused an unexpected shiver.

"Good morning, Ambassador," Metaxas said, leading the Italian into the lounge with its desk and couches. Grazzi seated himself on the green divan.

Grazzi was a large man with a round face and a sizable double chin. His hair was receding at the forehead, and he squinted through his round glasses. "He looks determined," thought Metaxas.

Lela Metaxas heard the men's deep voices but could not distinguish their words. The conversation seemed calm, but then increased in tempo and volume. She heard the angry voice of her husband shout "*Ochi!*" and a sudden loud noise, which she later learned was the palm of her husband's hand striking the top of his desk.

The door to the lounge opened and Lela heard the men walking toward the front door. As soon as Grazzi was gone, Metaxas returned to their bedroom. Now he was the one with the determined look.

"We are at war; I must dress quickly."*

This scene and some of the dialogue was described by Lela Metaxas in a letter.

Chapter 2
At War!

October 28, 1940

Henri Algava was as surprised as everyone else.

The newspaperman on the corner of Tsimiski Street was yelling something about war with Italy. Several small groups of people were on the street reading the Thessaloniki newspapers and their discussions were animated.

Henri quickly walked up to the man selling the newspapers. "War with Italy?"

"Yes, sir. Buy a paper?"

Henri saw the headline in big capital letters: DEFEND WHAT IS HOLY AND HOME. There was a picture of King George II and Prime Minister Metaxas with a smaller headline: "Greek Forces Defend the Fatherland."

Henri gave the man a few *drachmas.** "We are at war!" thought Henri. As Henri bought the paper, his cousin Aaron spotted him on the other side of the busy street and called out his name.

_____

Drachmas: The Greek currency of the time.

"Henri! Hey, Henri!" Henri looked up from the newspaper and saw Aaron through his round gold-frame glasses. Aaron crossed the street's morning flow of cars, horse-drawn wagons, and pedestrians, and ran up. "Henri! Did you read the news? We're at war with Il Duce!"

"Yes, I just bought the paper...I haven't read it yet..."

Aaron was excited. "Remember when the Italians sank the *Elli* back in August? Those bastards were trying to push us into war! And then there were all the Italian planes flying across our borders...probably spying on our defenses!"

"It's unbelievable!" said Henri.

"They invaded before their ultimatum expired," Aaron continued, "invaded before their own deadline!"

"Treacherous, just like Hitler," thought Henri.

"Everyone could guess this would happen," said Aaron. "They took Albania and now they want Greece!"

"The paper says Metaxas met with Grazzi," said Henri.

"Yes, and he told him '*Ochi!*' That stupid pig! They can't push the Greeks around!"

"Did he really say that?" Henri asked, surprised.

"Yes! It's war!'"

Henri felt his stomach tighten. "We can't have a war!"

"Like it or not," Aaron replied, seeing Henri's startled look.

"But Allegra and I have a baby! Andreas is just 10 months old..."

"I know," said Aaron in a softer voice, "and Sofia and I were planning to have a child soon, too, you know. Maybe now we won't."

"What if we're called into the army? What about our families? I guess rationing will start...we'd better buy supplies!"

"If the Italians aren't held," said Aaron, "they could be here in about a day. The fighting is only 250 kilometers away."

"Occupation by that pompous ass would be outrageous!" Henri said.

"Two Italian divisions are in the Pindus Mountains," said Aaron. "Those passes are rugged, and winter is coming. If our troops can hold them there, the winter will destroy them."

"Aaron," said Henri, "I need to get home. Give my love to Sophia..." Henri turned abruptly and ran toward home, to his wife and child in their apartment at 93 Tsimiski. The fighting had come to Greece after all!

Chapter 3
The Last Peaceful Moments

October 28, 1940

The windows were wet with the morning's intermittent rain, the sun obscured by the thick clouds filling the late October sky. Allegra turned her eyes from the high rain-streaked windows, removing the whistling teapot from the stove.

"Myriam," she called, "a single sugar?"

"Yes, my dear," her mother-in-law replied from the dining room. "She's the perfect grand-Mamá," thought Allegra, "round and fun! How lucky we are..."

Allegra poured three cups of tea and added a single lump to one. "None for you, I know, Daisyka," Allegra said, a bit louder to be heard over the laughter from the next room.

"Thank you, Allegra!" called Daisyka, laughter in her voice. Henri's cousin was in the next room with Myriam, playing with baby Andreas. For her 19 years, she had an attractive personality exhibiting grace, intellect and a caring nature.

"It sounds like everyone's having a good time!" The third cup was hers, also without sugar. Allegra was a tall handsome woman with stylishly short light-brown hair, and her figure was well-cut. A smile formed on her lips as she remembered Henri's compliment about her figure this morning. Placing the teacups on saucers and then on a tray, Allegra carried the tea to the elegant dining room table with its formal wood-carved chairs and burgundy seat cushions.

"He is getting fat!" laughed Myriam, Andreas's stocky grandmother. Myriam preferred her graying hair in a bun; in public she concealed it with a colorful floral scarf.

Allegra smiled. "Better him than me," she said, and set the tray on the table.

Daisyka was holding Andreas in her arms and smiling, and the baby was smiling back, reaching for a strand of her long golden hair with his chubby hands.

"Oh, you like that, do you?" said Daisyka, and Andreas cooed and laughed.

"Here, give him to me," said Allegra, and she took her son in her arms and prepared to feed him.

"It was cold last night," said Myriam, reaching for her tea. "I'm glad the apartment is so warm now." She was seated near the ornate metal stove glowing with heat.

"You and Avram were cold?" asked Allegra. "Were you cold, Daisyka?"

"Oh," said the young woman, "I was warm. I fell asleep and didn't wake until the morning."

"The blessings of youth," said Myriam. "It must be my old bones. Avram was up early today. He said he was going to the taverna for some coffee and maybe some breakfast."

"Henri left early, too, to go to the office and finish some orders," said Allegra.

The gramophone on the tiled side table, under one of the tapestries that adorned the walls, was playing *Ladino** music, and the sound of the lutes, zithers and hand drums filled the apartment with the exotic, playful sounds of a lovely Sephardic song.

"The music is so delightful!" said Allegra, gently swirling around the dining room, her skirt twisting about her as she danced with her baby, Andreas smiling and laughing at her pleasure and antics.

The music was instrumental because Henri had set a firm rule: No one was to speak Ladino near Andreas, ever.

Ladino: The unique music and language the Sephardic Jews brought with them to Greece when they were evicted from Spain in the 15th century. With few exceptions, anyone speaking Ladino would be identified as Jewish. The language would prove deadly...

"We've been in Thessaloniki for centuries! He should be a Greek," Henri had said. "I want my son to speak Greek and be as Greek as all the other boys." This is the way it was. Everyone spoke Greek around Andreas instead of the familiar Ladino.

"Henri won't be back until later," Allegra said, reaching for her tea, taking a quick sip.

"And Avram," said Myriam, "he won't be back until dinner. He loves to talk! He has so many friends they should make him the mayor of Thessaloniki!"

They laughed at the thought, and Allegra felt pride for him. Her father-in-law was very popular, and known for his kindness. Often called *Avram Houvarda,** he was always helping others through a hard time, or collecting money for people in trouble. Avram was an inspiration to many.

"Even though it's raining, today is such a beautiful day!" said Allegra, still swirling with Andreas in her arms. "Let's not listen to the news this morning."

"A wonderful idea," Myriam chimed in. "The news frightens me."

"Me, too," said Allegra, slowing her waltz. Her heart was always heavy when she thought of the chaos and terror

---

Avram Houvarda: Avram the Generous.

millions were suffering. Today all her loved ones were safe and her baby was sweet and healthy. Allegra felt instantly better.

Allegra glanced at the Halston radio on the table, made far away in the United States. They owned several because Henri imported radios, radio parts, and automotive parts, too.

"Henri said that Nicos came by just before the Sabbath with a few orders to fill," added Allegra.

"That's good, good," Myriam responded. "My boy is building his business, a blessing from God."

"Yes, thanks to God. And Nicos has also been very kind to us."

"He is another blessing," said Myriam, "giving Henri a good start." Nicos Efcarpides taught Henri the import-export business, trusting him to sign legal papers when he was hunting in the Pindus Mountains, and even gave Henri some of his own accounts. The two men were great friends.

Allegra stood up with Andreas in her arms, and stepped over to Daisyka. "Here, darling," she said. "Please take Andreas to his crib...I'll be there in a moment."

Daisyka took the baby. "Yes," she said. "Come on,

Andriko!"* and off they went to the baby's room.

"She's a good one," said Myriam. "So good with the baby."

"Yes, she's a treasure. She'll be a good wife and mother... and she is so beautiful."

They heard a key in the door.

"Oh, that must be Henri!" said Allegra. "He's back early," she thought as she walked to the front door to greet her husband.

The door opened and Allegra saw Henri's face. She knew at once that something was terribly wrong.

_____

Andriko: Little Andreas.

Chapter 4
Death to Il Duce!

October 28, 1940

In his taverna close to the White Tower on Thessaloniki's waterfront, Aleko turned up the volume on the radio. Lots of men had gathered to talk about the invasion and listen to the 9:00 a.m. broadcast.

"Since 5:30 this morning, the enemy has been attacking our vanguard on the Greek-Albanian border. Our forces are defending the Fatherland."

"Maybe we'll have more news now," said Avram to his two friends, Stefanos and Kostas. They looked up from their table in the back of the taverna and stared expectantly at the radio on its shelf.

The announcer's deep voice filled the room as the men quieted down to listen.

"This morning, 28 October 1940, Italian military units invaded Greek territory. Infantry, tanks and artillery have been reported entering Epirus from locations within Albania.

"The size of the Italian forces is not yet known. Early reports indicate that at least six columns of enemy troops have crossed the Albanian border over a 100-kilometer front, from

the coastal area north of Igoumenitsa to the northern Pindus Mountains.

"The Greek High Command is moving troops into position to stop the invasion. We will have more news as information becomes available."

"What? Is that all?" shouted a man at one of the tables. Others cried their disappointment, too, demanding more news.

As though at their request, the announcer continued.

"The Ministry of Foreign Affairs announced that Prime Minister Metaxas met with Italian Ambassador Emanuele Grazzi shortly after three o'clock this morning. Ambassador Grazzi delivered a three-hour ultimatum from Italian Prime Minister Benito Mussolini to Mr. Metaxas demanding that the Italian army occupy strategic Greek sites unopposed. Mr. Metaxas refused the ultimatum, resulting in this morning's invasion of our northern border."

The men in the taverna shouted *"Ochi! Ochi!"* Angry and loud, they pounded the tables with their fists, fury in their eyes, the room shaking with their rage.

"Italian military forces began their attack at 5:30 this morning, a half hour before the three-hour ultimatum was due to expire."

"Mussolini can go to Hell!" shouted someone as other insults were hurled at the innocent radio.

"Prime Minister Metaxas calls on all Greek men to defend the Fatherland and fight to your death."

The men cheered and shouted with enthusiasm, and then the "Hymn to Liberty"* blared from the radio. Everyone stood and sang, their voices filling the room with passion and patriotism.

"We will return with more news as it becomes available," and then patriotic songs and hymns continued playing. Aleko lowered the volume as the taverna exploded with angry shouts and loud conversations.

Some of the bravos in the taverna began posturing.

"I'm enlisting today! Who will join me?" shouted a burly young man with broad shoulders and a square jaw.

"I will," shouted another. "The Italians will regret their blunder! Who is with us?" One after the other, the angry men pledged their honor, each more passionate than the last.

One man with biceps bulging through his shirt sleeves pulled a long fishing knife out of its sheath, describing how he would fillet the Italians he caught, and the men roared their approval.

"Do they think they can just take our country and rape our women like the Turks?" shouted another, and the

_____

"Hymn to Liberty" is the Greek national anthem.

room burst with the sound of the men shouting "*Ochi! Ochi!* No! Never!"

The men's violent expressions continued for a while, but eventually the taverna began to empty. Avram, Stefanos and Kostas were still seated, talking among themselves, and Aleko joined them. Stefanos was a man in his mid-thirties, small in size with thick black hair contrasting sharply with the white-haired men at the table. "I told you," he said, "the Italians want to rule the world with Hitler. It was only a matter of time."

"You're right," said Kostas the milkman. "I saw it coming, too."

"We all saw it," added Aleko. "Metaxas and the King must have known Mussolini wouldn't stop with Albania."

"Yes," Avram joined in, "but we also know Mussolini wouldn't attack unless he was sure he could beat us." Avram quietly moved the *komboloi** beads on the string in his hand, one at a time, feeling each bead pass between his fingers.

"Say," said Kostas, "can you imagine being awakened by the Italian ambassador at three o'clock in the morning?

_____

Komboloi: "Worry beads" are a string of beads manipulated by one or two hands, used to pass the time. They have no religious or ceremonial purpose.

17

He looks like a beast... That must have been a scare!" The men laughed.

"What will Hitler think when we chase the Italian ass back across the border?" said Kostas.

"May they both drop dead from the evil eye," replied Aleko, and all the men nodded.

Stefanos spoke up. "I need to go," he said. "I'm late and Sultana will skin me if I miss morning service, much like that hero with the knife."

The seated men laughed as he stood up.

"I better go, too," said Kostas.

"Yes, yes, and me as well. You'll be here all by yourself, Aleko," said Avram.

"Oh," mused Aleko, "not for long. This war will be good for business."

The friends stepped through the taverna's front door into the damp morning air. A strong wind was blowing in from the sea, a wind that would not soon stop.

Chapter 5
The Shadows of a Dark Future

October 28, 1940

Henri touched the *mezuzah** and stepped into their apartment, a tight jaw and serious eyes replacing his morning smile.

"What is it, Henri?" asked Allegra, alarmed.

"I've heard some bad news."

Allegra took a quick short breath and steeled herself.

"Where are Mother and Father?" asked Henri.

"Mamá is in the dining room and Avram is probably at the taverna."

Henri took his wife's hand. "I want to tell you both what I've heard," and Henri led Allegra into the dining room where Myriam was sitting on the stylish couch by the tall windows overlooking Tsimiski Street.

"Hello, Mamá," Henri said.

Mezuzah: A small decorative case containing religious text, attached to a doorpost.

Myriam suddenly realized Henry looked serious. "What is it?" she said with alarm.

Henri and Allegra heard her fear and knew she was thinking something terrible had happened to Avram.

Henri quickly said, "No, Mamá, it's not about *Babá*."*

"What, then?" asked Allegra.

Henri unfolded the morning's newspaper and held it up. Allegra quickly read the threatening headline and her hand flew to her face in surprise.

"Oh, my God!" she exclaimed.

"What? What?" Myriam asked. She couldn't read Greek, but she saw the photos of the Greek king and the Prime Minister, and the big black headlines. Her first thought was there had been an assassination.

"The Italians invaded our homeland this morning, Mamá," said Henri.

Allegra felt a chill on her skin as she tried to take a deep breath but couldn't.

Henri looked at his mother's face, and saw fear in her eyes as well. He went to his mother and sat beside her, his arm around her shoulders.

Babá: Father.

"I'm all right," said Myriam. "Go. Be with your wife and little boy." Henri gave his mother a quick hug and walked down the hall with Allegra.

The nursery was quiet in the half-light, a few toys scattered on the carpets. Several framed pictures of flowers, bright butterflies and colorful birds hung on the walls. "Everything feels so fragile," he thought.

Daisyka was sitting on the floor, startled by the sudden interruption. Allegra took Andreas in her arms.

"What shall we do? Will we be okay?" asked Allegra.

"Yes," replied Henri. "Everything will be fine," knowing his words promised little. Every happiness they had ever known was now in the shadows of a dark future they could not see.

"The Italians invaded this morning," Henri said to Daisyka. She looked at him with surprise, and then looked away, scared.

"Where are they?" asked Daisyka numbly.

"The soldiers are in the Pindus Mountains," Henri replied. "They're about 250 kilometers away."

"They could be here soon," Allegra said.

"Yes, that's possible," Henri answered, "and we must consider what to do."

"Should we buy extra food and kerosene?" asked Allegra.

"Yes," said Henri, "and anything else we might need like extra blankets, candles, and fuel."

Henri remembered the bundle of Greek currency hidden in the back of the armoire, along with his stash of gold coins. There was also Allegra's jewelry, and the silverware, and the silver candlesticks.

"My baby," thought Allegra. "Will we be safe?"

"I want to go," said Daisyka. "I want to be with my mother."

"Yes, Daisyka, I'll take you back," said Henri. "Gather some things from your room and we'll leave in a few minutes." Daisyka left to get ready.

"We need to buy supplies tomorrow when the markets open," said Allegra. "Let's both go. We can leave Andreas with your mother, and you and I will buy beans, flour, rice, corn, and kerosene."

"Yes," Henri answered. "We need to have enough for all of us. Supplies will get tight."

"Henri," Allegra said with a heavy voice, "we have to think of Andreas. Nothing is more important than our baby."

Cradling their son in her arms, she looked at Andreas, at their healthy, happy son and said a prayer. "Please, God, please protect Andreas from all harm and help him grow into a good and righteous man, a joy to his family and a blessing to his community."

"Amen," said Henri, looking first at his son and then Allegra. "Damn Mussolini!" he thought, as fear changed to rage. "Damn that bastard!" Henri was surprised his fists were clenched. He heard the front door close with a muffled sound and left the nursery to greet his father.

Avram had returned. "Hello, *pedí mou*,"* he said. "You've heard the news?"

Henri gave his father a warm hug. "Yes, Babá. I just told Allegra, Mamá, and Daisyka. Daisyka wants to go home to be with her family; I'm going to take her back now."

"Good idea," said the elder Algava, hanging his hat on the coat rack. Henri was struck by how gray his father's hair was, and how worn this wonderful man looked on this terrible day.

"How are Mamá and Allegra?" Avram asked.

"Upset, of course. It's easy to think the worst."

"I know. Where is your mother?"

Pedí mou: My child.

"In the dining room. She'll be glad to see you. We need to buy extra food and fuel."

"I was thinking the same thing. Everything is closed today, so we'll have to go early tomorrow. Do you have extra cash?"

"Yes, I have some paper money and some gold coins."

"Me, too. We should go to the bank if it's open." Avram gave his son a hug. "I don't know what's coming," he said, "but we'll see it through."

Later, after taking Daisyka to her mother's home, the swaying trolley took Henri back to another trolley he'd ridden in Leipzig, Germany, in 1937.

> *"Oh, my God," he said to himself. "Look at that!" Henri saw signs in shop windows stating "Juden Verboten!"* and "Juden sind hier nicht erwünscht!"**
>
> *Henri was surprised by all the Nazi flags draping the buildings and streets, swastikas evident everywhere. Buying a newspaper, the anti-Jewish news and commentary was dreadful.*
>
> *"All the Jews should move," he'd told Allegra when he returned. "No one should live like that. I think it's*

"Juden Verboten!": "Jews Forbidden!"

"Juden sind hier nicht erwünscht!": "Jews are not wanted here!"

going to get worse." And it had, with the murderous rampage on Kristallnacht.*

"Could that ever happen here?" he thought. "No, that's Hitler's Germany and he'll never send his storm troopers to Thessaloniki." Now confident the Greeks would stop the foolish blustering Mussolini, Henri dismissed the thought.

He stepped into the doorway of 93 Tsimiski, climbed the stairs and stood outside his apartment door; he saw their mezuzah on the doorframe.

The mezuzah's blue and gold ceramic case had a Jewish Star of David at the top, a large זש,* an image of the walls of Jerusalem, and the word "Yisrael" at the bottom.

Kristallnacht: "Crystal Night" or "The Night of the Broken Glass," November 9-10, 1938. Over 1,000 synagogues were damaged, rioters looted over 7,000 Jewish businesses, over 90 Jews were murdered, and Jewish schools, hospitals, homes and cemeteries were vandalized, often by neighbors. About 30,000 Jewish men were arrested and sent to concentration camps.

 זש: *Shin* is a Hebrew letter that represents *Shaddai*, spelled *Shin, Dalet, Yud* signifying *Shomer Dalet Yisrael* (Guardian of the doors of Israel). Inside the mezuzah is a rolled parchment scroll inscribed with the *Shema*, which also begins with *shin*, and is the most important Jewish prayer. The Hebrew word *shema* has many meanings relating to "hear," "understand," "pay attention," and "be willing." In this case, *shema* is the first word in the central daily prayer that states, "Hear, O Israel: the LORD our God, the LORD is one."

Inside the case was the *klaf*,* and Henri automatically recited its first verse from the *Torah*,* beginning with the words "Hear, O Israel, the LORD our God, the LORD is One."

"I wonder if our *mezuzah* will keep the Angel of Death from entering our home," thought Henri, as he touched the *mezuzah* with his fingers, then slipped his key into the lock, turned the knob and opened the door.

_____

Klaf: The parchment on which the Hebrew verses of the Shema Yisrael were written.

Torah: The law of God as given to Moses; the first five books of Hebrew scripture.

Chapter 6
The Angel of Death

November 2, 1940

Allegra was restless. She was in a deep sleep, but her body was agitated by the dream. Henri was also in a deep sleep but relaxed and still.

Allegra's agitation grew as the dream took shape, as she visited some other dimension of knowing, a realm of metaphor, wisdom and Truth.

> *A factory. Tobacco leaves. Oily tobacco leaves. A great din. Long lines of people. People dressed in gray and black overcoats.*

> *Women, young girls, men of all ages. Young men. Old men. Beautiful women. Boys. Long hair, short hair. Hats, no hats. Big oily tobacco leaves. Walking into the factory. People wanting to go into the factory.*

> *People moving forward in a strange procession, single file. Now quiet and serious, solemn. Unaware of their own funeral procession.*

> *I want to go, too.*

> *No! Not you! Not you! You, and you, and you, but not you, Allegra. Not you! No, Allegra... Not you!*

But...

No! Ochi! Ochi! Not you!

The people. Into the tobacco leaf factory...coming out of the factory...carried out, wrapped in white shrouds. Hundreds and hundreds... White shrouds without end. Nothing but white shrouds carried out of the factory.

Allegra woke with fear gripping her heart! Cold sweat clothed her body, her bedclothes soaked, the sheets damp.

"Oh, my God!" she said, in a muffled half-voice. The bedroom was dark, but a little pale light was coming in from the street lights behind the draped windows. Allegra felt a powerful chill run through her.

The dream was still heavy upon her, the horror of the images still fresh. In those early moments of waking, the dream carried her from the dimension of sleep into the half-conscious awareness of waking life.

A weight was on her chest, resisting her breathing, a shrill alarm ringing in her mind, the terror holding her speechless in the dark room, overwhelming her with dread and the force of the hideous vision. Helpless, frozen, she could not speak, a captive trying to pull away, fighting the grip of the dream. With extreme force of will, Allegra regained her strength and turned toward Henri to rouse him.

"Henri!"

There was no response. Allegra's chill went deeper as the dream worked on her mind and she feared her husband was a corpse lying beside her.

"Henri!" Her voice was louder now, her will more assertive, panic pushing aside the fog of the dream.

"Henri, wake up!"

Henri moaned softly and began to stir, slowly returning to awareness.

"Henri!" This time Henri exhaled an extended moan and his head turned on the pillow. Allegra felt relief that her husband was alive, slowly coming to her from across the far frontiers of sleep.

Allegra became more urgent to wake him and share the dream so its power would relinquish its hold.

Henri's consciousness began to materialize.

"Yes..." he murmured.

"Henri, wake up. Wake up!"

He was doing his best to comply. Disoriented and startled, he responded sleepily. "Yes? What is it? What's the matter?"

"I had the most horrible dream. Listen to me."

"Yes."

"I don't know how to describe it except I was outside a factory. It was a tobacco leaf factory. Inside were piles and piles of tobacco leaves. Outside the factory were long lines of people."

"Yes," Henri said sleepily.

"Everyone wanted to go into the factory. Everybody could go except me. I wanted to go like everybody else, but a voice told me, 'Not you, not you!'"

"Not you?"

"Yes, everybody could go, but not me. And then I saw that everybody was coming out of the factory on the other side, but instead of people, they were dead bodies. Everybody was coming out of the factory ready for the cemetery, dressed in shrouds!"

Henri was silent. He thought about what Allegra said. "So they were all dead?"

"Yes! All the people that went in came out dead. All of them."

Startled, Henri was now fully awake. "What does it mean?"

"I don't know," she said, "but it's important."

"Yes," Henri confirmed. "Whatever it means, the dream said you'll be safe."

"Maybe I'm just upset about the war," Allegra said hopefully. "Maybe it's because I'm afraid about the invasion..." her voice trailed off.

Henri moved closer to her and found the sheets were wet and cold. He hugged her, Allegra grateful for his warmth.

"Maybe that's all it is," said Henri. "Maybe it's nothing at all."

Chapter 7
Air Attack!

November 2, 1940

Standing at the second floor window of his radio and auto parts office, Henri watched the stormy sky. Gray rain clouds blocked the sun, but the clouds were thinning. Henri's face was dark like the sky. The pressed collar of his white shirt was stiff and irritating, and his tie was too tight. He could hear the plaintive cry of seagulls begging passersby for bits of food and bullying each other for the few morsels they were thrown. It was mid-morning and they were hungry.

Henri was taking a break from the tedious paperwork of cancelled orders. All his buyers were cautious because of the war. "Even Michalos," he said to himself. The cancelled order from his associate lay on top of the stack. Michalos and Henri had done business for years, often enjoying cups of Greek coffee at the café by the bank.

Henri turned away from the window and saw the newspaper on his desk. Five days since the invasion and Greek troops were being pushed back. There was also the threat of bombing; the Greek army had deployed antiaircraft guns around the city.

"It's foolish to keep Allegra and Andreas here," he thought. "It's not safe. What about Elek and Yosha?

They live on a farm outside Volos.* Allegra and Andreas would be safe there." A friend from the old days when they attended *Ecole des Frères* and *Lycee Francais*,* Elek now owned a large olive orchard on the outskirts of the town.

Though the idea of sending his wife and son away made him feel empty and sad, it was somewhat bearable because they'd be safe.

His thoughts were interrupted by the sound of the bell above the front door downstairs. Someone had just entered, and Henri descended the stairs.

"Nicos!" Henri said. "It's wonderful to see you!"

"Hello, Henri! It's good to see you, too, my friend."

Nicos was stout with a wide girth, but wasn't fat. He had a muscular build, and carried himself well. A closely trimmed black moustache complemented his prominent nose. Henri admired his friend's carefully fitted suit and the gray trilby with the green and black duck feather tucked inside its black ribbon. A clever and successful businessman, Nicos spoke five languages. He had done well and now owned an apartment overlooking

---

Volos: A port city in Thessaly about 200 kilometers south of Thessaloniki.

Ecole des Frères and *Lycee Francais*: Two schools in Thessaloniki.

Liberty Square in the prestigious part of downtown Thessaloniki.

"Has business slowed much, Henri?" asked Nicos in his deep voice. "My orders have dropped off quickly. Everyone wants to hold on to their cash."

Henri nodded. "Very discouraging, Nicos. I've lost about a dozen orders, and I have a full inventory. I was just on the phone with Michalos and he said he had to cancel his order for 200 radios."

"I know," said Nicos. "For now we just need to be patient."

"Yes...but I'm worried! I'm thinking about sending Allegra and Andreas away. We have some friends in Volos where they'd be safe, safer than here."

"Good idea," agreed Nicos. "I'm planning to send Sousanna to my cousin in Crete, but have faith, Henri. Mussolini is a loud fool...and it's November. I've hunted game there, and in the winter those mountains are almost impassable. I'm betting our army will give Il Duce's men a good beating. Have you heard the news about those village women?"

"Yes! Pulling cannons up to the ridges! They're amazing!"

"I read they're rolling rocks down the slopes, crushing

the *Bersaglieri*!* Mussolini must be having nightmares."

"I'm glad we're fighting the Italians and not the Germans."

"The Germans... Heaven forbid." Nicos became grave, his forehead furrowed. "That would be most unpleasant..." Henri and Nicos thought about Thessaloniki's 56,000 Jews. Their eyes met, and both men nodded.

"Well, on the bright side," said Nicos, "you have a lot of inventory. That may be an advantage. Radio and auto parts should soon be in demand. If supplies are cut off, you'll make a fortune!"

"That's a thought," Henri replied, "but still..."

Suddenly they heard a loud high siren. It took a moment to realize what it meant.

"Air raid!" Henri said incredulously, looking at Nicos.

"Where's the nearest shelter?" asked Nicos.

"Across the street! The bank!"

Henri and Nicos ran for the front door and were quickly in the street. "Planes!" Henri shouted, looking up at the sky.

Bersaglieri: Specialized Italian combat troops.

Suddenly they heard the "Pom! Pom! Pom! Pom!" of the antiaircraft batteries.

"Come on!" yelled Henri, running through the street, crowded with people, the droning engines of the airplanes sounded closer and louder, rumbling Henri's chest.

The siren was urgent as everyone rushed and pushed through the bank's doors. Henri, Nicos and the others ran through the lobby and down the stairs into a large room filled with file cabinets and boxes.

Heart beating rapidly, Henri took a place by the wall, wondering what would happen, Nicos beside him. A mother with her baby, frightened but brave, was quieting her crying daughter.

Five meters under the street, Henri could still hear the muffled sound of airplanes and the steady staccato of the antiaircraft guns. Everyone's eyes were on the ceiling, wondering what was happening.

Henri could hardly breathe. He said a prayer for Allegra and Andreas. "Please, God, keep them safe!" He heard the sound of dull explosions as dust began to drift down from the ceiling.

"How foolish!" he said to himself. "If God gives me a second chance," he swore to himself, "I'm sending them to Volos today!"

The sound of the bombers was suddenly much louder and Henri heard the whistling shrieks of falling bombs! Henri crouched at the base of the wall, covering his head with his arms, waiting for the blast. Some of the women began to scream and a man cried out, "Mother of God!", and then the first bomb hit.

The bomb must have exploded a block or two away and then there was another booming thud, and another, and another! Henri pushed himself into the wall as the ground shook, the explosions pounding the earth. The sound was deafening and the underground room seemed to jump as chunks of the ceiling fell on him... and then it was over. Henri couldn't hear, as though his ears were plugged, and his head was throbbing.

"Nicos! Are you all right?" Nicos was covered in bits of plaster and dust.

"Yes. And you?"

"In one piece." Henri could taste the dust in his mouth. He was shaken but alive. The baby was crying loudly, and her mother was rocking the infant. People were standing up slowly, half expecting another assault...but there was no more whistling from above.

"That was close," said Nicos, half-smiling, dusting the debris from his suit.

Henri couldn't answer. His mouth was too dry. The crying baby made him miss Andreas.

"It must have been the docks they were after," said Nicos. "One of the joys of having offices near the waterfront."

Henri found his voice. "I need to see Allegra," he said, "...see if they're all right..."

"Yes, let's go up," said Nicos, lightly dusting off his trilby. "I'm lucky I was wearing the gray one today," he said with a smile.

People were slowly making their way out of the basement room toward the stairs in the hallway.

"Are you all right, Ma'am?" Henri asked the young mother.

In a state of shock, she replied, "Yes, thank you."

"May I help you?"

"No," she replied slowly to prevent a cascade of tears, "we're fine. We're going home. We'll be safe there."

The idea of being safe seemed absurd. Nicos stepped aside to allow her to pass with her baby, and then he and Henri followed.

The floor by the stairs was covered with debris. As they passed the room next door, Nicos stiffened.

"Look!" he said to Henri.

Henri's eyes opened wide. Powder still drifting from a hole in the ceiling, an unexploded bomb was wedged diagonally in the floor, its nose buried in concrete.

"Oh my God," Henri croaked. They quickly mounted the stairs and exited the bank.

Henri and Nicos smelled the pungent smoke of burning wood, and saw a collapsed building across the street. A crowd had gathered, and a policeman was helping several men pull bodies from the damaged building.

"That's where Michalos works!" shouted Henri. He ran over to the crowd and felt sick when he saw Michalos lying lifeless in the street.

"He was a good man," said Nicos softly. "We'll visit his widow and children and give our respects."

"Yes," was all Henri could say, his constricted throat blocking more words. He had to get home to Allegra and his baby. Nothing else mattered.

* * *

By the docks, Marcos Hombitis stood at the edge of the crater.

There wasn't much to see, but he was interested in the impact the bombs would have made had they hit the dockyard. The crater was about 20 feet across and 6 feet deep. Nearby were three other holes from this morning's bombing. "We were lucky," Marcos thought. Straightening up, stretching his tall frame and broad shoulders, he took off his cap and ran his fingers through his black and gray hair.

"If our fighters hadn't chased those bombers, the damage would have been a lot worse," Marcos said to Yannis, his assistant.

"They got close," replied Yannis.

"Let's go back to the office," said Marcos. "I've seen everything I need to see. I want to check on the damage downtown. I have some friends there and want to find out if they're all right." He and Yannis walked quickly back to the customs office.

Marcos was thinking of Henri, Nicos, Michalos and a few other merchants in the import–export business. Some were Jews, some were Greek Orthodox like himself, but it made no difference. Marcos was their faithful friend.

He despised the demented hate and cruelty of Hitler, Mussolini, and Franco. Marcos wasn't a Communist, but he had no love for Fascists. He was quite happy simply being an honorable Greek.

"See you later," he said to Yannis.

Marcos heard the sound of an airplane...he looked up. It was a single plane, high above Thessaloniki. He knew it would be a long time before he heard that sound without concern.

Chapter 8
Safe?

November 2, 1940

Henri ran up Tsimiski Street toward home, eyes focused ahead, his mind in a jumble. "Are they all right?" was all he could think. Nothing was safe, and nothing would ever be safe again until this frightening, ugly war was over.

Turning the corner, he saw the street was as normal as when he left in the morning. Slowing to a walk, out of breath, Henri felt such relief that he sagged, filled with gratitude.

"Oh, my God," he sobbed. "Thank you, thank you!"

He reached the doorway of 93 Tsimiski and ran up the stairs to their second floor apartment, kissed his fingers and touched them to the *mezuzah*. His hands trembling, Henri could not get his key in the lock.

From inside, a voice called out, "Who is it?" It was Allegra, and Henri felt another wave of relief and gratitude that his dear wife was safe. Safe!

"It's me!"

"Henri! Wait a moment," and in an instant she had

turned the lock and the door swung open. Henri grabbed her in his arms and held her, his heart beating wildly with relief. Allegra held him tightly and they were silent for a moment, safe in each other's arms. Henri knew they were unsafe, but now he needed to draw from her strength.

"Darling, why are you so upset?" Then she noticed the disarray of his shirt and tie, the powder on his suit, his disheveled hair...

"Henri! Oh, my God," she cried, realizing. "We heard the sirens and explosions but couldn't tell where the bombs were falling."

"I was with Nicos when the air raid started. We ran to the bank."

Henri told her about the bombs falling and shaking the ground, about the dud in the next room, and seeing Michalos dead. Allegra hugged him close, sobbing into his jacket.

"I want to see Andreas. I want to hold him," Henri said. Henri and Allegra went to the nursery, and Henri held Andreas to his chest, the warmth of his son surprising him. Henri knew he would do anything to protect Allegra and Andreas.

The afternoon passed in earnest conversation. "It's decided, then," concluded Henri. "I'll call Elek in Volos and find out if he can shelter you, Andreas, and Mamá. Avram and I will stay here."

Avram stood up. He'd been sitting on the sofa near Myriam, under the tall windows that now held the last light of day.

"It's a good plan," he said. "Call Elek. I'll help Mamá and Allegra gather the things they'll need."

"Thank you, Babá."

In a few minutes, Henri found his family in the living room, already stacking clothing and supplies. "It's arranged. Elek and Yosha welcome you with open arms!"

"Thank God," said Myriam and Allegra at the same time. "May God bless them," added Allegra.

Henri glanced at his father and saw relief in his eyes, and felt his own relief. Allegra, Andreas, and Henri's mother were leaving tonight.

Chapter 9
Heroes Fight Like Greeks

March 23, 1941

After nearly 4½ months of battle, the Greek army had pushed the Italians out of the mountains, and now most of the Greek army was on the Albanian border. The Italian spring offensive had ended in failure, embarrassing Mussolini. To support the war, many Greek troops had been pulled from the Metaxas Line, a defensive front of fortifications along the border with Bulgaria.

Prime Minister Metaxas suddenly died in late January 1941 and was replaced by Alexandros Koryzis, a former governor of the Bank of Greece. The government was under the control of the Greek king, King George II, with Koryzis acting as figurehead. Patriotic fervor was high, inspired by the popular Greek singer Sofia Vembo, the "Songstress of Victory." Commenting on the courage of the Greek soldiers, Winston Churchill said, "...until now we would say that the Greeks fight like heroes. From now on we will say that heroes fight like Greeks."

A light breeze suggested the arrival of March rain. Henri was in his office downstairs; Avram had stopped by on his way to Aleko's taverna.

"Babá," Henri said, "have you seen today's paper?"

"More good news from the front?" asked Avram lightheartedly. "The last I heard, our army was about to cross into Albania and the Italians were in retreat. Is there any better news than that?"

Henri laughed. "No, but it is actually a treat to read the papers these days. The only way the news could get any better is if I started getting new orders and our family came home."

"I miss them, too," said the elder Algava, "and I'm thrilled they'll be home in a few days."

"It's been a long time," Henri sighed.

A song began on the radio. "Isn't that Allegra's friend?" asked Avram.

"Yes, that's Sofia Vembo!" Henri said, turning up the volume. The sultry voice of the patriotic singer filled the room.

> *"Mothers are searching to find their children, their children who vowed to win and return...but for those who are gone and are now wrapped in glory, we should be happy, and none of us cry!*
>
> *Children, children of Greece who are fighting a tough fight on the mountains, Children, to the sweet Virgin Mary we all pray you return!*

For those who love and stay awake for someone, bitterness is not proper for a fair Greek woman...

Greek women of Zaloggo from the cities and rural areas, women from Plaka, however bitter our pain, we proudly stand like the women of Souli. With the branches of victory, we are expecting you, Children!"*

"She has a beautiful voice," Avram said when the song was over. "I'll see you tonight, *pedí mou,*" he said, and left.

Henri was turning the pages of the morning paper when the bell above the door signaled a visitor. In stepped two men.

One was a Greek army major in full uniform, and the other was Henri's friend and customs broker, Marcos Hombitis. The major was wearing wool breaches that flared at the knees with the legs seated inside the tall brown boots. Henri noticed the French service pistol in his side holster. The major's uniform looked worn but clean and though his boots were polished, they couldn't fully hide the scuff marks of serious use.

"Henri!" said Marcos, his deep voice filling the room. "How have you been?"

"Good," said Henri happily. "It's always good to see you, Marcos." Henri took his friend's hand and shook it.

Children of Greece: Sofia Vembo, paraphrased.

"And how are you?" he asked, feeling the strength in his friend's grip.

"Good, thank you, and feeling better every day our army pushes back the Italians!"

If we weren't losing good men," rejoined Henri, looking at the major, "I'd read the news with pleasure."

The major smiled politely and briefly.

"Henri, I would like you to meet Major Stamatis. The major asked me this morning about batteries for trucks. Since I knew you had a good inventory, I felt you could help with his requisition."

"Of course."

"Major," Marcos continued, "this is Henri Algava. Henri, Major Stamatis."

"I'm pleased to meet you, Major," Henri said, extending a hand. "How can I help?"

The major took Henri's hand firmly, replying with a slight Thracian accent, "A pleasure, *Kýrios* Algava." The officer was terse, but polite.

"I've been sent by my colonel to requisition truck batteries and battery parts," Major Stamatis began. "I

Kýrios: Mr.

48

need to know how many batteries you have, and how many battery plates and separators."

"Of course, Major. I probably don't have as many as you'd like, but I'm happy to tell you what I do have." Henri went to his file cabinet and pulled out a folder of inventory.

Henri showed the major his list and the major looked closely.

"Over 500 batteries, almost 800 battery plates, and a little more than 600 battery separators."

Henri saw the major's eyebrows go up in appreciation.

"This is excellent, *Kýrios* Algava," said Major Stamatis. "I'll have you to thank when I'm a colonel," he said with a smile. "The Greek army will appreciate acquiring all these items."

"Thank you, Major," said Henri. "I'm glad to help."

"I'll return later today with men and a truck," said the major, "and take delivery."

"Very good."

The major extended his hand and the two men shook. "Thank you, *Kýrios* Algava. Your country is grateful."

The major turned toward Marcos and said, "*Kýrios*

Hombitis, I wish to thank you as well. My command appreciates your introduction to *Kýrios* Algava and this excellent supply."

"My pleasure," said Marcos.

"*Kýrios* Algava," said the major, "I look forward to seeing you this afternoon. Gentlemen, good day," and the major turned and left the office, the little bell above the door ringing him out.

"Well," reflected Marcos, "it looks like you're out of the battery business, Henri."

"Yes, it does. All I've got now are radio and auto parts."

Marcos smiled. "I'll see what I can do about getting those sold for you, too!"

"I'm in your debt, Marcos." Those words would ring loud before long, in a way Henri could never imagine.

That afternoon Major Stamatis returned with three men and a truck, and they quickly carried out all the requisitioned supplies. Major Stamatis signed and dated the receipt, taking a copy.

As a soldier carried out the last crate, Henri looked at the empty space in his storeroom. For a moment, only the little bell's echo remained.

Chapter 10
Enlisted

March 24, 1941

Henri got new orders, but not the kind he wanted. Sitting on the train in a sour mood, Henri had been traveling for several hours already. The train was taking forever to travel the 600 or so kilometers from Thessaloniki to the port of Nafplion, southwest of Athens.

It all had happened so quickly. Soon after the Greek major had left with his supplies, a messenger came with orders. Henri was to report to Nafplion the next day for military service. He had to scramble, and Avram agreed to help at the office. Today was March 24, Henri's sixth wedding anniversary. As the train slowly swayed along, Henri reflected on last night's conversation.

> "Hello, Polyagapiménos,"* Allegra said. "We're so excited! We'll be home with you in two days!"

> "I'm glad you're all coming home," he said, but he could not disguise the disappointment in his voice.

> "Henri, what's wrong?" Allegra felt a chill.

Polyagapiménos: Beloved, Darling.

"Are you all right? Has anything happened to
Avram?"

"No, we're both fine...but I have some
unbelievable news. I've just received orders
to report to Nafplion for military training. I
leave in the morning."

"What? That's impossible!"

"I wish it was. I feel horrible. I wanted to
call and wish you a happy anniversary, but
instead..." Henri's voice trailed off.

"What bad luck," he thought. "Just two days..." Henri
silently swore things couldn't get any worse, and then he
decided they probably could.

"Oh, Honey! They aren't going to make you
fight, are they?" Allegra's voice was rising in
alarm.

"They might. If this war continues, a lot of
soldiers will be needed."

"Oh, my God!" and Henri had tried to console
her, but it was futile.

Now, staring out the dirty train window for hours on
end, Henri's thoughts turned to happier days with
Allegra. He remembered the night almost two years ago

when they decided to visit New York City to attend the grand opening of the 1939 World's Fair.

> "Let's do it!" Allegra said to Henri." It will be a fabulous trip!"
>
> "All right, I'll get the ship's tickets this week. When they're confirmed, I'll wire the hotel for our reservations. Nicos knows New York and he can recommend a good one."
>
> "I'm so excited!" said Allegra.
>
> "Me, too," Henri said with a big smile, feeling the glow of happiness, seeing his bride of four years so exhilarated. "New York City! Our second honeymoon..."
>
> "I'll start packing now," said Allegra as she pulled away from him, and then playfully whirled back into his arms laughing and kissing him again.
>
> "You'll...what?" and then Henri laughed, too.

The train stopped at a station. Men got up to find a toilet, stretch their legs, and maybe get some food. Women and boys outside the train's windows were calling out to the men on board, holding up oranges, boiled eggs, and pastries for sale.

"I'll take one," Henri called to a boy selling *pasteli*.* "How much?"

"Three *drachmas*," said the boy. "Get two!"

"Give me two," and Henri passed the coins down to the boy, taking the sweets.

"*Efcharistó*,"* said Henri.

"*Parakaló*,"* the boy replied, pocketing the coins and moving along the train to find other open windows.

Henri devoured them both in a moment. Men were starting to board, and Henri settled in and let his thoughts drift again.

> *"What a shame we can't go," he'd said to Allegra. "Hitler invading Poland... It's too dangerous to cross the Atlantic. I know this is such a huge disappointment!"*
>
> *"Henri, you're right, of course," Allegra said, and Henri heard the calmness in her tone. "It's just not a good time for us to go right now."*

"Well," thought Henri, "it wasn't to be, but the day will come when the three of us will go to New York."

The train continued south, its seats filled with men

Pasteli: Sesame seed candy.

Efcharistó: Thank you.

Parakaló: You're welcome.

destined for battle training as Henri remembered meeting Allegra for the first time.

> "Nicos, how can I ever thank you?" Henri said. "You've given me practically your best accounts!"

> "You've earned them, Henri. In the last two years you've made a lot of money for my company and I'm a wealthy man; I always show my gratitude."

> "And now you're making me a wealthy man, Nicos. I owe it all to you."

> "I'll take a little credit," laughed Nicos, "but it's really you. You were clever and worked hard, and really, Henri, the debt is mine."

A half-smile of pleasure formed on Henri's face, remembering the day he told his parents.

> "I think we should move," Henri said to Avram and Myriam. "I know a nice little place on Tsimiski Street."

> "Tsimiski?" said Avram. "You must be kidding! And what will you use for money?"

> "Money? How much money do you think we need?"

"Henri," said Myriam, "save your money. That's the best advice."

"That's good advice, Mamá, but money is for spending also."

"Listen to your mother," rejoined Avram. "She knows."

"It's time we moved out of the Vardar,"* Henri insisted. "I saw this nice apartment, and there is plenty of room there for the three of us."

"You must be out of your mind," said Avram. "What would we be doing on Tsimiski?"

"I think a young upcoming businessman like me should have a nice place to live."

"That's a good idea, Henri," replied Avram, "but wait until you have the money, then you should enjoy such a blessing."

Henri pulled out a key from his pocket and put it on the kitchen table. "I bought an apartment at 93 Tsimiski. Let's move there today," he said, his eyes sparkling.

Vardar: A neighborhood working-class district in Thessaloniki.

"What?" said his father, his mouth dropping open.

"Henri!" his mother shouted.

Henri laughed involuntarily at the memory, and suddenly remembered where he was as the train swayed more than usual around a long curve.

The new apartment was too big for the three of them, so Henri took in a renter. A nice young couple with a young son moved into the extra bedroom. Victoria and Stavros Nicolaides knew Allegra's family, and had been friends for many years. It wasn't long before Victoria started talking to Henri about getting married.

"I know a girl who would be exactly right for you," Henri remembered her saying.

"Forget it, don't talk to me about getting married," Henri replied.

"I know her like I know you. You have many things in common..."

"I'm not interested."

"Henri! How can you say that?" his mother had joined in.

"Mamá! Stop. I'm too busy."

"Too busy? What are you too busy with? Too busy to have a nice wife and a family?"

"Stop it, please."

"You should listen to Victoria. She says she knows a nice girl from a good family. Why won't you listen?"

There was no stopping his mother, and then his father got into it, too.

"Yes, son," Avram said. "Make yourself happy, make your mother happy...make ME happy. What will it take just to see what she looks like? She might be just the right one for you."

Henri resisted, but their attack was relentless. One night, after repeated solicitations over several weeks, Avram broke into tears at the thought of his son being a miserable bachelor all his life.

"Why won't you?" said Avram. "Do you want to go to your grave a bachelor? Everyone is getting married except my son. All of my friends have grandbabies, but not me. My son wants to be miserable. He wants ME to be miserable. What will happen to our

family? Who will carry the family name?
Henri, why won't you just go and see this
girl?"

Henri relented.

The train whistle blew loud and long, almost disrupting
Henri's recollections. It was dark outside the train
windows, and all Henri could see was the glare of lights
from an occasional village, or the sudden flare of a
match as one of the men lit up a cigarette.

"Nicos, I need your help."

"Anything, Henri. What can I do?"

"I need you to spy for me."

Nicos smiled and his eyebrows went up. "You
need a spy? Who is the girl?" Nicos loved
intrigue, of course. He was glad to go on this
errand.

"Supposedly there is this beautiful woman I
should court and probably marry. My renter,
Victoria, says we are a perfect match. I need
you to take a look at her for me. My mother
and father won't leave me alone until I see
her and personally have a fright."

"Ah, Henri, my young man, it's about time
you found your better half. I said better half,

not bitter half!" Nicos said, barely holding back his laughter.

"You can laugh all you like," Henri retorted, "but I still need this favor so my mother and father will give me some peace!"

"I'm glad to, my friend. Where can I find your future betrothed?"

Henri ignored his comment. "Her name is Allegra Carasso, and her father owns the dye factory in town. I think she…"

"The Carasso family?"

"Yes, you know them?"

"Know them? Henri, where have you been? They are a very wealthy family. You should be so lucky!"

"That's as may be, but I have the right to marry a woman who won't shatter a mirror."

"I see the handwriting on the wall," said Nicos with a knowing smile. "I'll go over there today or tomorrow and see if I can spy on this mysterious Allegra."

It wasn't long before Nicos returned with his report. "I don't know, Henri," Nicos said. "I went to the office with the pretext of inquiring about dyes for one of my clients. There was this absolutely awful looking woman behind the desk."

"I thought so," said Henri.

"So I asked her if she was in charge," continued Nicos, with a glint in his eyes. "She was short and plump, but I know you have a fetish for women like that, so I wasn't dismayed."

"Oh, please," Henri said without humor.

"But before this radiant goddess could reply..." and Henri could hear the laughter in his friend's voice just waiting to bust, "this tall, elegant, and good-looking youngish woman came out from behind the shop door."

Suddenly Nicos had Henri's attention.

"I must say, Henri, I was very impressed, and you know I'm not easily impressed by anyone...except you, of course." The moment was too keen and both Henri and Nicos burst out laughing.

"Youngish?" asked Henri when he could control himself. "What does that mean? Certainly she isn't my grandmother's age, I hope."

"Well," Nicos began philosophically, "she is not recently out of the eggshell, but neither is she an old buzzard. If I were to guess, and I know you're going to make me guess, I would say she is just past 20. A young woman like her has probably been courted by a few men, and I imagine she's been kissed, but not more than that."

Henri reflected. "Not more than kissed? How does Nicos know these things?"

In the meantime, Allegra had also been approached by Victoria.

"Allegra, I know these three young men in my building. One is in business with his father, in glassware, and business is good, very good, but he's too fat."

"El godrito!"* Allegra's father, Mordechai, had said, and Allegra and her sisters laughed.

"And I know another," Victoria continued. "He is the director of a camp for children, and he is nice, but he's not for you." Allegra's sisters, Mathilde, Rosa, and Marika all giggled as Allegra waited to hear what was next.

_____

El godrito: "The little fatty" in Ladino.

"But there is a third one," Victoria went on, "and this young man...he's clean, studious, you should see the books he has, and he is a very good son."

"Maybe..." thought Allegra. "I'm almost 24 and most of my friends are already married with children. He has to look nice though, and have good manners."

Allegra reflected on her less-than-stellar romantic history. There had been suitors but each one was unacceptable to her father. The latest had been Zared, an employee in her father's factory. He claimed he was in love with her, and when she rejected him he swore that if she got engaged, he would kill her and then kill her fiancé. Love, passion, murder... It was with relief when Zared engaged another woman...after he was fired.

Looking out the train window, still lost in thought, Henri remembered that Victoria had arranged a meeting of the two families at *Bechtsinar*, a lovely public garden on the outskirts of Thessaloniki not far from the harbor, overlooking the bay.

Henri smiled when he thought of how both he and Allegra had each arranged code words with their parents, to tell whether the meeting was favorable or not.

"Remember, Allegra," her mother said, "I'll ask you if you've given the keys to your sister, Mathilde. If you like the young man, say yes. If he's not the one, just say no."

Henri liked what he saw. Nicos had been correct; Allegra was a beautiful young woman and she carried herself with poise and grace.

Allegra was equally charmed. She liked the way Henri answered her father's questions, and she could see he was well-mannered and had a good head.

As they were enjoying their tea, Allegra's mother, Doudoun, asked the big question, "Allegra, did you give the keys to Mathilde?"

Allegra asked, "What do you mean?" forgetting this was the secret code. Doudoun was astonished!

Henri laughed to himself as the train lurched slightly.

"Oh!" Allegra recovered. "Yes, yes, I did," she answered, surprised with herself.

Henri had also responded to his secret code in the affirmative, and as Victoria knew these codes beforehand, she said, "My dears, I am happy to say we have a match!"

Drinks were ordered, and congratulations were given and accepted. Allegra and Henri were engaged! It had happened as fast as that.

After drinks, Henri escorted Allegra to another place for the first time without her parents or her younger brother Pepo as chaperones so they could have time alone. Thinking ahead, Henri had decided to bring Allegra to the Astoria Beta on Salaminos Street, the most fashionable café in town.

"Please allow me to buy you a drink," Henri said.

"I'd like that very much," Allegra said, and she ordered a Bay Breeze.*

"That'll be fun," Henri commented. "I'll have a Brown Derby,"* he told the waiter, and then they fell into a delightful conversation, sitting together, talking, exchanging views, getting to know each other.

The band was playing "Parlami d'amore Mariu", and that's how "Speak to Me of Love, Maria" became their song. It was a big hit at the time, and Henri brought Allegra to the elegant ballroom floor for their first dance.

Bay Breeze and Brown Derby: Two stylish drinks of the time.

A happy memory.

The train slowed as it entered the camp terminal and came to a halt. "Everyone out!" yelled a sergeant, and Henri's life in the army had begun.

Chapter 11
Home Again

March 25, 1941

Allegra was so glad to be home. It was as she'd left it, except Henri was gone and she missed him terribly.

"How ironic!" she thought bitterly as she changed Andreas's diapers. "Just before we return, Henri is drafted..." Sadness pulled at her heart, and she pushed the thought of fear for his safety from her mind. "Be brave, Allegra," she told herself. "Many have suffered worse." She snapped the safety pin in place and picked up her squirming baby boy.

"Now how does that feel?" she said, smiling at her son in his fresh diaper. "Don't you feel good?" Andreas smiled at his mother, making happy sounds.

Myriam walked into the nursery. "How is my baby grandson?" she asked, walking up to the pair of them. Smiling at Andreas, she tickled him on his belly and Andreas laughed again.

"Such a happy baby!" Allegra said to her son, and then she said a silent prayer for him, and quickly added another for Henri.

"What could be keeping Avram and Daisyka?" Myriam

wondered. "I thought they'd be home by now."

"Today is March 25, Mamá. It's Greek Independence Day. There are probably a lot of people using the trolleys."

"I wish Henri was here," said Myriam. "We could all go watch the parade," and then she realized what she'd said, and looked at Allegra apologetically.

"Oh! I miss him!" Allegra said aloud, surprised her thoughts were audible.

"I know you do, dear," soothed Myriam. "He is in God's hands, and he is safe."

"I hope so," Allegra said. "I just want him here with us." She heard the front door opening, and the sound of two voices.

"That must be Avram returning with Daisyka," Allegra said.

In a moment Daisyka's bright energetic presence appeared at the nursery door.

"Hello, Allegra!" Daisyka said cheerfully, "Hello, Myriam!" Daisyka was dressed in a bright yellow floral frock and a cream blouse with puffed shoulders.

"It is so good to see you," Allegra said. "You look so pretty today!"

"Hello, dear," echoed Myriam.

"Thank you," Daisyka replied. Her eyes sought Andreas and she smiled at him. "Hello, Andreas!"

Andreas smiled broadly at the young golden-haired woman. "Daisyka!" he said.

"Look, he remembers me!" exclaimed Daisyka.

"Oh, yes," said Allegra. "You're his favorite!"

"Can I hold him?" asked Daisyka, and in a moment Andreas was settled in her arms as Daisyka waltzed him over to the nursery's window.

"I'm so glad you're back, Daisyka. It has been a long time without you!" Allegra said, relieved to let the young woman take Andreas and play. It was a blessing that she lived with them and minded Andreas during the day. "Your room is just as you left it, but we changed the linens for you."

"Thank you!" said Daisyka, smiling at Allegra, and then turned her smile toward Andreas.

Avram poked his head inside the nursery. "Hello, everyone," he said cheerfully in his deep voice. "He's so big now, isn't he, Daisyka?" Avram felt a deep warmth for his young grandson.

"Yes, he's a big boy now!" Daisyka said, happy to be home.

"Avram," asked Myriam, "will you be staying for lunch?"

"Yes," replied Avram. "Then after my nap I'm going to Aleko's for my afternoon coffee. What are we having for lunch?" Avram's belly had a sudden interest.

"I'll make a nice vegetable stew. There were some fresh zucchinis and tomatoes at the market. I also got a nice eggplant and some peppers."

"Did you also buy some olives and *feta*?"* Avram asked hopefully.

"Yes!" laughed Myriam. "I knew you would ask!" Avram smiled and Allegra laughed with her mother-in-law. "We also have fresh bread, cheese, olives, *horiatiki salata*,* and *retsina*.* You will have a good lunch, Babá," Allegra said. Avram's smile broadened considerably.

"Always with the belly," chuckled Myriam.

"Well," responded Avram, "don't tell Henri, but I missed your cooking. We did well in your absence, but you two are the best cooks in Thessaloniki." Avram knew how to

---

Feta: A pungent cheese.

Horiatiki salata: A traditional Greek salad.

Retsina: A resin-flavored wine.

apply sugar to get what he wanted. A good meal was so much better when someone else cooked it.

Allegra and Myriam laughed, but they knew his strategy and didn't mind. "I wonder what Henri is eating today," thought Allegra. She imagined Henri living in the barracks, training in the rain, firing weapons, and being drilled for combat. "Dear God," she prayed again, "please take good care of him." She caught herself as a sob rose within her. "Please God, please! Keep Henri safe and bring him home to me soon!"

The phone rang…it was Henri! "Hello, Darling!" she said, trying to stay calm.

"Hello!" said Henri. "You're home!"

"Yes, but it's not home without you. I miss you!"

"I miss you, too. Is everything all right there?"

"Yes, we're all fine," said Allegra. "Avram just brought Daisyka over, and she's playing with Andreas. Your son is getting so big, Henri!"

"I know," Henri said, unable to completely hide his sadness. "And my mother and father?"

"They are good! Myriam bought some fresh vegetables from the market. We're making a stew for lunch. I wish you were here to enjoy it with us. I want to feed you."

"You do, my love. You're feeding my heart."

"I love you, Henri. Always remember…"

"I will, Honey. I have to go…there's a long line here. Please give Andreas a big hug from his Babá, and tell him I love him."

"Yes, my darling, I will."

"I'll call in a few days. Take care of yourself and Andreas."

"You be careful! I'm worried!"

"I'll be all right," Henri said. "Goodbye. God's blessings on you and Andreas."

"And on you! Goodbye, Henri." And he was gone.

* * *

After his late afternoon nap, Avram walked along the streets in the cool air of early evening toward the White Tower and Aleko's taverna. Dozens of Greek flags hung from balconies and flagpoles, and one was even suspended from clotheslines above the street. *Bouzouki**
and martial music wafted through the damp streets in equal measure.

Bouzouki: Traditional Greek music is played on this plucked instrument that is related to the lute.

He stepped inside his friend's warm taverna. "Welcome, Avram!" Aleko called out. Several men looked up and greeted him, and to all he replied, "*Yiasou!** How is everyone?"

Avram chose one of the tables near his friends, loosened his heavy sweater and sat, the chair squeaking a bit.

"Avram," joked Costas Papapavlou, "did you have too much lunch today? You may need a stronger chair!"

"I will have a special chair made for you," Aleko added, "so I don't lose my thin profits with broken furniture!"

All the men laughed. Avram was a dear friend, and they loved to poke at him. Avram knew how to give it back.

"It is true I may need a special chair," he replied, "or how shall I carry the weight of all your foolishness?" The men laughed again, happy that Avram was with them. Aleko went to the bar to make a thick Greek coffee for Avram.

"Aleko!" called Stefanos the court clerk, "I want another!"

"And me, too!" cried Kosmas the electrician.

As Aleko walked past the radio, Costas yelled across the room, "Turn it up, Aleko! That's Sofia!"

Yiasou!: Your health!

Sofia Vembo was singing *"Children of Greece,"* and the men became quiet, listening to her soulful voice calling them to fight for liberty and "come back again with the branches of victory."

Stefanos pulled out a handkerchief when the music ended, wiped his eyes, and blew his nose loudly. "What a voice," he said. "I swear to you, when she sings 'I love you' in a song, I begin to love even my mother-in-law."

The men erupted with laughter. "And I've met his mother-in-law!" shouted Costas. "I'd rather kiss the tax man!" The laughter burst out again, and they laughed until their sides ached.

"Mother of God," said Stefanos, finally catching his breath. "Don't tell Sultana about that...," as the room roared again.

"This has been a great Independence Day," said Kosmas. "Our soldiers have made a fool of Il Duce with half the men. We might just push the bastards all the way out of Albania."

"He was a fool before we made him a fool," said Kostas.

"That's true," added Aleko. "He was an empty braggart. Beating the Ethiopians? The Albanians? How hard could that be? But the Greeks? There he ran into a steel backbone and courage."

"Even so," added Avram, "there is a greater threat." The

men nodded. They knew what Avram was going to say. "Hitler won't let Mussolini lose. I don't know if we could hold back the Germans if they crossed the borders."

"I don't think Hitler will invade us," said Costas. "He might supply the Italians, maybe send a few divisions to support the lines, but Hitler is too busy with all his other wars. We're too small and too far away to matter to him."

"Maybe," said Avram. "I hope you're right."

Stefanos lit a cigarette, picked up his coffee cup and lightly swirled its contents. "I also hope you're right," he said, "but there's only so much Herr Hitler will take. It wouldn't surprise me if we woke one day to see Nazi flags in our streets."

The cheerful happy mood was gone, the men's faces turned dour.

"There was a general call-up just the other day," said Avram. "Henri was drafted and he's in Nafplion right now."

"Really?" asked Kosmas, surprised.

"Yes, that's so," said Kostas. "Five of our union electricians were called up."

"In spite of our victories," Aleko said, "a lot of men are dead or injured. I heard a soldier on leave say the posts on the Bulgarian frontier are depleted."

"My nephew and two of his friends were bused to Nafplion yesterday," Costas said. "A lot of families are in trouble."

"It's too bad we lost Metaxas,"* added Kosmas. "He was a tough old bull. I liked the way he stood up to Il Duce."

"He was a strong leader. Koryzis* is just a puppet," said Kostas.

"He's doing well enough so far," Aleko mused. "He's only been prime minister for two months..." The talk quieted, the men lost in the thoughts of a future they could not see.

"Tell us about Andreas," Stefanos suddenly said to Avram, changing the subject to a happier topic. "Is that cheerful little grandson of yours running circles around you yet?" This brought the smiles back to the men's faces.

"Andreas..." Avram said with obvious pleasure. "Andreas is 15 months now...a big boy, and it's so good to have him home again. He started walking about two months ago, and just this morning he was reading the paper and discussing..."

The men laughed and drowned him out with their noise. It was a sweet moment, one they would long remember.

Metaxas: The deceased prime minister.

Koryzis: The new prime minister.

Chapter 12
Military Camp

March 25, 1941

Henri hung up the phone and stepped away, feeling the pit in his stomach. "They're home," he thought, "and I'm not!" The day looked bleak, even though it was Independence Day.

"Hey, Henri!" greeted Aaron. His cousin from Thessaloniki was walking toward him across the drill field.

"Hi, Aaron," replied Henri.

"I see you've got the sickness."

"Sickness?"

"Every recruit feels homesick."

"I just got off the phone with Allegra..."

"That will do it," Aaron added.

"If I was home," Henri said, "Allegra would make a special lunch, and maybe we'd see the parade, hear the cannons, and celebrate a little."

"Ah, the joys of civilian life. I've been here two weeks and it's all I can think about, except when the sergeant is making me run through the obstacle course."

Henri shook his head; this was something he was not looking forward to.

"I know you miss them," Aaron said. "What can I do to cheer you up?"

"I wish there was something you could do, but there isn't." Henri scratched his neck, the brown woolen uniform making him itchy.

"I miss Sofia, too." Aaron said with sympathy. "This is serious, Henri. We're stuck here until we're sent where they need us."

"My whole life is in Thessaloniki," Henri said, "and I may never get back there alive. What if I never see Allegra or Andreas again?"

"Put that thought out of your head, my friend," he said. "Think like that and you'll get into big trouble fast."

Henri shook off the thought, feeling the thin edge between the arms of the love of his life, or the sudden grip of death.

More than that, he now fully realized he was a small part of the immense upheaval engulfing millions across Europe...and this tidal wave of barbarism and inhumanity had finally claimed him and everybody he loved. Henri clenched his teeth against the terrifying thought.

"Come on, Henri," Aaron suggested, "let's get some food."

"The food is awful. Last night's dinner was like animal scraps. I don't know what they were serving, but it was salty and fatty and smelled bad."

"Must have been the hash," Aaron commented lightheartedly. "Not one of the better choices. It will, however, give you stamina for the long days of training resuming tomorrow."

"I'm surprised they're giving us today off."

"Me, too. With a war on, I figure every day is important."

"Privates," boomed a voice behind them, "today would be a good day to write your families, or your sweethearts. You won't have time tomorrow," said Sergeant Manikas, a tall burly soldier with dark hair and a wiry black mustache growing past the corners of his mouth.

"Yes, Sergeant," replied Aaron.

"Algava," the sergeant continued. "I don't want to see you in line tomorrow at the clinic."

Henri looked at Sergeant Manikas. "Why is that,

Sergeant?" asked Henri.

"We might be kicking the Italians' asses," the sergeant said with a smirk, "but we need more men than we have. You're not going to get a medical exam as your ticket out of here."

"Yes, Sergeant."

"Tell your friend he can save himself a lot of time and trouble, Ganis," and the sergeant walked off to intimidate others.

"Don't listen to what he says," said Aaron. "You'll see, there'll be a long line tomorrow morning."

"What should we do about food?" asked Henri. "I need something healthy, not that hash garbage."

"We can leave the base, so let's go to a taverna not far from here. Lots of soldiers go. The local tavernas are owned by farmers, so there's usually lots of fresh food."

"Sounds good," said Henri.

"I can promise a lot of fresh oranges. This is orange country, and they're really juicy and sweet."

The two men disappeared across the field and soon arrived at a taverna full of recruits enjoying the farmer's public house.

"You were right," said Henri. There was an abundance of oranges, piles of bread, and cheese, coffee, wine, olives, *baklava*,* along with the delicious fragrance of stew with spring vegetables. Henri had his Independence Day feast after all.

The day passed and the cold empty night came, and then came a day of fatigue, and then another and another, taking orders, turning right and turning left, rifle practice, running, jumping, climbing and whatever else Sergeant Manikas thought was in their best interests. A week went by, and then a second, and Henri felt his body becoming stronger.

Then, suddenly, it was a surprise to wake one morning and learn that the Germans had attacked through Bulgaria, and were pummeling the Metaxas Line* with artillery and dive bombers. In three short days the whole northern defense had collapsed and the Nazi flag was flying in Thessaloniki.

Baklava: A sweet pastry made with honey and nuts.

Metaxas Line: A defensive military line of fortifications protecting Greece's northern border with Bulgaria.

Chapter 13
Swastikas on Tsimiski Street

April 8, 1941

The German invasion on April 6 was sudden and swift. Unwilling to let Mussolini fail because of military concerns about southern European exposure, Hitler sent Stukas* and artillery to pummel the Metaxas Line. In spite of extremely determined resistance by the depleted Greek army over a three-day period, the Wehrmacht* and panzers* finally pushed into northern Greece. Some Greek forts held on, but were bypassed by the advancing German army, managing to hold their positions until heavy German guns obliterated them.

The German army occupied Thessaloniki on April 8, 1941, and the next day, on April 9, the Greek Second Army surrendered unconditionally. German Field Marshal List made plans to move his Twelfth Army south into central Greece, and then on to Athens.

Germany's attack of Greece in support of the ineffective Italian forces delayed the invasion of the Soviet Union until late June, and may have cost Hitler the war...

Stukas: German warplanes used for dive-bombing and ground-attack.

Wehrmacht: The German Army.

Panzers: German tanks.

German tanks and personnel carriers, troop trucks, staff cars and motorcycles moved into and through Thessaloniki, occupying without resistance, taking control of its streets and intersections, waterfront and dockyards, banks, government buildings, police headquarters, newspapers, radio stations...the Germans rolled into the city, absorbing it like a giant wave from the sea.

"How?" Allegra said to Avram. "How has everything changed so quickly? Just last week, no...just four days ago we were safe!"

Slumped in his chair, Avram replied. "What do they want from us? Olive oil?"

Stunned, Allegra realized how illusory their safety had been. "We were never safe. Never! I've been living in a dream. How foolish of me!" she thought.

The unwelcome sounds of loud motorcycles on the street outside and the sound of shouting men made the fear clutch at her heart. It was hard to breathe.

"*Schnell!*"* commanded a voice below her window. Allegra looked down, peering from the window's corner behind the lacy curtain. What she saw took her breath away and filled her with horror. A German army truck was parked on the sidewalk and soldiers were jumping

---

Schnell: Hurry!

out the back. The soldiers were commanded by a big sergeant, and he was loud and angry.

"Oh, my God!" she thought. "They're really here!" It was shocking to see German soldiers so close to her home and her baby...her Jewish baby.

Allegra felt sick and wanted to throw up. She knew Hitler and the Germans blamed the Jews for decades of misery...and here they were, right outside her window! "What am I to do?"

A feeling of helplessness consumed her and she felt faint, the rising red fog flooding her brain, but she fought and pushed the scream away from her lips. Forcing herself to breathe, she came back from the edge of the abyss.

Shaky, she fell onto the sofa, her mind numb. Feeling the slumbering coals within her blow into embers, a heat grew into a fire of resolve to fight and endure whatever hardships lay ahead.

Avram came into the room and saw Allegra on the sofa. "Are you all right?"

Allegra spoke softly. "I will be all right," she replied. "I believe all of us will be all right."

Avram went to the window and looked down on the activity below. "Night has fallen in the middle of the day," was all he said.

As he left the room, Myriam appeared. "Go to Allegra," he softly advised. "She needs you." He walked to the front door of the apartment, put on his heavy sweater and hat, and left. He was going to Aleko's to learn what the others knew.

Myriam went to Allegra in the semi-darkened room and sat beside her, putting her arm around Allegra's shoulder. "I'm all right, Mother," Allegra said, quietly. Myriam held her, silently.

Chapter 14
*"Saloniki ist in deutscher Hand!"**

April 9, 1941

Henri felt like someone had reached into his chest and yanked out his heart.

"The Nazis are in Thessaloniki!" he thought. "What's happening to Allegra and Andreas? My mother, and my father...?"

"My God, Henri," said Aaron. "How did this happen?"

"I don't know! I want to go home and be with Allegra and Andreas."

"Do that," said Aaron, "and you'll be shot as a deserter."

"I didn't say I would," replied Henri.

"Besides," added Aaron, "even if we did get out of camp, the whole German Army is coming this way."

"There's nothing we can do," Henri said dismally. "I tried

**Saloniki ist in deutscher Hand!*": "Thessaloniki is in German hands!" These words were spoken by an announcer in a German newsreel showing panzers, trucks, and German troops occupying Thessaloniki.

calling Allegra, but the lines are down. I couldn't get through."

"The Germans probably cut them," Aaron guessed, "or our troops are blowing up bridges, roads, communications…"

Henri shook his head in bitter dismay, hopelessness in his eyes. "There's absolutely nothing we can do."

"We better report to the sergeant or he'll kick our ass," Aaron advised.

"It's already been kicked," said Henri, and the two men headed off to find their unit.

For the next two weeks, Sergeant Manikas and Lietenant Petinos drilled the unit from before dawn until long after dark, preparing them for combat with bayonet and target practice.

One thought was consistent. "Will I ever see Allegra and Andreas again?" Henri wondered. Henri felt he was being prepared for the slaughter. "What chance do I have against veteran German shock troops with combat experience?"

The news blackout at the camp was complete, but at night Henri, Aaron and the others went to the local taverna and listened to the Athens Radio broadcasts. The German army was rapidly approaching, consuming everything in its path. Though the British were resisting, it was too late. The *Luftwaffe** had fought the RAF* over Athens and silenced them, and the *Wehrmacht* would soon be on the outskirts of Athens. The situation was hopeless, and the knot in Henri's stomach grew bigger and tighter as the disaster came closer.

* * *

Something was wrong. In the semi-dark, Henri couldn't tell what it was, but it wasn't good. He sat up in his bunk. The other men were breathing heavily. Sleepy, Henri held up his watch and saw the slender fluorescent hands pointing to 4:30 a.m.

Surprised that Sergeant Manikas hadn't come bursting in, booming his usual "Wake up, Troops! Five minutes to formation!" created Henri's further confusion.

He got up, slipped on his pants, shoes, military jacket and cap, and opened the barrack's door half expecting to run into Sergeant Manikas, but the sergeant was not there.

The entire camp was quiet. No one was around except a few early risers like Henri. He entered Aaron's barracks and found his sleeping cousin.

Luftwaffe: The German Air Force.
RAF: The British Royal Air Force.

"Aaron! Wake up," Henri whispered, pushing on his cousin's shoulder. Henri shook his shoulder again.

"Wake up!"

"What is it?" Aaron began to rouse.

"It's me, Henri," he said in a low voice, not quite a whisper. "Get dressed. Something's wrong."

"What's wrong?"

"I don't know, but get up! Get dressed. We need to go."

"Go where?"

"Just get up. All I know is we have to go."

Aaron slipped out of bed, fumbling in the dark, and followed Henri outside. It was chilly and damp, and their eyes began to tear up.

"What's going on?" Aaron asked when they passed through the door.

"It's about five o'clock and the camp is too quiet."

"You got me up..." Aaron started to complain, and then, "You're right, something's wrong." He stopped and looked around. "Where is everybody?"

"I don't know. Manikas didn't wake us up, and I don't see any..."

"Officers! There aren't any officers?"

"Yes, I think they're gone! Let's check..."

Headquarters was empty. No one was making breakfasts in the mess hall, and the medical facility was abandoned...everyone except the sleeping troops had disappeared!

"We better go, too," said Henri, "right away!"

"I'm going to change out of this uniform," said Aaron. "Let's get into our civilian clothes."

"Good idea," Henri agreed. "Meet back here."

A few minutes later Henri and Aaron hopped the fence and blended into the darkness, the lights of the training camp receding behind them as they ran across the dew-drenched fields and vanished.

The light green leaves from the foliage above their heads provided cool shade from the late morning sun. Henri and Aaron had favored the fields and woods as they cut through the countryside.

"What do you think, Henri?" asked Aaron.

"I never expected to be hiding under olive trees on the Sabbath," he said, scanning the hills, reassuring himself no one was watching them.

"I'm glad we decided not to go to Nafplion. There will probably be a lot of men going there once they realize the officers abandoned them."

"Yes, that was smart."

"And I'm glad you've got a friend in Athens."

"Maurice will put us up," said Henri. "You can see the Acropolis from his rooftop. His apartment faces the west side, a beautiful view. Allegra and I went to Athens for our honeymoon. I have happy memories."

"I look forward to it." Aaron changed the subject. "Before we get started again, we should decide if we're going to Athens by land or sea."

"Both are dangerous. With the German army moving south, do you think we'll run into refugees?"

"I doubt it," replied Aaron. "I think people will stay indoors."

"Even so, it would be faster by sea. We could be in Athens in a few hours instead of days."

"But if we go by sea we're more exposed. On land we can hide better," Aaron countered.

"What do you think we should do?"

"Let's flip a coin," suggested Aaron.

Henri reached into his pocket and pulled out a 10 *drachma* coin. "Here's one."

"Let's see it," said Aaron.

"What? You think it's got two heads?"

"No!" laughed Aaron. "I want to see the coin you're betting our lives on."

Henri tossed him the silver 10 *drachma* coin.

Aaron looked at it and said, "Ten *drachmas*? You want me to bet my life on a 10 *drachma* coin?"

"Do you have better?" asked Henri.

Aaron reached into his pocket and pulled out a few coins. Looking in his palm, he selected one. "Shall we bet our lives on a 20 *drachma* coin?"

Henri laughed nervously. "All right, then. How about heads by land and tails by sea?"

"Yes," said Aaron. "Ready?"

"Go ahead. Flip."

They watched as the little coin rapidly spun their fate between heads and tails.

Chapter 15
Perilous Escape

April 26, 1941

The German advance on Athens was slowed by British, Greek and Allied army units fighting and destroying bridges and roads as they retreated. It was evident the Allies would be unable to stop the German advance. Meanwhile, in Thessaloniki, German officers set up administrative offices in key buildings. German troops on leave walked about without weapons since resistance was nonexistent.

Aleko brought coffees to the three men talking quietly at the table in the back. They stopped for a moment and nodded appreciation.

"It's not the best," said Aleko, "but it's the best I have. The only beans in Thessaloniki are the ones people are hoarding."

"I guess it's going to be a while until we have real coffee again," said Kosmas.

"Another reason to hate the Germans," said Marcos. He smoothed his long black mustache with his fingers, then picked up the cup of chickpea coffee, taking a tepid sip. He tried not to make a face. "I don't know which I miss more," he said, "the coffee or the sugar."

"Well," added Avram, "at least for now our cigarettes aren't rationed." He took out his pack of *Papastratos Numero Ena** and offered them to the others.

"This will make the coffee taste better," Marcos reflected as he pulled one from the pack. "Thank you."

"I'd like one," said Kosmas.

"Take," offered Avram. "For you?" Avram asked Aleko.

Aleko shook his head. "Thanks."

Avram struck a match and Marcos and Kosmas leaned forward to light up.

"At least the tobacco is good." Marcos Hombitis breathed in a long draw of smoke, and slowly let it out. His face relaxed. "I got a visit today from Lieutenant Scheidel."

"What about?" asked Kosmas.

"He came into the customs office wanting to see my files on who's been importing radios."*

Papastratos Numero Ena: A popular brand of cigarettes.

Radios: Radios and newspapers were the primary sources of news and information. The Germans wanted to confiscate all the radios so citizens could not learn what was happening outside their immediate area, making their propaganda the only source of information.

Avram looked at Marcos. "What did you tell him?"

"I told him I couldn't find the files. I made an excuse, and he said he'd be back. He was convincing about that. I can only delay him so long. If Henri has any supplies left, you should sell them as soon as possible."

"Thank you, Marcos."

Kosmas spoke up. "What kind of supplies does Henri have? Our electrician's union might be able to take those off your hands."

"I know Henri has some radio parts, and auto parts, too. I'll get you an inventory list."

Marcos nodded. "I can hold off the little Nazi another day or two."

"I'll bring the list today," Avram said to Kosmas.

"Good," Kosmas replied. "If the union can't buy everything, maybe I can find others who will."

✳ ✳ ✳

It was dark as Henri and Aaron approached the outskirts of Epidaurus after hiking up and down soggy, hilly meadows. A few rides in farm trucks had saved them from blistered feet and the sun-baking heat of a spring day. Their last ride at sunset brought them to the end of their 50-kilometer trip, sweat chilling their lower backs as the day's heat yielded to the cool offshore breeze.

"We're almost there," Aaron said in a parched voice.

"Yes," Henri answered. He was reflecting on the irony that all his physical training had only served the single purpose of helping him flee the army he had been expected to serve. "Although," he thought, "if I didn't have the training, I might not have made it to Epidaurus in one day."

"If we get a ship tonight," Aaron said, "we could be in Athens by morning."

"I hope we do," replied Henri. "It's only 40 kilometers to Piraeus* but it saves about two days of travel."

They followed the road down the hill into the village, winding past quiet homes, a few lights to guide their way. At the docks, a few fishermen stood near the swaying boats, talking quietly. The tang of the briny sea filled Henri's nostrils.

"*Kalispéra*,"* said Henri.

"*Kalispéra*," replied one of the fishermen.

Piraeus: A port city 11 kilometers south of Athens.
Kalispéra: Good evening.

"My friend and I want to go to Piraeus tonight. Do you know anyone who can take us there?"

"Yes," the man said. He was tall and thin and had a full dark beard. "I'm sailing in two hours; we'll be there by dawn." He adjusted his fisherman's cap. "It will cost you 4,000 *drachmas* each."

"4,000 each? That's pretty steep."

"It's a dangerous night," said the man.

Henri understood there was no room to negotiate. If they wanted to cross tonight, they would have to pay.

"That much money," said Henri, "and you leave us almost nothing on the other side." Henri did not expect the man to lower his price, but didn't want him to think he could raise it higher.

"It is your choice not to go."

"I want to talk with my friend," said Henri evenly.

"As you wish."

Henri and Aaron conferred in the dark. "I don't see that we have much choice," said Aaron.

"I agree. We have the cash. Let's take our chances. We've done well so far." Henri returned to the group of sailors.

"All right. We won't have enough for a pair of coffees when we get there, but we'll go with you. Is this the boat?" asked Henri.

"The coffee isn't any good anyway," the captain said. "Yes, this is my ship. What are your names?"

"I am Henri Algava."

"I'm Aaron Ganis."

"I'm Stephanos Liakos," the captain said. The men drew closer and shook hands. Henri could see he was weather-worn, and everything about Liakos felt serious. "It will be a long night and a dangerous trip. Do you see the taverna there?" the captain asked. "Stay there and I will come for you. Don't drink too much or you may regret it."

The two men with Liakos laughed lightly.

Henri smiled. "Thanks for the advice. We'll be all right."

"You can pay me when you board."

"Good. We'll be waiting," said Henri, and he and Aaron went to get food and something to drink as the evening sky darkened.

It was a moonless sky. Captain Liakos ordered his men to

release the mooring lines of the *Mikri Omorfiá** and push off from the Epidaurus dock. The ship's engine made a steady thrumming sound as the *Little Beauty* headed into the darkness with about 30 passengers.

"It's crowded," Henri said to Aaron.

"I hope we don't sink."

The air was cool, and became colder as the little ship picked up speed; the shoreline with its few twinkling lights receded. As the little ship cleared the harbor, the order was given to extinguish all lights, including cigarettes. Only the few sparks rising from the ship's smokestack were visible.

"I'm staying on deck," said Aaron. "They're all throwing up down below."

"I love a sea cruise," joked Henri. "Breathe that fresh air!" The salty breeze on his face and the sound of the little ship carving the waters was refreshing.

An hour later, just after midnight, they heard the sound of airplanes overhead. Liakos slowed his ship in the middle of the open sea.

"Michos!" he ordered, "Cover the smokestack!"

———————

Mikri Omorfiá: Little Beauty.

Michos grabbed some empty burlap bags they had for this purpose and threw a bucket of seawater on them. Climbing onto the pilot house, he draped the wet cloth over the top of the smokestack, allowing the smoke to rise but dousing the sparks.

Liachos shifted gears and the ship resumed its speed. Henri heard more planes rumbling in the sky nearby, their droning engines a terrifying threat. "There's only darkness to conceal us," he thought, his heart beating quickly.

"Those are dive bombers," said Aaron. "They may see us, but more frightening are the German patrol boats. They will sink us. Keep your eyes on the surface of the water."

Mixing with the thunder of the airplanes' engines were distant, sudden explosions, the night sky lighting up erratically like a lightning storm, their little boat briefly appearing and disappearing in the darkness.

"My God!" cried Aaron, "they're bombing our naval base on Salamis!"

Henri saw the flashes and heard the muffled explosions. They were about 20 kilometers away and the explosions grew louder and more frightening as their little ship plowed past the island under attack.

"We might be seen," said Henri. Looking up, he saw Liachos through the bridge window during the flashes. Henri said an earnest prayer.

The explosions grew louder and more frightening. Only a dozen kilometers offshore, everyone could see the bombardment as the German dive bombers obliterated the port, sudden flashes of light briefly brightening the night, the sound of distant thudding explosions rolling across the black water toward them.

Soon after, Henri turned to Aaron. "It looks like this is as close as we're going to get," relieved that the ship was pulling away. But then they saw explosions in front of their ship, and knew what it meant. "Now they're bombing Piraeus!" Henri exclaimed.

By the time dawn arrived, the *Mikri Omorfiá* was south of Piraeus, tying up to a dock on the tiny island of Koulouri. *Stukas* were dive-bombing the port; the whistling bombs and steady explosions only a few kilometers away made Henri realize how lucky he and Aaron were to be alive.

"Thank you, Captain," Henri said as he and Aaron disembarked, uncertain what would happen next.

"Lord Jesus have mercy on you," said Liakos.

"And on you," Henri said, as he stepped off the *Little Beauty* onto the quay.

"Let's go," said Aaron. "We can be in Athens in about two hours."

Chapter 16
A Changing Landscape

April 25, 1941

Soon after the German occupation began, the calculated isolation and destruction of Thessaloniki's Jewish community started. Anti-Jewish sentiments were encouraged, and all Jewish newspapers were prohibited and replaced with two pro-Nazi daily newspapers, "New Europe" and "Evening Press." New Europe blamed the Jews for Germany's difficulties and reestablished the EEE,* the anti-Semitic organization that had attacked and burned down Camp Campbell ten years before.

New Europe soon announced that all Jews were required to turn in their radios. Members of the Jewish Community Council were arrested and the Council replaced. Rabbi Tzvi Koretz,* the Grand Rabbi of Thessaloniki, was arrested by the Gestapo on charges of conspiring with Jewish communities in other countries and sent to a concentration camp in Vienna.

Allegra was stunned. She couldn't believe what she was seeing. The large sign in the bakery window read "No Jews Allowed."

EEE: *Ethniki Enosis Ellados*, the National Union of Greece.

Rabbi Tzvi Koretz: See next page.

Allegra's stomach tightened and she felt her face grow red with insult. Caught off guard, she felt humiliated. The feeling was quick and sharp, and she was angry!

Allegra opened the bakery's door and stepped inside.

"*Kyría* Algava..." said Lavinia, the baker's wife, standing behind the counter just inside the door. Allegra saw Lavinia's surprise, and the short plump woman's embarrassment was evident.

"Good morning, *Kyría* Houvarda," Allegra said, measuring the woman. Allegra's eyes met hers, and Lavinia looked away quickly, uncertain what to do. The other customers in the store grew quiet, realizing, watching, anticipating... "I see you have some very nice pastries this morning," Allegra said with difficulty, keeping her voice steady and firm.

"*Kyría* Algava..." Lavinia began. She stopped, not knowing what to say. The room was absolutely quiet.

Kyría: Mrs.

Rabbi Tzvi Koretz: A controversial figure, he was brought to Thessaloniki by the city's Jewish leaders who wanted a more modern approach to Judaism. Soon after the German invasion, the rabbi was imprisoned, later released to preside over the Jewish community during the deportations. Rabbi Koretz was sent to Bergen-Belson and died of typhus three months after its liberation by the Russians. He was suspected of being a collaborator by deliberately misleading the Jewish community, though this remains unsubstantiated.

Allegra softened when she saw Lavinia's distress. "We've been good customers and friends for years," Allegra began, looking for the words to express her hurt and disappointment.

"I know, I know..." Lavinia replied, almost in tears. "But what am I to do? What can I do?" and the tears began rolling down her face.

Allegra looked away from Lavinia's face and saw the faces of the other customers in the bakery. Some were blank, some were cruel, some looked away. No one stood up to intervene.

Looking back at Lavinia, their eyes met one final time. "It's all right," Allegra said. "I understand." Allegra turned and stepped out of the bakery, the door closing behind her with the sound of permanence, a sound she would remember the rest of her life.

* * *

Three hours later, Aaron and Henri stood outside Maurice's apartment building on Figalios Street in Athens. It had taken longer than expected to travel the 11 kilometers. Several towers of heavy smoke were visible when they looked back toward the port. German warplanes flew overhead, their raucous engines a menacing reminder of the immediate threat bearing down on Athens.

It was not quite 8:00 a.m. when Henri rang the bell of

his friend's apartment. Henri and Aaron heard a window open above their heads, and there was Maurice, leaning out to see.

"Henri? My God, what are you doing here? Don't tell me, I'll be right down!"

They could hear the sound of footsteps rapidly descending and in a moment the door flung open and Maurice grabbed Henri for a big hug.

"How good to see you!" Maurice loudly proclaimed. He looked quickly at Aaron. "Both of you!" and then, as if he was only now seeing more than just their faces, Maurice said, "Look at you! What happened? Were you in the fighting at the port? Are you all right?"

Before they could answer, Maurice had looked them over from top to bottom.

"Thank God you're not hurt!" he said. "Come upstairs! This is your friend? My name is Maurice. Both of you can take a bath, put on some fresh clothes, and I have lots of bread and cheese and grapes and I made *moussaka** last night. There's plenty!"

"Thank you, Maurice. It's so good to see you!" said Henri, and Aaron quickly agreed.

Moussaka: A special Greek entrée typically made of eggplant, meat and tomato sauce.

"Come on, come on," urged Maurice. "Come upstairs and I'll start the bathwater. It looks like you can both use some scrubbing."

Maurice quickly had the water heating and a welcome spread of *feta*, crackers, grapes, and bread. As the water heated and Maurice warmed the oven for the *moussaka*, the men sat at Maurice's table by the window, facing the Acropolis.* The Parthenon* had a beautiful glow in the early morning sunlight, its 2,000 year old magnificence proudly dominating the view.

"Do you remember, Maurice, when I introduced you to my bride?"

"It is the highlight of my life!" Maurice boomed. "How is Allegra? And your son? I would love to see them, but with this invasion..."

"With God's blessing, the day will come. The last I heard, Allegra and Andreas were fine."

"I remember when we met at the café and enjoyed a bottle." Maurice winked at Aaron "...or two! We toasted your long life and happiness!"

"It was a wonderful time," said Henri. "I remember I took Allegra to the Parthenon." He turned to Aaron and explained. "It was our honeymoon, about six years ago,

_____

Acropolis: The ancient citadel in Athens, site of the Parthenon.

Parthenon: An ancient temple from the fifth century B.C. dedicated to the goddess Athena, the city's patron.

remember? You were at our wedding. We had our photo taken on the Acropolis."

"I think I saw that photo," reflected Aaron. "Isn't that the one in your dining room?"

"Yes, that's right. Well, it was a wonderful week here in Athens. We went out dining and dancing, stayed at a lovely hotel, were treated like royalty by Maurice..."

"You deserve it, Henri," Maurice said as he checked the moussaka.

"...and we toured the city and saw all the sights! It was marvelous." Henri smiled at a memory or two...

Maurice was busy with the hot water, heating several pots, and the cheerful *bouzouki* music from the radio was pleasant. Enjoying the food, they were all surprised when the music suddenly stopped in the middle of a song.

Glancing up from the stove, Maurice looked at the lights in his apartment, but the bulbs were still lit. "It's not the power..." he said in a wondering voice.

After a few moments of silence, the radio began playing the national anthem, "The Hymn to Liberty." When the anthem ended, a station announcer read an official statement; everyone was to stay in their homes until further notice.

Maurice, Henri and Aaron looked at each other, surprised.

"What's that?" asked Aaron, hearing a deep rumbling outside that was growing louder. Maurice looked out the window and up and down the street but saw nothing.

"Let's go to the roof," he said and led the way. From above they could see the white jumble of apartment buildings filling the landscape.

"They're still bombing the port," Henri said, seeing the plumes of smoke in the bright blue sky. Several airplanes were flying over the city

"That's the *Luftwaffe*," said Maurice.

Henri was the first to spot the advancing army. "Look over there!" he pointed. The squeaking of the metal treads and wheels rose above the ponderous sound of heavy engines. Motorcycles and armored cars rolled past cafés and stores. The German army had entered the city with no resistance.

A few minutes later Maurice spotted German soldiers on the Acropolis. Henri's throat tightened as he saw the blue-and-white Greek flag struck from the flagpole and the German war flag with its ugly black swastika raised in its place.

The feeling of loss was tremendous, their beloved

Athens under the heel of the Nazis was too awful for words. Maurice threw his cigarette down and crushed it with his foot. "Those bastards."

"We need to get back to Thessaloniki," said Aaron. "We should leave before we get stuck here."

"Yes," agreed Maurice. "The sooner you leave, the better for all of us."

"We need to figure out how to get home," mused Henri.

"I'll ask around," said Maurice. "I have a few friends who truck up to Thessaloniki. Maybe they can get you a ride. I'll see what I can do."

"That would be great!"

"It's nothing, Henri," Maurice replied. "I would do anything for you. You are my friend." Maurice laughed, "I was brought up by a good mother and father, and they taught me to always help a friend in need!"

The three men laughed.

"I'm hungry!" Maurice grinned. "Come on. Let's get some food! Oh! The bath water is probably cold by now!" and he led them from the roof.

Not far away, the flag with its sinister black swastika fluttered in the ghostly breeze that flowed across the high rocky citadel and the ancient Greek temple.

* * *

The truck carrying Henri and Aaron was noisy and belched smelly fumes. Vasos, the driver, enjoyed the curving bumpy roads as he sang, mangling the melodies and lyrics of popular songs.

"*Ba*,"* thought Henri, "this guy sings like a rooster!" but he chuckled at the driver's antics and good humor.

Vasos slowed the truck as they approached a check point. "Get your papers out," he said. "These animals will want to see them."

They rolled up and stopped. Vasos rolled down his window and cheerfully greeted the German soldier. "*Kalimera!*"*

"Where are you going?" the soldier asked.

Vasos replied in German. "Thessaloniki. We have a load of building supplies."

The soldier took their papers and studied them as another soldier looked in the back.

"All right," he said, returning the papers. "There will be

Ba: A common Greek interjection showing admiration, amazement, refusal and sarcasm.

Kalimera: Good morning.

detours. Roads and bridges have been destroyed. On your way."

The truck was waved through and Vasos resumed his cheery nature. Lighting another cigarette, he said, "Did you know I used to be a deckhand? I worked on freighters bound for India and Africa. That was before I sold carpets at the Grand Bazaar in Istanbul." There was a twinkle in his eyes.

Aaron easily saw through him. "Really? Tell us about that," and the next few hours passed in good humor. Henri told his story about the time he was apprenticed to a famous chef in Paris, and Aaron topped that with his balloon race over the Alps. There was a lot of laughter, and the miles and hours fell steadily away. Endless delays for check points, troop convoys moving south, and constant detours to bypass broken bridges and damaged roads turned a single day's journey into eight.

"Allegra...how is she? Andreas?" This was Henri's constant thought. His anxiety made it difficult to keep still as the truck slowly traveled north, but at last the bumpy, smelly journey came to an end.

Relieved to be home, what they saw no longer looked like home. German troops were everywhere, strolling the sidewalks without weapons. An occasional troop truck with the *Balkenkreuz** insignia drove by; a flag with a swastika hung from a government building.

Vasos dropped them near the White Tower and waved a cheerful farewell, and Henri and Aaron parted company. "Goodbye, good luck!" and each headed off to learn the fate of his family.

Henri's steps soon brought him to Tsimiski Street. Agitated, not knowing what to expect, he entered the building and walked up the stairs to the second floor. Home! Or was this still home? Was his family inside these walls?

Henri took a deep breath and knocked on the door.

Balkenkreuz: The military cross that was the emblem of the Wehrmacht.

Chapter 17
Cat and Mouse

May 5, 1941

"Who is it?" said a voice within.

"Allegra! It's me!"

The door opened instantly and Allegra ran into his arms. "Henri!" and she held him tightly. Unable to speak, Henri gratefully held her. He smelled her soft fragrance, her hair tickling his cheek as he felt the tears streaming down his face. They held each other like that for a long moment, and then Allegra kissed him and pulled him inside their apartment.

"I was so worried!" She said, tears subsiding.

"I tried to call you many times," said Henri, "but the phone lines are dead. I couldn't reach you."

"I know, dear," Allegra replied. "We tried to reach you, too, but we couldn't. Oh, darling, I'm so glad you're home and safe! It's been almost three months since I kissed you!"

She hugged him again, and kissed him again, and he felt her love, strong and deep.

After another welcome moment holding her, Henri asked, "How is Andreas? How are my parents?"

"Come look," said Allegra, and she took Henri by the hand and led him to the nursery. Before Allegra and Henri could get there, Myriam, hearing the commotion, came out of her room to greet her son.

"Henri!"

"Mamá!" he said and they hugged.

"Are you all right?" Myriam asked.

"I'm fine," Henri replied. "I'm still in one piece!"

"*Doxa to Theo!*"* his mother said.

"Come to the nursery," Allegra said, and pulled Henri by the hand.

"Yes! Yes!" said Myriam. "Go see your son! He is almost a man!" she laughed.

In the nursery at last, Henri saw Andreas...almost a year and a half old...and Andreas recognized his father immediately. "Babá!" Andreas called from his crib.

Henri reached over and picked him up, high above his head, and then to his chest.

Doxa to Theo!: Glory to God!

"Andreas," Henri said, "what a big boy you are! I missed you!" and Andreas reached for his father's face with his little boy hands, and laughed, and touched his father's cheek and mouth and nose and forehead happily.
As Henri smiled, Allegra's arm around his waist and Myriam smiling at the door, the four of them, happy again, for the moment.

✳ ✳ ✳

"So that's what I did," said Avram, explaining how he sold all of Henri's remaining radio and auto parts inventory, making quite a bit of cash for his son.

"That was so smart of you!" said Henri.

"Well, I did have a little help. Marcos Hombitis and Kosmas...you really have them to thank," finished Avram.

"To your health!" said Henri, lifting his cup of coffee in gratitude to the men at the taverna's table.

"*Yiasou*," said Marcos with a smile.

"My pleasure," said Kosmas. "Those radio parts and auto supplies will come in handy, and they're safely hidden, I assure you."

The men looked at each other and smiled slyly.

"Now when that ugly pup, Lieutenant Scheidel, comes by, he can examine your empty office and storeroom as much as he likes, even until the day Hitler shaves off his moustache!" Marcos said with a grin, stroking his own thick *moustakia*.* The men at the table chuckled to think about the eternally damned lieutenant.

"Yes," added Avram. "He's been by three times already, I heard."

"How do you know?" asked Henri.

"Takis, the building manager," Avram replied. "He said a German lieutenant was looking for you..."

Henri felt a chill...

"...so Takis told the lieutenant you never came back from the war."

The men chuckled again, amused by the little joke.

"So what will you do now?" asked Aleko.

"I may become your very best customer," replied Henri.

"Not possible," said Aleko. "Your father already has that honor!"

The men smiled, enjoying the ribbing.

Moustakia: Mustache.

"I have an idea," said Marcos, "so you can make some money and maybe a living. I know a few men in the textile trade who have large inventories of British cloth... You should talk to them. They might give you a good price on quantities, and you can open another shop and sell the fabrics at retail."

"That's a good idea," Henri speculated.

"I like it," said Avram. "When can you put Henri in touch with these people?"

"Give me a day or two," replied Marcos. "I'll see if they're interested, and then arrange a meeting. What do you think, Henri?"

"Yes, let's get started," Henri decided. "I want to get back into business!"

* * *

"Of course, *Kýrios* Straka," Henri said. "These are very good prices. I think you'll be pleased with this purchase. Imports from the English mills are excellent quality."

"I like the subtle design," said *Kýrios* Straka. "The suit will look very fashionable, I think."

"I agree. It's a good choice. Shall I have your cloth delivered to your tailor, or would you prefer *Kýrios* Papadakis to send for them?"

"Yes, if you don't mind, please have him send someone. That would be very kind of you," *Kýrios* Straka concluded.

"Very well. And I hope you will come again when you want more suits. I'll be happy to give you my best prices," said Henri, showing his customer to the front door.

"Good day," *Kýrios* Straka said pleasantly, but his demeanor changed as two German soldiers entered the shop. *Kýrios* Straka left in sudden haste.

Henri noticed with alarm that the German soldiers were accompanied by Panos, one of Henri's commissioned salesmen. The fool had brought German soldiers into his shop!

"Gentlemen," Henri began in his best German, hoping his voice was steady. "How can I help you?"

"*Kýrios* Algava," said Panos, "may I introduce Private Oberhauser and Private Wahrmann? I met them at a taverna on Mitropoleos Street. They want to buy some special cloth and have their suits made. Gentlemen, this is Mr. Algava."

"I'd be delighted to show you my best cloth," Henri said. Henri's mind was racing. His only thought was to get these soldiers out of his shop as fast as possible. He was furious with Panos, but could say nothing.

"What are you interested in?" Henri asked. "I have some

very fine cloth imported from England, or perhaps you would like some excellent local cloth."

The two soldiers stepped forward, looking about the shop, assessing the quantity and quality of Henri's inventory.

"We don't want any local cloth," said Private Oberhauser. "Isn't that right, Steffen? We want the English fabric."

"Yes, Albert. We want the best." The soldier looked at Henri, studying his face.

"Very well, gentlemen," said Henri. "Let me show you what I have." Panos was unaware of the cat and mouse game being played in front of him. Henri proceeded to display his best British cloth, the soldiers taking their time, looking carefully at everything.

"How many meters of cloth will I need?" asked Private Oberhauser.

"Both of you are about two meters tall, so I think you should buy three and a half meters of cloth; I suggest four meters to be on the safe side."

The Germans looked closely at Henri and went back to examining the stacks of cloth growing on the counter. When Henri had laid out more than a dozen bolts, Private Wahrmann had seen enough.

"You are a Jew, yes?" Private Wahrmann asked. "I heard

that Jews charge too much."

"How much will you expect us to pay for four meters of cloth," asked Private Oberhauser, "especially since we only need three and a half meters?"

Panos suddenly understood the danger, and now looked panicky. What had at first seemed like a good idea for a nice commission was now an obvious end to his relationship with Henri. He thought seriously about running for the door.

Henri forced himself to keep his mind clear. "Of course I will give you a very good price," he said. "I will sell the fabric to you at pre-war prices, much less than they would cost today, a very good value for you."

The two soldiers looked at each other and looked back at Henri.

"Yes," Private Oberhauser said, "we want the lowest price."

"Make sure you give us your best price, Jew," said the other soldier. The threat made Henri's throat dry and he had to steel himself to keep his hands and voice steady.

"I think you will be very pleased," said Henri. "I normally sell this cloth for 2,000 *drachmas* per meter, but I will be pleased to let you have it for 2,000 *drachmas* for all four meters."

"That is a good deal," said Private Wahrmann. "What do you think, Albert?"

"*Ach, ja,*"* replied Private Oberhauser with a big smile. "I think it is a very good deal."

"*Das ist gut,*"* Private Wahrmann confirmed. "Wrap it up for us, Jew."

"Of course," replied Henri, glad the transaction was almost done. He quickly cut the four meters of cloth for each soldier and wrapped the two sets in brown paper.

"Here you are, gentlemen," said Henri.

"Thank you," said Private Oberhauser, picking up his package and walking to the door.

"Yes," said Private Wahrmann. "Goodbye."

"You have not paid for the cloth yet," replied Henri, looking at the soldier without wavering.

"Oh!" said Private Wahrmann. "Albert, we haven't paid the Jew yet. Come back and pay the Jew."

Private Oberhauser was by the front door, where Panos was standing, looking down at his shoes.

Ach, ja: Oh, yes.
Das ist gut: This is good.

"How could we forget, Steffen?" he said. "The Jew must always be paid."

The two German soldiers looked at Henri and laughed, and then dug into their pants for their billfolds.

They each took out a quantity of bills and threw them on the counter.

"Here, Jew," said Private Wahrmann. He leaned forward threateningly, "Maybe we will come back tomorrow, *ja*?"

Henri looked down to avoid a fight.

"Thank you, Jew," Private Wahrmann said snidely, and both soldiers turned and walked toward the door.

"And thank you," Private Wahrmann said to Panos. "You helped us find a really good deal," and both soldiers stepped through the doorway laughing loudly.

Henri felt his knees would buckle, and his heart was beating rapidly at this near disaster; he could not speak.

"I am so sorry," Panos started to say, and not able to think of anything more, he quickly left the store, closing the door behind him. Henri was alone.

But not for long.

Chapter 18
Incarcerated

May 26, 1941

The German military often collected prisoners from the jails and executed them in reprisal for partisan resistance activities. The number of Greek citizens shot in retribution varied, usually at the whim of the Nazi officer in charge.

Henri's door opened less than 30 minutes later, and a German underofficer of the *Feldgendarmerie** in a field gray uniform stepped into the fabric shop. A rifle was slung over his shoulder.

"You are Henri Algava?" he said, looking at Henri.

Henri knew this was trouble. "Yes."

"Come with me," the underofficer said in a stony voice.

"Where?" Henri asked.

"To army headquarters."

"Headquarters? Why do they want to see me?"

Feldgendarmerie: Military field police.

"That's not my concern. Take your hat and coat and let's go."

Henri felt a lump in his throat. The thought of running occurred, but there was nowhere to run. Henri gathered his coat and hat and followed the soldier onto the street, locking the door behind him.

Army headquarters was only two blocks away. The underofficer escorted Henri along the street until they came to Liberty Square. They entered the large building that until recently was the Ionian Bank. Now a large red Nazi flag was hanging from the second floor above the front entrance.

The underofficer ushered Henri to a receiving desk.

"*Herr Oberleutnant*,"* the underofficer said sharply to the First Lieutenant, giving the officer his orders.

The First Lieutenant looked at Henri, smirked, looked at the papers and dismissed the guard. There were about a dozen soldiers and officers in the lobby, some on errands, some having a smoke, and some just standing about waiting.

"Henri Algava, the Jew?" the lieutenant asked. "Show me your papers."

Herr Oberleutnant: The title of a Senior or First Lieutenant in the Wehrmacht.

"I am Henri Algava." Henri pulled out his identification papers and gave them to the lieutenant.

"Are you a Jew?"

"Yes, I am Jewish."

"Well, Henri Algava the Jew, you have been accused of a crime."

"A crime? What crime?"

"Corporal Schmidt," the Senior Lieutenant called to a soldier standing nearby, "take this Jew to interrogation room five."

They walked down a short hall. The corporal opened a door, and Henri stepped within as the corporal followed, closing the door behind them.

It was a large room. Sitting at the table was an army captain, evidently the officer in charge of the investigation. Next to him sat a Greek interpreter. Standing by the wall were Private Oberhauser and Private Wahrmann. The two sets of fabrics they had purchased were displayed on the table.

Henri could feel his heart beating rapidly, and his skin felt cold.

The Greek interpreter was expressionless, translating the officer's words into Greek. "*Hauptmann** Kreisel has

---

Hauptmann: Captain.

some questions for you," the interpreter began, looking at Henri through his thick glasses. "You are Henri Algava, the fabric merchant?"

The two German soldiers were suppressing their smiles.

"Yes, I am Henri Algava."

"Did you sell this fabric to these two soldiers?"

"Yes."

"What did you charge for the cloth?"

"The fee was 2,000 *drachmas* for four meters of cloth. They each bought four meters."

"Privates Oberhauser and Wahrmann claim you charged too much money for the value of this fabric. What do you say to this accusation?"

Henri was dumbfounded. He had given the soldiers a price far below his own cost. Henri now understood the soldiers wanted to have some fun and send a Jew to jail.

Henri spoke to the interpreter. "You're a Greek from Thessaloniki. You know perfectly well that the fee they paid is much lower than normal."

The interpreter looked at Henri, and his face showed no emotion. "No, I don't know. I'm just a translator, and that's what the soldiers said. I am just translating."

"Tell the officer that the soldiers paid a quarter of the value of the fabric."

The interpreter spoke to *Hauptmann* Kreisel. Kreisel stared at Henri. The two soldiers kept a straight face, but Henri could see they were amused.

The captain spoke to the interpreter, and the interpreter said, "We don't believe anything a Jew says."

"But it's the truth!" cried Henri.

The officer said something, and the corporal that had brought Henri into the interrogation room stepped up to Henri, and grasped him by the arm in a tight grip.

The interpreter said, "You are being arrested as a black marketeer. You will be detained until your trial."

"What? My trial?" Henri blurted, but there was no further discussion because the corporal forcefully led Henri out of the room, past the smirking soldiers.

Down the hall they went, and down a flight of stairs into the basement. The air was cool and damp, and smelled musty. The corporal delivered Henri to a guard, and the guard led Henri to a dark cell, locking the door behind him. There was nothing except a dirty cot and a smelly pail for waste.

As Henri stood in the semi-dark, he could see dried blood on the floor.

"Someone was beaten here, or brought here after being beaten," Henri thought.

The jailer's post was a few meters from Henri's cell, and Henri could hear him grumbling "*Juden...Juden...*"* in a disturbing manner. He was in a perilous situation. "No one knows I'm here," he thought. "I could be murdered and nobody would ever know."

✱ ✱ ✱

A few hours later a different corporal came with papers, and the guard opened Henri's cell. "*Schweinehund...* "* the guard said as Henri went up the stairs.

Henri was taken to an office, and *Hauptmann* Kreisel addressed the corporal.

"You are being handed over to the Greek police because you sold cloth to soldiers of the German *Reich** at an exorbitant price," the interpreter explained. Henri knew it was futile to object and kept quiet.

"The captain wants the police to bring you to court and condemned as a speculator."

Juden: Jews.
Schweinehund: A curse word meaning "pig dog."
Reich: Empire.

"Condemned?" Henri thought. "Not tried, but condemned!"

Hauptmann Kreisel was observing Henri, his right and left hands pressing each other at the fingertips, casually interested in Henri's reaction. Henri remained stoic under Kreisel's gaze.

Escorted onto the street, Henri saw his friend, Kosmas, and called out.

"Kosmas! Tell my father I'm being taken to the police station!"

Kosmas nodded and turned to carry the message. Inside the station, the corporal gave the Greek police officer some papers, and left. Henri was taken to a cell with other prisoners. There was nothing to do but wait.

❋ ❋ ❋

A Greek policeman brought Nicos to the cell. "Henri!" said Nicos Efcarpides. Henri's heart leapt with relief, seeing his friend and mentor. "Don't worry, Henri. We'll get you out of here."

"I'm innocent!" Henri said.

"Of course you are. Don't worry about a thing. Kosmas told me and I came right away."

"Does Allegra know?"

"I think so. Kosmas was on his way to tell her, and your father. You'll have to go to court, Henri," Nicos advised. "But I will get you a good attorney and we'll get you out of here."

"When?" asked Henri. "I can be shot at any time!* The longer I'm in jail, the more chance I'll be killed."

"I don't know," Nicos said. "It depends how fast your trial comes up."

"Their orders are to convict me, Nicos."

"I know, I know... We'll get you out of here. I'll talk to Gregos. I'll see him right now and ask him to be your attorney. He'll come talk to you."

"I need to get out of here quickly."

"Yes, we'll get you out as fast as we can," Nicos promised. "In the meantime, I'll speak with Captain Kanelos. He's a personal friend; I'll see about getting you a better cell."

"Thank you, Nicos."

Nicos left and Henri was shortly brought to a cell that wasn't so filthy and dark.

Soon Allegra and Avram came, bringing food. Though

The Nazis would collect prisoners and execute them as reprisals for resistance activities and sabotage.

Allegra's edgy eyes showed she was frightened, Henri saw how brave she was. He had to be brave for her.

"You'll see," he told her, "I'll be free soon. Nicos will make it happen," though his distracted look told Allegra he was not completely convinced.

When they left, Henri was alone with his troubled thoughts, exhausted. It had been a long day, and he fell asleep praying the partisans were sleeping tonight, too.

Chapter 19
Convicted

May 27, 1941

In the morning a Greek police officer came for him.

"Where are you taking me?"

"To a cell in the courthouse," said the officer. "You will remain there until your trial."

By the end of the day, Gregos Athas, Henri's attorney, arrived with Nicos and Avram to discuss Henri's situation.

"Gregos!" Henri exclaimed. "I'm so glad to see you!"

"Courage, my friend," Gregos replied. "We will get you out."

"We have some good news," added Nicos. "Tell him, Gregos."

"I spoke with a big importer in the textile market, and asked him to check the current prices for the goods you sold." Everyone was listening closely to Gregos.

"When I told him the price you charged the two soldiers, he started laughing. The price they paid was ridiculous."

"Of course it was," said Henri. "They got the fabric almost for free."

"That's what he said," Gregos continued. "But that really doesn't make any difference. I looked at the court papers, and the Germans want you brought to trial and convicted."

"What can be done?" asked Avram.

"We can't do anything about that," Gregos continued. "The Greek court has to convict you or the German command will go after the judges."

"But Henri is innocent!" Avram exclaimed.

"Yes. Remember, though, our only imperative is to get Henri out of jail, and quickly. Given the circumstances, there's only one thing we can do."

"What's that?" asked Henri.

"The court needs to convict you to satisfy the army commander. We're going to let the court convict you."

"What?" interrupted Avram.

"I know how it sounds, but let me finish. We want the court to convict you of a lesser offense so your punishment will be 60 days or less in jail."

"I don't want to be here for 60 days," Henri complained. "That's too long! I could be shot in reprisal."

"You won't be here that long," Gregos said calmly. "If I can get you convicted of a lesser offense and you receive a 60 day sentence, you have the option of paying the court a fee for the 60 days and buying your freedom."

"Ransom, you mean."

"Call it what you like... It gets you out of danger and it's the best choice we have."

"What are my chances of getting convicted of a lesser offense?" asked Henri.

"Nothing is certain, of course," said Gregos, "but I hope you'll trust me. I'll bring in character witnesses and textile importers who can verify the prices, and I can make a convincing case you're not a black marketer."

"It's risky," said Avram, "but I don't see a better choice. What do you think, Nicos?"

Nicos thought for a moment, and then said, "I don't like it, but I agree it looks like our best option. The court has to convict. The judges will never stand up to the German command." He turned to Henri. "What do you think, Henri?"

Henri felt sick. "Gambling on being set free by placating the Germans, who put me here in the first place…it's a serious risk," he thought. "But the alternative is worse. I might never leave here alive."

"I don't like it either," Henri said aloud, "but I don't see a choice." After a long sigh… "All right, Gregos, my life is in your hands."

* * *

Hauptmann Kreisel met with the three Greek judges at his office in army headquarters, and the interpreter translated his demands.

"The Third Reich has determined that the people whose cases you are reviewing today are enemies of the State. They will be convicted."

The judges were motionless, their eyes on *Hauptmann* Kreisel.

"Do you have any questions about what you are expected to do?"

The judges shook their heads.

"Then I expect to see these Jews convicted."

"Yes, *Hauptmann* Kreisel," said one of the judges. "The Jews are guilty, and will be convicted."

"Very well," said the German captain. "You are dismissed."

✳ ✳ ✳

Late in the day the case against Henri Algava was brought before the judges. Gregos invited one character witness after another to affirm that Henri was a good citizen, a good husband and father, and an honest businessman. Nicos, Marcos and Costas all testified on Henri's behalf, and several Greek Orthodox merchants from the textile business verified Henri had greatly undercharged the German soldiers. Gregos argued for the Court to find Henri innocent of intentional fraud, but guilty of the lesser offense of theft.

The judges listened without emotion, conferred, and rendered their immediate decision.

"Henri Algava, you are guilty of theft. The Court sentences you to 60 days in jail."

Escorted out of the courtroom, Henri was taken to the police station where Gregos spoke with the officer in charge. The fee for buying a single day's release from jail was 1,000 *drachmas*. Gregos immediately paid the 60,000 *drachmas* fee.

After a week behind bars, Henri stepped outside with Gregos, into the late afternoon sunshine.

"Gregos…" Henri began.

"Don't say a word, my friend," Gregos responded. "You're out of danger."

"Yes, thank you," Henri said, wondering for how long.

Chapter 20
Baba Yorgo

June 18, 1941

The German occupation is now just over two months old. Under the authority of a commission called the Nazi Jewish Affairs Commission, also known as the Rosenberg Commando, Jewish libraries and archives have been plundered and literally tons of Torah scrolls, Jewish books, and religious artifacts and art were seized and shipped to Germany. The rabbis cried when the Torahs and books were taken; nothing mattered more than the sacred texts...

German soldiers have no qualms about pilfering the merchandise in Jewish stores, taking anything they wish. All Jewish organizations are banned and community buildings are seized for use by the German military. The best Jewish homes are expropriated, and some Jewish families are forced to house German soldiers. Jews are prohibited from meeting, from going to cafés and cinemas, and banned from many stores...while their own are boycotted. Jewish bookstores are closed and their owners arrested.

"I think he's very handsome," said Evanghelia.

"I do, too, but he's too old for you," said Daisyka.

"No! He's just the right age."

"But he's 26 and you're only 19!"

"I don't care. I think he's perfect."

"Well, I think he's perfectly too old."

"Nonsense, Daisyka. I thought you were my friend!"

"I am, and that's why I'm telling you. You need a younger suitor."

"I disagree. I'm going to see a palm reader tomorrow, and I know he'll say that Nicholas is right for me!"

Allegra, in the next room, overhearing Evanghelia, joined the two young women seated at the dining room table. "You're going to see a palm reader?" asked Allegra.

"Yes, *Kyría* Algava. I've seen him before and he told me I would meet an older man who would become my husband."

"What is this reader's name, and where is he?" inquired Allegra, curious.

Evanghelia smiled, glad that *Kyría* Algava, whom she respected, was interested. "His name is Baba Yorgo. He's not far from here. He lives in the district."

"How do you know him?" asked Allegra.

"I heard about him a few months ago when I was

cleaning Dr. Matarasso's house. *Kyría* Matarasso's guest was telling how he reads cards and palms. I've gone to him a few times," said Evanghelia with a mischievous smile.

"You didn't tell me!" said Daisyka, surprised by her girlfriend's boldness.

"Oh, yes," added Evanghelia, "and that's why I know Nicholas is the one for me."

"What? The palm reader said his name?" asked Allegra.

"Well, not exactly, but he did say I would marry an older man."

"That doesn't mean it's Nicholas!" Daisyka interjected.

"Well, that's why I want to go back tomorrow!" replied Evanghelia, slightly annoyed, but also pleased with all the attention.

"Henri has been talking about missing three suits from his closet. He gave a number of them away, and I think he gave these three to the *kaffejee*,* but he doesn't remember doing that. This could be a chance for him to find out what really happened to those suits," said Allegra.

Kaffejee: A person who makes and sends coffee to people in offices.

"Do you want to come with me?" asked Evanghelia hopefully.

"Yes! I've always been interested in fortune tellers. And I know Henri wants to find out about those missing suits. Would you mind if Henri comes, too?"

"Not at all. I'd like that."

"Then we shall all go together."

It was a bright and pleasant day. Allegra and Henri were walking with Evanghelia who was in a happy mood... happy because she knew the soothsayer would confirm Nicholas as her future husband.

"I've always liked this part of town," said Henri. "The old buildings, a bit dilapidated now but full of history. Just think of all the people who lived here..."

"I like the old neighborhoods, too. It's quite rustic now," commented Allegra.

"The sidewalk is ending," said Henri. "Be careful on the cobblestones."

In a few minutes they arrived at *Arslan Han,** an old

Arslan Han: Turkish for Lion's Shelter.

inn for wagon drivers. The bottom floor was a stable for horses and there was a yard for wagons. Above the stables was the inn with its bare rooms, each with a bed, a table, and a chair or two. Unkempt, the red paint was peeling from the worn wooden exterior.

"Here we are!" said Evanghelia.

"I've been here before," Henri said with surprise.

"You have?" asked Allegra.

"Well, not the inn," replied Henri, "but in this building. This is where Eugenios Karras has his automotive parts store. He was once a good customer of mine. I wonder how he's doing."

Before Allegra could answer, Evanghelia said, "Baba Yorgo has a room upstairs," and she led the way.

It was dark inside, with the pleasant fragrance of sweet hay mixed with the pungent odor of manure. The stables were warm with the heat of the horses' bodies, the gentle sounds of flaring nostrils and shifting hooves familiar and soothing as the horses pulled on the hay and slowly ground the golden stalks.

"Look at the horses, Henri," said Allegra as they climbed the squeaky stairs behind the young woman to the dismal floor above.

The sounds of the horses followed them as they walked

down the hallway. Evanghelia stopped before one of the doors and knocked softly.

"Hallo," said a high thin voice from within. "Come... come..."

Evanghelia opened the door and stepped in.

"Hello, Baba Yorgo," she said.

"Hallo. Is good to see you, my child."

"Baba Yorgo, I brought two friends."

"Let me see, let them come."

Allegra and Henri stepped into the dimly-lit room, the floor covered with a Turkish carpet. A small man sat upon an embroidered pillow, his legs folded underneath.

"Welcome, welcome. Come. Please sit."

Baba Yorgo wore a wool peasant shirt and comfortable loose trousers. His hair was covered with a red scarf, and a pendant on a simple silver chain hung from his neck.

"These are my friends," said Evanghelia.

"You are welcome," said the little man. "I have been expecting you. I am glad you came."

Allegra stepped forward. "I am Allegra, and this is my husband Henri."

"Please, come and sit. I am Baba Yorgo. Welcome. Forgive me for not rising. My legs do not work as once they did."

Evanghelia sat next to the Yogi, eager in her childlike way to learn more about the future she desired. Allegra and Henri sat on the cushions. The dingy walls were covered by mandala tapestries and religious scenes of the Buddha; in a corner was a small altar with a statue of the Buddha, and crystals, candles and incense.

Baba Yorgo spoke first with Evanghelia; his tarot cards showing conflict ahead for herself, her future husband, and their two children. They would find a path through their troubles if they kept a promise to an elder in a distant city. This left Evanghelia in a pensive mood as Baba Yorgo now turned his attention to Allegra.

"Now, Allegra, what do you wish to know?" She felt the mystic's full attention.

"Baba Yorgo, this may be a small matter, but Henri has lost three suits. He thinks they were stolen. I think he gave them to a friend. Could you tell us what happened to them?"

The seer looked at her and then moved his hand, dismissing the issue. "Look, you lost three suits, but you'll gain ten. Forget them. You lost them. Finished. Don't think about it."

Henri was going to say something, but saw it wasn't

worth the trouble.

Baba Yorgo looked at Henri. "Never mind the missing suits. But I do have a message for you. I see your wife. You have a wonderful wife. This woman is a good companion, and she's a good soul, and she's good for you. Listen to her and you will live long."

Henri smiled. "Thank you, Baba Yorgo...I see you are a wise man."

Baba Yorgo turned to Allegra. "Do you want me to tell you what the cards say?" he asked.

"No."

"Give me your hand," Baba Yorgo spread her palm and studied the lines, their meaning inescapably clear. He said, "What is it you want to do? Do you think you can save the world?"

Allegra was silent, but surprised.

"It's impossible. You cannot do what you want to do. You can save a few, but you cannot save the world."

Allegra knew what Baba Yorgo meant and she felt the sorrow in her heart.

Baba Yorgo then said to Allegra, "Thessaloniki is too small for you. You are born to live in a big country."

This also surprised Allegra. Thessaloniki was her home and she had lived nowhere else. "Too small?" thought Allegra. "Does he mean I should live in Athens?"

"You will see," said Baba Yorgo, as though he was reading her thoughts. "This is all I can tell you."

The audience was concluded. Allegra smiled at Baba Yorgo, and he smiled back. "Thank you. May I come again?"

"Yes, yes, again. You will come," Baba Yorgo said in his falsetto voice.

Everyone rose, the donations given. Baba Yorgo put his palms together and bowed from the waist. "Go with God's blessings of peace and health," he said as they left and closed the door.

No one spoke a word until they had descended into the warm dark stable. "I've never been to a mystic before," said Henri. "He certainly thought highly of you, Allegra."

"Yes," added Evanghelia. "I wonder what he meant about Thessaloniki being too small."

"I wonder also," Allegra considered. "There was his comment about not being able to save the world."

"He certainly had that right. You're always helping others. You have a generous heart."

"The better to love you with, my dear."

"And you!" Allegra said to Evanghelia. "Two babies!"

Evanghelia smiled broadly, delighted with her prospects.

"Do you have an elder living in a distant city?" asked Henri.

"My mother's sister lives in Bern," Evanghelia replied. "I haven't seen her in years." Marrying Nicholas was all she had on her mind, and she couldn't wait to tell the good news to Daisyka when they got home.

Stepping into the sunlight, Henri saw Eugenios Karras standing in front of his automobile parts shop.

"Eugenios!" he called.

"It's good to see you, Henri," Eugenios replied. "I heard you went out of business. Where will I get the supplies I need?" he half-joked.

"I was drafted," replied Henri, "and my father sold the stock. Get in touch with Marcos Hombitis, the customs broker. He may be able to help."

The walk home included a refreshing stop at a café for beverages and a light dessert. Their waiter hesitated, then thought better of asking if they were Jewish.

In his quiet room at *Arslan Han*, Baba Yorgo did a

cleansing ceremony. Impressions of deep despair and desperate circumstances lingered. The mists did not part sufficiently to know the outcome, their path treacherous and uncertain. He sent a prayer after them, a prayer to guard against the great evils that lay ahead.

Chapter 21
Black Sabbath at Liberty Square

July 11, 1942

A year passed. From the summer of 1941 to the summer of 1942, time moved slowly. After his brief imprisonment by the Germans, Henri stopped all commercial activities, and he and Avram spent their days at Aleko's taverna near the White Tower visiting quietly with friends, listening to the war news on the radio, and watching German soldiers patrol the streets of Thessaloniki.

Abuse against the Jews quieted after the initial anti-Semitic activities, providing a false feeling of security. Several wealthy Jewish families fled to Athens, which was under the more lenient control of the Italians, and some Jews began to disappear into the mountains, to fight later with the partisans harbored in remote villages.

Greek soldiers who had fought the Italians surrendered their weapons and were allowed to return to their homes. Max Merten, a captain representing the German civil administration as the German military governor, issued decrees and gave orders to the Greek puppet officials.

After the war with Italy, Greece's economy was crushed, and the German occupation of Greece continued with devastating economic effect. With the decrease in agricultural production and the destruction of roads and rail lines, severe food shortages caused the Great Famine. The German army stripped the Greeks of everything they produced and fed themselves with the stolen wheat, dairy, fruits, nuts and fish. Whatever was not consumed by the army was shipped to Germany.

During the winter of 1941–1942, about 60 Jews died from hunger each day, and the general population suffered similarly. Many died in the streets and were loaded onto horse-drawn wagons. When limited aid did arrive in February 1942, most of the food was delivered to government and black-market traders who sold the desperately needed commodities at highly inflated prices.

Outside Greece's borders, by late 1941 German troops were within 11 miles of Moscow. Rommel and his Afrika Corps were battling in North Africa and the Japanese attacked Pearl Harbor. In early 1942, Leningrad was under siege, General Doolittle raided Tokyo, and the Battle of the Coral Sea gave the United States its first strategic victory. Both England and Germany were bombing each other continually. Hitler was furious that almost all of Lübeck's medieval town center was destroyed; in revenge, he ordered the bombing of British historic sites in York, Bath, Canterbury, and others.

Though the German authorities did not outwardly increase the persecution of the Jewish population more than they had already, the winter was cold and food was scarce. The death rate rose five times higher than normal, and few newborn babies survived. Medicine was scarce, and tuberculosis and malaria began to spread. Because lice had become such a serious ailment, authorities advised everyone to shave their heads.

At the end of January 1942, the Nazis allowed Rabbi Koretz to return as Chief Rabbi. He had been in a concentration camp in Vienna since mid-April 1941 and his return was greeted with suspicion.

As the spring turned into the summer of 1942, Henri and Allegra's family lived on their savings, and in spite of their own hardships, gave food and money to those who were desperate. Allegra did what she could, even making a suit for a rabbinical student whose only clothes were almost rags. Long days in the café were met with both patience and anxiety, but there was little to do except appreciate what they had. Their health was good, and there was no end to the love they felt for each other.

Andreas was now two and a half years old and Allegra gave thanks every day that there was food so he could grow strong and healthy. Many times a day Allegra stopped what she was doing to admire Andreas and thank God for her beautiful young son.

"Chrisso mou!" she would say. "My golden one!" and she would hug Andreas and tell Andreas how much she loved him, dancing with him across the wooden floor and carpets of their apartment on Tsimiski Street, holding him to her chest, and Andreas would laugh.

* * *

"Allegra, have you heard the news?"

"What news?"

"The *Evening Press* says all Jewish men between 18 and 50 must report to Liberty Square this Saturday at 8:00 a.m. The order was given by General von Krenzski, the commander of the German army."

"Report for what?" asked Allegra, alarmed.

"To register for work details. They're assigning numbers."

"I don't want you to go."

"Neither do I," said Henri, "but I could get in serious trouble. If I don't get a number, that's proof I didn't obey the order."

"I don't care. You're not going," said Allegra. "I have a bad feeling about this."

"Me, too, but the army has a file on me. They'll know if I don't show up."

"I've got an idea," said Allegra. "Nicos has an apartment that overlooks Liberty Square. Ask him if we can watch what happens from his terrace."

"Good idea. I'll ask him."

"We can watch what happens without being in the middle of it."

* * *

It was eight o'clock Saturday, and the still morning air was heating up. A bright blue sky free of clouds suggested it was going to be a hot summer day.

Allegra, Henri, and Nicos were standing on the second floor terrace overlooking Liberty Square. Thousands of Jewish men and teenage boys were in the square across the street from the former Ionian Bank and the Hotel Ritz, now being used by the German army. A huge red flag with its swastika hung from a flagpole above the building's entrance.

"I don't like the feel of this," said Allegra.

"Neither do I," commented Nicos.

"No matter what you're thinking," said Henri, "I could be in serious trouble. I can't be arrested again."

"If we have to, we'll find a doctor to verify you were sick. Remember what you saw in Leipzig...how they treated the Jews when the Nazis took over."

Thousands of Jewish men in their Sabbath clothes waited for instructions. Suddenly German soldiers and sailors began giving orders, clubbing the Jewish men, forcing them to stand in straight lines.

"Oh my God!" gasped Allegra. Henri couldn't believe what he was seeing, and Nicos was dumbfounded.

"I swear to you, Henri. If you go down there, I'm going to jump!" Allegra moved toward the edge of the terrace. Henri knew she was serious.

"I'm not going, Allegra. You don't have to worry."

Nicos didn't know which was more astounding, the display of brutality or Allegra's threat to leap from the terrace.

For hours the beatings continued. Forced to stand still in the ever-increasing heat, the Jewish men and teenage boys were beaten with clubs and fists if they shielded themselves from the sun or brushed at a fly. Some were severely beaten; others were forced into squatting positions and attacked if they fell over. Still others were threatened at gunpoint. None of the Greek spectators protested.

When the men fainted, they were kicked until they regained their feet. Some were forced to roll on the ground like barrels, or perform demeaning calisthenics. From some of the balconies above the square, German women were applauding, taking photographs and laughing with their Nazi escorts.

"I can't watch anymore," said Allegra. "I feel sick. Please take me home." Allegra cried in Henri's arms.

The next day, in the taverna, Henri learned that Saturday's registration hadn't been finished; the Nazis would never know he hadn't been there.

"Hello, Henri," said *Kýrios* Amon, an elderly Greek Henri knew from the fabric shop. "I read the paper today. This is unbelievable! Were you there? Did you see this atrocity?"

"Yes, I was there. I saw what happened. It's all true. Fortunately, I was at a distance. As you can imagine, I was horrified."

"The Germans are barbarians, a nation of evil people. Hitler and his Nazis are criminals and must be destroyed. Have you been registered?"

"Registration is rescheduled for tomorrow," said Henri. "I really don't know what to do."

"Henri, don't you worry," *Kýrios* Amon said. "I have a friend, Dr. Kostopoulos. He knows the German system and how to get around things. I have no doubt he'll find a way to get you registered without risk. I'll talk to him today; he can probably get you listed as an invalid."

"Do you think so?" asked Henri eagerly.

"Yes, I think it can be arranged. It will take some money,

of course, but if it works out, you'll be registered and released from all work."

"Thank you! You may have just saved my life," Henri said.

"I'm happy to help, Henri. Let's meet here tomorrow and I'll take you to the doctor to introduce you."

✳ ✳ ✳

"Thank God you have your number," Allegra said with relief.

"Yes, and I'm registered as an invalid."

"What did it cost?"

"The doctor said he would have to pay some Greek officials. I gave him six gold coins and eight meters of British cloth."

"It's worth it," said Allegra. "I also have some news. I spoke with Kyria Aglaia today. Kosta, one of her nephews, is working at the airport for the Germans. He said he'd heard that Jews were going to be forced to rebuild damaged roads. The Nazis are going to make a new road from Thessaloniki to Katerini and Larissa."

"Oh, no," groaned Henri. "That's about 150 kilometers!"

"And you won't be involved. God is protecting us,"

Allegra said. "She told me something else. Kosta says the Germans want to hire more young Jewish men at the airport. Kosta gets paid, and he goes home every night. The work is really easy. Most of the day the men are lying in the shade."

"That's great news... Who can we send there?" asked Henri.

"I'm going to tell my cousin Larry, and my two other cousins. I might be able to get my nephews there, too."

"Great! I'll see your brother Pepo and tell him about Dr. Kostopoulos...he should get registered as an invalid, too."

Over the next few days Allegra contacted her close friends so their sons could circumvent the Nazi slave labor crews. "Send them to me!" said Kosta when he heard Allegra knew young men they could save. Their mothers blessed Allegra because now their sons were safe from having to break stones under a burning sun, living in tents, eating bad food, and being beaten by German soldiers and the construction supervisors from Croatia and other regions.

Allegra had Henri send Kosta a suit as a gift, and Kosta's friend received a nice wristwatch; they were grateful. Assigning men to the airport cost money to arrange, and when a family couldn't afford to pay in full, Henri covered the balance. Allegra saved over a dozen young men.

"We have to help *Theíos* Isaac," Allegra said, worried. "His number was called, but he's crippled. He can barely walk."

"Where is he now?" Henri asked.

"He's at a work camp waiting to be transported to a road crew."

"There isn't much time! Go see Kyria Aglaia and tell her. She might know what we could do."

Allegra visited Kyria Aglaia at once. "It will cost a lot more money," said Kyria Aglaia, "but I can talk to one of my renters, Colonel Anastos; he's a retired Greek officer, and he'll know how to get your uncle transferred quickly."

That afternoon Henri paid the ransom to the Greek authorities. By the evening he and Allegra were at the work camp with Isaac's papers. They found Isaac in line with a sack on his shoulder, about to board a truck.

"Isaac!"

"Allegra? What are you doing here?"

"You're coming with us!" Allegra pulled Isaac out of the line.

Theíos: Uncle.

"But the money!" cried *Theíos* Isaac when he heard the story. "You paid so much money!"

"Don't worry about it," said Henri. "The money is nothing." They brought Isaac home, and the next day he reported to the airport.

The long hot summer continued. Almost every day a new set of registration numbers was published in the Nazi-friendly newspaper, *New Europe*, ordering Jews to report for slave labor.

"Henri, your number is not in the paper," Henri's Greek friends often reported.

"No, not yet. Not yet."

"When will you be called?"

"I don't know. Soon, I guess," he said.

Henri never told his story to anybody.

Chapter 22
A Half Million Graves

December 7, 1942

*Thessaloniki's Jewish cemetery was the largest Jewish
cemetery in the world and had grown to over 85 acres with
more than half a million tombs. At one time the cemetery
had been well outside the city walls, but as Thessaloniki
grew, the cemetery became encompassed until it was
practically in the middle of the city. Because Jewish law does
not allow the movement of graves, the cemetery's location
created a difficult problem for the Jewish and Christian
communities. One contentious issue was that the Aristotle
University of Thessaloniki bordered one side of the cemetery
and was unable to expand its facilities.*

*The Nazis knew the cemetery was a major concern and
they used this to their advantage by offering the Jewish
community a chance to free the Jewish slave laborers...in
return for a large sum of money and the surrender of the
cemetery. The Germans slyly arranged the pressure to come
from the Christian community, not the German command.
The Jewish community had no choice but to accept the offer,
and bought the release of 4,000 forced laborers.*

*The Christian city government quickly took advantage of this
opportunity and the next day sent 500 workers to begin the
destruction of all the tombs. Within a few weeks the entire
cemetery had been demolished; grave robbers stole artifacts*

and gold teeth from among the bones and skulls. Centuries-old Jewish gravestones were used to pave streets and for the construction of homes, churches, urinals, and a swimming pool for German soldiers.

"Please do this for me, Henri," said Avram, with tears in his eyes.

Henri looked at his father and could not deny him. Henri was in near tears himself, upset with the magnitude of what his father asked. "How was it possible?" Henri thought.

"Of course, Babá," Henri replied calmly. "I will do what you ask."

"Thank you," the old man said. "I just cannot do it myself."

"The sooner I go, the better. They are opening the graves now, and I'm not sure what section they're working on."

"Henri, be careful. There will probably be looters and I don't want you getting hurt. If you can't do this safely, I don't want you to do it at all."

"I'll be all right, Babá. Don't worry. I'll take care of myself," said Henri as he stood up to go.

"God bless you, son."

Henri leaned over his father, and gently kissed him on both cheeks. Henri was surprised to taste the old man's tears.

"God bless us both."

Henri walked out of the dining room and down the hall toward the nursery. When he got there, Andreas was turning pages of a book with Daisyka. Andreas heard his footsteps, and the young boy looked up and saw his father. A big smile blossomed on the boy's face.

"Babá!" Andreas called, happy to see his father.

"Andriko *mou*!"* Henri replied, equally delighted. "How is my Andriko today? Are you having fun with Daisyka?" Henri asked as he bent over and scooped his son into his arms.

Andreas laughed as he flew through the air.

Henri held Andreas against his chest and kissed his son on the forehead.

"I love you very much, Andriko. Always remember that. I have to go out for a little while," he said to Andreas, "but when I come back, I will have a little treat for you."

———————

Mou: My, as in "My Andriko!"

Andreas smiled and burst into a laugh. Henri smiled with joy. He set Andreas down on the floor next to Daisyka. "It's almost time for your nap," he said. "I'll be back before dinner."

"Babá!" called Andreas.

"Goodbye, Andriko. I love you."

Henri walked down the hall to the front door, putting on his hat, coat and gloves as he prepared for the cool wet December weather waiting outside.

Henri stood at the edge of the massive Jewish cemetery sprawling before him. The crypts and headstones extended for thousands of meters in all directions, a vast city of gravestones marking the remains of Jewish men, women, and children buried here during the past 450 years.

At one end of the enormous cemetery a small army of several hundred Greek workers were busy with shovels and pickaxes, tearing up the gravesites, pillaging for treasure. Henri watched with a mix of astonishment and horror as Thessaloniki's Jewish history was being destroyed before his eyes, forever.

"Dear Lord, please protect me," Henri whispered, realizing the ravenous workers would demolish the cemetery quickly, feeling nausea at its imminent death.

Forcing aside his feelings and thoughts, Henri induced a state of numbness. He knew where *Theíos* Abraham's grave was, and he walked through the rows of memorial stones and marble crypts. The fragrance of moist soil and the decay of autumn's vegetation were strong in his nostrils, his shoes wet from the raindrops caught by the grass and weeds that poked between the graves.

Other Jews were carrying shovels, too, moving among the hundreds of thousands of memorial stones. In several places small groups were gathered to exhume an ancestor's remains. As Henri walked between the stones, his eyes caught the names of the graves' inhabitants in Hebrew, Ladino, and French. He twisted and turned through the centuries, through the labyrinth of marble and stone. Henri briefly remembered Allegra's dream, the long line of people exiting the factory carrying shrouded corpses.

He arrived at his father's brother's gravesite. "Abraham Algava" the stone letters read "1873–1917." As he began pushing aside the giant stone sitting on top of the grave, Henri remembered a distant summer chasing chickens and ducks in the yard behind the house of his *theíos*. The ground beneath the raised stone revealed a large curling earthworm, surprised at being discovered. Henri scooped up the earthworm with the shovel and gently placed it to the side. He then began to sink the shovel into the soft flesh of the earth. A light drizzle began to fall.

What are a man's thoughts as he digs in the grave of another? Time was suspended as the shovel excavated the years. Henri thought of his son and how someday Andriko would see his own father's remains settled into the earth...as Henri would someday see Avram's.

Henri moved the earth more gently, and within the hour the remains of *Theíos* Abraham were reverently gathered into a jute sack. There, upon a gaping grave in the midst of a half-million other graves, Henri finally let his feelings overwhelm him, and he cried and cried, his hot salty tears flowing endlessly, streaming down his cheeks into the open earth.

Chapter 23
34434 and 34435

February 21, 1943

In the beginning of 1943, the situation changed radically. A group of SD officers* pushed away the Wehrmacht authorities and began their plan for the elimination of the Jews. Orders were given that all Jews over the age of five must wear the yellow Star of David, and must move to designated ghettos by February 25. As Jews moved out of their homes to relocate in the ghettos, non-Jews were allowed to take over their homes and property.

Jews were no longer allowed to use public telephones or public transportation. The Jewish community was informed through Chief Rabbi Koretz that this internal migration was to establish a self-administered Jewish entity within the city with its own mayor and Chamber of Commerce. A Jewish Militia was appointed, and all Jewish citizens were required to complete a detailed form describing their assets. There was talk about emigration to Krakow, Poland.

Henri was next. They had waited for nearly three hours to get their yellow Stars of David and identification cards.

SD officers: *Sicherheitsdienst* (Security Service), or SD, was an intelligence organization of the Nazi Party, regarded as a sister organization of the Gestapo.

The big room overflowed with people; children were crying, and several elders were sitting on the floor in line. It was February, and people were coughing and sneezing; Henri hoped Andreas and Allegra would not get sick.

Allegra was holding Andreas. Henri turned to her and smiled bravely. "It will be all right," he said. Henri knew his words did not reassure her. She looked at him and gave a weak smile.

"Next," said the seated man at the table, looking at Henri from under bushy black eyebrows. "Your names?"

"I am Henri Algava. This is my wife Allegra and our son Andreas."

"Algava...," the clerk said. "I saw your name earlier." He turned a few pages in the ledger, the names carefully entered by the synagogue's staff.

Henri winced as a child started screaming and crying in the line behind him. He looked quickly at Allegra and saw her patiently taking everything in stride. "How beautiful she is," he thought, seeing her soft face and the delicate curl of her hair. And then, because everything seemed so immediately fragile, he thought, "What will happen to us?"

Resting his head on his mother's shoulder, Andreas's big liquid eyes watched the clerk's finger moving down the long list of names.

"Here you are," said the clerk, startling Henri out of his reflections. "Henri Algava, 93 Tsimiski Street?"

"Yes, that's right."

"Show me your identification."

The man looked at Henri's papers briefly and handed them back. He then reached into a cardboard box and pulled out two yellow Star of David patches.

"Here. Sew the star onto the front left side of your jacket. If you're stopped by the authorities and aren't wearing the star, you'll be in serious trouble. The second star is an extra, or you can sew it onto a different jacket. Any questions?" The number on his star was 34434.

"Does my son have to wear a star?"

"No. He's under five. He doesn't wear one."

Henri looked at Allegra. He sensed she was thinking about the long lines of people in her dream, carried out wrapped in shrouds.

The little man looked at Allegra. "You are Allegra Algava?"

"Yes."

"Show me your identification."

Allegra saw Henri's concerned look. "It will be all right," she thought, trying to tell him with her eyes. "We'll get through this, all of us will get through this," and she said a silent prayer.

The man at the table gave Allegra her papers and the two stars. The number on her star was 34435.

"Sew the patches on the front left side of your coat. If you're caught without your Star of David, you will be severely punished."

Andreas began moving in his mother's arms, tired of waiting for so long.

"That's all," the seated man said. "Next."

"Go, Mamá," Andreas said.

Henri and Allegra stepped aside to make room for Avram and Myriam.

"We'll wait for you," said Henri.

"No, son. You go home. You have the baby. We'll be home soon," said Avram, turning his attention to the seated man.

"Yes," said Allegra. "Let's go home, Henri."

"Here, give me Andreas," said Henri, reaching for his son, fitting Andreas into his arms. "Andriko *mou*," he said, "what a good boy you are! So very patient!" Henri gave his son a kiss on the soft cheek.

Together, across the large room, past the long lines of people and through the doors onto the chilly street, they stepped into the cold winter weather, walking into a stiff angry wind, a wind that had just begun to blow.

Chapter 24
Nightfall

February 20, 1943

The German Military Command of Thessaloniki, following the orders of Sonderkommando Wisliceny,* issued orders that all Jews must be expelled from vocational organizations such as labor unions. The orders were signed by Dr. Max Merten, the Military Governor of Thessaloniki.

Henri felt the sudden cold inside his shirt as he took off his coat and folded it so the yellow star wouldn't show. Avram did the same, and both men entered Aleko's taverna. Henri relaxed when he felt the warmth and saw the smiles of his friends. There were no German soldiers in the room.

Aleko was the first to greet them. "*Yiasou!* Come in, come in. It's good to see you! Take a table. I'll be right with you."

Henri and his father took a seat near the rear wall and put their coats on one of the chairs, careful to keep them

---

Sonderkommando Wisliceny: Dieter Wisliceny was a member of the Nazi SS and a leading figure in the Holocaust. After the war, his testimony helped convict Adolph Eichmann. Wisliceny was found guilty of war crimes and executed in 1948.

folded. In a moment, Aleko was placing two hot cups of ersatz coffee on their table.

"Do you think you really needed to do that?" asked Aleko, indicating their folded coats. "You're among friends here."

"How could we be sure there weren't soldiers here tonight?" said Avram.

Henri nodded and smiled at Albert Confortes, a longtime friend, seated at a nearby table. His coat was also carefully folded.

"You're right," said Aleko. He lowered his voice and leaned forward. "I don't think of you as Jews, only as good friends."

Avram put his hand on top of Aleko's. "You're a dear friend, too." Aleko smiled, his eyes turning soft. He nodded slightly. "I'll be back," he said, leaving to serve others.

As Henri lifted the coffee to his lips, Marcos Hombitis came into the café, his eyes searching the room. Spotting Henri and Avram, he smiled, and walked over.

"Hello, my friends," he said. Henri and Avram welcomed him.

Marcos pulled out a chair and sat down. Aleko came up and poured a small glass of ouzo for him, and joined their table.

"I heard about the registration," Marcos said softly. "I am disgusted," he said, his bushy eyebrows sharpened in a frown. He spat at the floor. "These Nazis are pigs."

Henri and Avram agreed. "I don't know what they're going to do next," said Henri. "I saw some pretty terrible things when I was in Leipzig a few years ago…"

Henri remembered seeing Jewish men being beaten with clubs on the city's streets by the Brownshirts,* one man covered in blood as if he'd been hit by a car. Jews were being bullied and pushed along the street past shops with posters of large-nosed, ugly, distorted Jewish faces, and many Jewish stores were empty and charred from looting and arson.

"Something terrible just happened to one of my family," said Henri. "We just heard about it today.

"What happened?" asked Marcos, wrapping his big hand around the glass of ouzo.

"Joseph was arrested. He's Allegra's cousin, one of the Carassos who own the dye factory. He was denounced by a competitor and now he's in jail."

Brownshirts: The SA or *Sturmabteilung* (German for "Assault Division") also known as Storm Troopers, a paramilitary organization in the Nazi Party known for violent intimidation.

"Unbelievable," Marcos said, his voice tense. "What can you do about it? Can you get him out?"

"We're going to see how much it will cost to buy his freedom."

"That's delicate business," Marcos observed.

"Expensive, too."

"The Nazis are insatiable. That Lieutenant Scheidel still keeps coming around asking about the missing list of radios."

"What do you tell him?" asked Henri, looking up quickly.

"I tell him what I always tell him," Marcos answered. "He should go talk to Mussolini."

"Mussolini?"

"Yes. When the Italians bombed our port two years ago, a lot of files went missing. I tell him I'm not responsible for what happened..." Marcos paused, a thin smile forming on his lips. "What he doesn't know is that I burned them."

Grins broke out around the table.

"That's good!" said Aleko. "I've been expecting them to come for mine. Now I don't have to worry!"

"Well, be mindful," said Marcos. "I saw them offloading a radio-locator truck this week. You should keep a lookout before you turn it on."

"Now the Nazis are taking whatever they want. They just walk into Jewish homes and take silverware, candlesticks, anything! And Jewish shops, too, helping themselves. No one stops them," Avram complained.

"Allegra and I have been giving everything away," said Henri.

"Don't give too much," cautioned Aleko. "If they come to your apartment, let them find something of value or it could go extra hard on you."

"They will come to your home, Henri. It's only a matter of time," said Marcos, looking Henri in the eyes.

But there was no time left.

Chapter 25
The Jewish Colony of the East

February 24, 1943

With sunken shoulders, Allegra stood in her living room. She was dressed to leave, wearing her unbuttoned winter overcoat with the large yellow star. She took one final look at her apartment, the home she had lived in for the last eight years. "This is where Andreas learned to walk," she thought.

The new owners were in the kitchen making breakfast. Allegra could hear Phedra Petracca with her children, Pello and Alida. Their father, Thanos, was cheerfully telling them something about the Jews moving out today. Allegra felt a sob rising inside her. "Oh, God, why is this happening to us?"

Allegra's eyes slowly took in the room for the last time. The big bookshelf was only half-filled. She and Henri had given away all the rest to their Christian friends. The beautiful oriental carpets on the floor...only a few remained now, all the others given as gifts to good friends like Nicos and Marcos, and many of Avram and Myriam's Greek Orthodox friends as well.

Lamps, tables, chairs, and vases once filled with beautiful flowers, all now either gone or left to the Petraccas. Allegra felt the tightness in her gut, realizing how shallowly she was breathing.

Suddenly there was commotion as Andreas, now two, came running into the room, Daisyka close behind.

"Mamá!" he cried out, running for her, oblivious to the massive changes in his life and the life of his family.

"Oh, my big boy!" Allegra responded, trying to be light-hearted. She scooped him up into her arms and held him, feeling the heat of his warm body next to hers, wriggling as he turned in her arms to look at Daisyka who was giving him a playful look. Andreas was giggling with excitement.

"I'm going to get you!" Daisyka said. Andreas wriggled even more wildly, and Allegra, at odds with her own feelings and Andreas's excitement, couldn't smile, couldn't summon any playfulness, and put Andreas down.

"Daisyka, are you and Andreas ready?" Allegra asked in a stern voice that caught Daisyka by surprise.

"Yes," Daisyka replied, the playfulness now gone from her face, too. "I only have to put on his coat and we're ready to go." Daisyka reached for Andreas who shrieked and backed into his mother's legs.

Confused with the flood of feelings, Allegra stepped back. "Please take Andreas into the other room," she requested, and Daisyka stretched out her hand to

Andreas, who quickly took it.

"The hardest part," thought Allegra "is letting go of the life we were supposed to have." The stabbing pain in her heart grew larger. "What will become of us, God?"

Allegra heard a key in the door and then the familiar sound of Henri entering the apartment. She walked over to the hallway to greet him.

"Hi, Honey." Henri's face was haggard.

Allegra fell into his arms and hugged him like she would never let go. She looked into Henri's eyes, and he could see how red they were.

"We'll be all right," he said in a strong voice. "I know it."

"Yes, I know," Allegra replied, but the knot in her stomach did not relinquish its hold.

"I found a man with a cart. He's downstairs. We need to bring our suitcases and boxes."

"Everything is ready," Allegra said, her voice cracking. "Andreas and Daisyka are ready, and Myriam and Avram, too, I think."

"Let's gather everything here by the door, and I can start carrying the boxes and suitcases down," Henri said, suddenly now all business. In moments their possessions began to gather in the hallway. Myriam and

Avram had very little, just a suitcase each and three boxes.

"It's just a few things," Myriam said in her sing-song Ladino. Henri noticed her eyes were reddish, too. "Mostly clothes and some linen. I'm bringing candles, my medicines and ointments..."

"It's all right, Mamá," Henri interrupted her. "Whatever you're bringing is fine." Henri looked at his father, and he could see the appreciation in his eyes.

"You know me," Avram added. "I don't need much."

"I'll get started," said Henri as he picked up a box and turned toward the front door.

"I'll help," said Avram, and he took a suitcase, following his son out the door.

Allegra looked at Myriam and they reached for each other. Allegra hugged Myriam tightly, the tears running down her cheeks; she felt Myriam's short sobbing breaths.

Henri and Avram returned and Allegra said, "I have something to say. I want all of us to know that no matter what happens, we are a family and whatever we do, we do it together. Nothing will change that, ever."

Then, with a final rush, the suitcases and boxes were moved downstairs and onto the waiting cart. "I'll get Andreas," said Allegra, and in a moment she had scooped up her energetic son and was descending the stairs with Daisyka.

Saying a quick goodbye to the strangers in his home, Henri heard the door lock behind him, the sound of the latch louder than he'd ever heard it before.

Henri walked down the stairs, aware as if for the first time, how loud his departing steps sounded on the familiar staircase. At the bottom, he opened the door and stepped outside. Tsimiski was busy today, hundreds of people carrying suitcases, packages, and belongings, the street full of Jews carrying their bundles or riding in loaded horse-drawn carts. In a moment Henri and his little family had joined the others, moving toward the ghetto, disappearing in the crowded street.

The man with the horse cart drove their belongings the two dozen blocks from Tsimiski to the apartments Henri had found on Afroditis Street. Allegra was seated in the front between the driver and Myriam, holding little Andreas on her lap. Henri, Avram and Daisyka walked alongside.

Three and four story wooden and stone buildings lined the street with peeling paint, worn bricks, windows held by dirty frames, and discolored rooftops with mossy shingles. People carried large rope-tied bundles on bicycles, or pushed carts piled high with the remnants of their homes. Allegra watched a man struggling with a cart laden with chairs, a mirror, stuffed bags of goods, blankets, and boxes as his wife and three children walked behind him, yellow stars on their coats. Dogs were barking and children were crying as families moved into the ghetto.

"This is the house," said Henri. The cart driver pulled to the curb before an old three-story brick and plaster building. Henri's eyes met Allegra's. Her familiar strength was a great reassurance. Allegra nodded, and he heard her silent words again, "We will all get through this."

Children were sitting and playing on the frayed wooden steps; Allegra's face fell as she saw their ragged clothing and gaunt eyes. Looking at his mother, Henri saw her disappointment, and her helpless acceptance saddened him.

"I'm all right, son," she said, looking down from the cart. She tried to smile, but couldn't. "Is this our home?"

"Yes, we have two rooms. It's the best I could find."

"It will be fine, I'm sure," Myriam said. "I'm grateful we don't have to share a room with another family."

"Wait here," Henri said to everyone. "Babá, please come with me," and he led his father up the few steps past the playing children and into the house.

Inside, the heavy fragrance of onions and cabbage filled the dark, filthy hallway, and they heard a baby crying loudly upstairs. Henri's heart sank again, as when he first found these rooms in the poor Vardar ghetto.

A few steps down the hallway, he opened the first door with one of the keys. Once a dining room, it wasn't tiny, but for his wife and son, and Daisyka, it was terrible...yet would have to do. A simple glass chandelier hung from the ceiling; Henri switched on the light and it sputtered, then held. In the dull light, the walls looked sallow, the floor was old stained wood, and there was no window.

"Your room is next door," he said to his father. "Here is your key."

"It will be fine, son."

A few moments later, Henri followed his father outside, his steps slow and heavy. Back in the sunshine, Henri squinted, the light hurting his eyes after the gloom of the apartment. "Let's get everything inside," said Henri.

Their belongings were pulled off the cart and deposited in their dismal rooms. Allegra began sorting bundles, suitcases, bedding and furnishings into the two tiny rooms. Outside, Henri paid the cart driver, and he drove off to find the next transient family.

"Oh, God," thought Allegra, "that we have to live here," her beautiful apartment on Tsimiski Street so far away and gone forever.

All photographs featuring the Algava family are from the author's private collection. Unless otherwise credited, photos of Thessaloniki during the war years are from the collection of Andreas Assael.

Henri Algava, 1931.

The Carasso Family, 1932.

Allegra Carasso in a long white dress she designed and sewed, 1934.

Henri and Allegra at their engagement reception, October 21, 1934.

The newly married couple in the synagogue, March 24, 1935.

Henri and Allegra on their wedding day.

Henri and Allegra at the Acropolis in Athens on their honeymoon, March 28, 1935.

Second floor apartment of Henri, Allegra, Avram, and Myriam Algava and the birthplace of Andreas Algava, until forced to move to the ghetto.

Allegra Carasso, 1938.

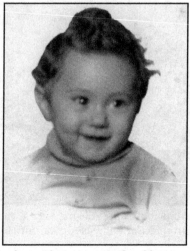

Andreas Algava, 14 months old, 1941
(two months before the German Army
occupied Thessaloniki).

Next to the harbor in Thessaloniki, a house bombed
by the Italian air force in early November 1940.

Once a Turkish prison, the White Tower, a landmark of
Thessaloniki as camouflaged by the Greeks.

German tanks rolling through the Galerius Arch.
(Credit: Sueddeutsche Zeitung Photo / Alamy Stock Photo)

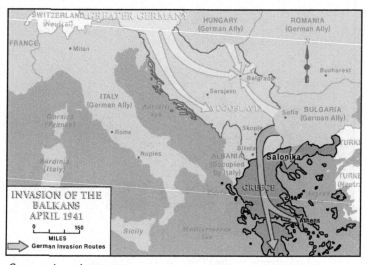

German invasion route.
(Credit: United States Holocaust Memorial Museum)

Two Greek soldiers arriving from Albania after defeat of the Greek Army (visible on the right is a German motorbike driving on Nikis Street).

The Wehrmacht band playing in Tsimiski Street at Aristotelous Square (in the middle is a German soldier playing the trombone who later photographed the Jews at Liberty Square).

After the capture of the city, German mountain troops have their boots polished by Greek children.

German guard in front of Kommandantur (German headquarters) building where Henri Algava was taken when he was arrested and interrogated.

The Jewish cemetery with the White Tower and the sea in the far distance.

Black Sabbath, July 11, 1942. The German authorities required the male Jewish population to stand many hours in Liberty Square under the hot sun to register for forced labor. Shown are two Greek police officers who were ordered to keep discipline.

During the registration, the Jews were forced to do exercises. In the background is the Ioniki Bank building where the registration documentation took place. In front stand a German navy under-officer and a Wehrmacht officer.

Brutalized in the extreme July heat, a Jewish man has collapsed in Liberty Square. A German soldier looks on smiling.
(Credit: Jewish Museum of Thessaloniki)

On April 20, 1943, a group of 300 Thessaloniki Jews arrived for forced labor in Karya. They were ordered to use their bare hands to construct a railroad spur, which would increase the traffic flow of the railway.

On the top of a hill in the north part of Thessaloniki, sits the famous Jedi Kule prison (built in the 9th century A.D.). Just below was the Algava family's first hiding place.

A group of five German soldiers walking by the sea on Nikis Street. In the distance is the Kommandantur building. On the left side is the Hotel Mediterranee used as the German air force headquarters. After the war, Henri found his first job working as an interpreter for the British advance force at this hotel.

Built in the 4th century A.D., the Galerius Arch is named after the Roman emperor. The Algavas were hidden approximately a block away from the Arch as their last location in hiding.

Second floor apartment of Nicos and Sousanna Efcarpides (overlooking Liberty Square).

ISRAELITISCHE KULTUSGEMEINDE SALONIKI
ΙΣΡΑΗΛΙΤΙΚΗ ΚΟΙΝΟΤΗΣ ΘΕΣΣΑΛΟΝΙΚΗΣ

PERSONAL - AUSWEIS
ΔΕΛΤΙΟΝ ΤΑΥΤΟΤΗΤΟΣ

Registernummer _____ 24435
'Αριθ. μητρώου

Familienname _____ Algava
'Επώνυμον

Name _____ Allegre
"Ονομα

Name des Vaters oder des Gatten _____ Aaron
"Ονομα πατρός ή συζύγου

Geburtsjahr _____ 1910
"Ετος γεννήσεως

Beruf _____ Οἰκουρά
'Επαγγέλμα

Adresse _____
Διεύθυνσις

Saloniki den 21 Φεβρουαρίου 1943
'Εν Θεσ)νίκη τῇ

DER PRÄSIDENT DER ISRAELITISCHEN KULTUSGEMEINDE
Ο ΠΡΟΕΔΡΟΣ ΤΗΣ ΙΣΡΑΗΛΙΤΙΚΗΣ ΚΟΙΝΟΤΗΤΟΣ

Guil. Gen. No. 3788 N

Allegra's Ausweis, February 21, 1943.

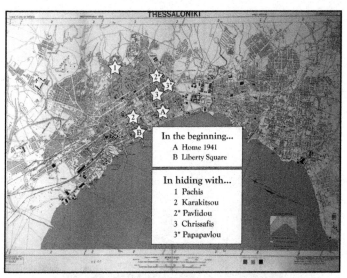

1943 Map of Thessaloniki, illustrating the Algava family's hiding places (* indicates where Avram and Myriam were hidden in a separate location).

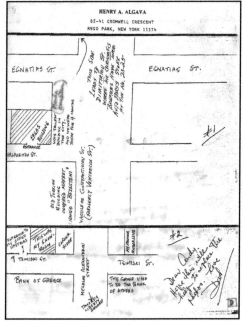

Henri Algava's hand-drawn representation of a few significant locations, 1990.

Henri in a sidecar with his brother-in-law Pepo behind the driver in Athens, 1945.

Henri and Allegra at Rockefeller Center, New York City, 1946.

An autographed program from a
Sophia Vembo performance in 1947.
The inscription reads: "To my good
and beloved friend Allegra. Vembo."

Myriam and Avram Algava in
Brooklyn, 1948.

March 11. 1943 — October 30, 1944

1943			1944		
	March	21		Jan.	31
	April	30		Feb.	29
	May	81		March	31
	July	30		April	30
	July	31		May	31
	August	31.		June	30
	Sept-	30		July	31
	Oct.	81		Aug.	31
	Nov.	30		sept.	30
	Dec.	31		Oct.	30
		296			304

304
296
Total 600 days.

Henri Algava's calculation of the number of days the family was in hiding, written in his own hand.

The Algava family in 2017: Drew, Michael Gow, Sabria, Andreas, Carin and Alisa. (Credit: domineyphotography.com)

* * *

Henri and Allegra were talking softly at the little table so Daisyka and Andreas didn't overhear their words. "I had another dream last night," said Allegra. "It was frightening." Henri looked at her closely, studying her face. His stomach tightened at her whispered words.

"I don't know how I got there, but I remember I was in the water, and my whole body was covered. I was drowning...dying! I needed air and was about to breathe the water and come to my end when a belt was thrown to me and I was pulled out! At the very last moment I was saved!"

"Oh..." said Henri, startled.

"I woke with an incredible sense of relief," she added. Allegra looked at her husband and saw the alarm in his eyes. "Do you see, Henri? It's another dream where I am saved from death." There was urgency in her voice.

Henri could feel her hands tightening around his. "I see," he said. "I feel something bad is about to happen."

"And look again at this magazine Alberto gave you the other day." Allegra placed a glossy magazine on the table. "Do you believe this?" she asked, her whispered voice rising.

Henri looked at it. The title of the magazine was *La Colonie Juive de L'Est*.* The front cover showed a picture

---

La Colonie Juive de L'Est: The Jewish Colony of the East.

of a smiling Jewish family, seemingly happy in their new surroundings. Henri shook his head as he opened the magazine, turning a few pages. He saw photographs of a thriving Jewish town with Jewish doctors, Jewish policemen, banks and stores run by Jews, and even a Jewish hospital. Good jobs were available, waiting for new arrivals. Jewish leaders were explaining the benefits of living in this exciting new land reserved just for Jews.

"This is propaganda," he said to his wife.

"That's right, Henri." Allegra's face was intense and she was speaking with the strength of her recent dream. "These are all lies. The Nazis want us to believe this, but none of it is true."

Henri looked into Allegra's eyes. "It all seems so real."

"Yes," Allegra agreed, lowering her voice again. "It does seem real, and yet we know it can't be. This magazine is a fantasy. I couldn't believe what Avram told us he heard Alberto saying in the taverna!"

"I know, it's unbelievable," Henri replied. "What was it? 'We are afraid for no reason... We are going to be well-treated in Poland.'"

"Impossible!"

"Yes, and then Alberto said, 'Who knows, maybe Hitler is our Messiah.'"

"He is mad," said Allegra, lifting an eyebrow.

There were some rustling noises in the hall outside the door. They recognized Avram's voice and in a moment Myriam and Avram were seated on two chairs beside the small table while Henri and Allegra sat on a suitcase and crate. "We don't feel safe here. I had another dream... Henri and I both feel something bad is about to happen soon."

Avram and Myriam looked at Allegra and Henri, and nodded their heads. "What do you think we should do?" asked Avram.

"We don't trust this information," Allegra said, slightly pushing the magazine on the table. "The idea of relocating Jews to a New Israel in Poland seems absurd."

"I don't know what to expect, but I don't trust the Germans," added Henri. "I think we need to leave here, soon."

"Where should we go?" asked Avram.

"What are our choices?" asked Myriam.

"We've heard some people are paying fishermen to take them south into the Italian zone...it would be expensive, but we could escape to Athens. Maurice could put us up for a few days until we found a place," offered Henri.

"I don't like that idea," countered Avram. "I've heard

it costs a fortune. I also heard some were denounced as they tried to board the boats and were shot by the Germans."

"We need to do something," said Henri. "If we stay here, we'll be deported..."

"...to a certain death," finished Allegra, her voice almost hissing. "Remember my dream? This thing is no good. All these people, they are not coming back."

"What chance do we have if we go into hiding here in Thessaloniki?"

"Where would we hide?" asked Myriam, alarmed.

"I don't know," replied Avram, "but I have friends. Henri and I have many friends. I believe they would help us somehow."

"If we hide, what are our odds of surviving? One percent?" Allegra looked at her husband and in-laws. "But if we are sent to the Colony, what would happen to us? It's worth taking a chance going into hiding because if we stay here...we have no chance at all!"

Silently the decision was made.

Chapter 26
Certain Arrangements

March 2, 1943

Henri walked quickly down the street, past the men and women dressed against the midwinter cold, their yellow Stars of David standing out against the heavy gray overcoats.

The wind made Henri draw inward and tighten his shoulders. Hands in his pockets, he pulled the fabric of his coat closer about his body, but it did little good. The wind pierced the cloth and he felt chilled, especially on his legs. A small group of street children ran up to him, the oldest about 14. His face was filthy and red from the cold; on his head was a flat woolen cap.

"Excuse me, Mister," the boy said to Henri. "Can you please give us some money? We want some soup." The boy was standing just far enough away in case Henri tried to cuff him. Henri could see how thin he was, how thin they all were, taut cheekbones showing below recessed eyes. Henri pulled out some money and gave it to the boy who quickly grabbed and ran, his gang close behind, their voices excited.

Henri reached his destination, a little taverna in the ghetto, not so different from Aleko's by the White Tower. Henri brushed past some men coming out, quickly pulling up their coat collars against the unrelenting wind blowing down the street. Gratefully stepping inside, the warmth felt almost like fire on his cold cheeks.

The room was crowded and smoky amid the familiar sound of Ladino voices. Marcos Hombitis was sitting at a table a few meters away, his glass in front of him, the ashtray holding several stubs.

Henri took off his coat with its star and walked over. "Hello, my friend," said Marcos in a voice that betrayed his concern. "It is good to see you."

"Thank you, Marcos. It's always good to see you, too. You've been waiting?"

"Not too long," replied Marcos. "I arrived a short while ago. I didn't know if there would be a problem getting through."

"Was there?"

"No. No one asked to see my papers."

"Good." Henri draped his coat over the back of his chair and caught the eye of a waiter.

"So," began Marcos, "aside from sharing a drink with an old friend, why did you want to see me?"

Henry leaned forward and whispered. "We've decided

we want to leave the ghetto and go into hiding." Henri's eyes searched Marcos's face for a sign of surprise or objection and saw neither.

"That's a good idea," Marcos said as he lit another cigarette. "You've heard the rumors?"

"We've heard some," said Henri. "We think it's propaganda about a New Israel near Kraków."

"When it comes to the Jews," reflected Marcos, "I wouldn't believe anything the Germans say." Marcos took a deep drag on his cigarette and blew it out slowly. "Do you have a plan?"

"This is why I wanted to talk to you. We're ready to go as soon as we have a destination. We thought about taking a fishing ship down the coast into the Italian sector, but that seems too risky."

"The Germans have been killing the Jews they've caught," Marcos frowned, thinking what might happen to his own wife and children if he was caught helping.

"We want to stay in Thessaloniki and pay rent to a family that would hide us. Maybe someplace on the edge of town, out of the way…" Henri's voice trailed off. "Do you know anybody who would help us?"

Marcos looked around the room for a moment, took another drag on his cigarette, and then looked at Henri. "I don't," he said, pausing, "but I could find someone. I have a lot of friends and can ask around."

"That would be very good," Henri said, sitting a little taller now that some weight was lifted. "We want to leave as soon as possible. It's not safe here."

"I understand. Actually, I just now thought of a farmer I know. He has an orchard in the *Kastra*.* I think he can be trusted...and if he can't help us, maybe he knows someone."

"Thank you, Marcos," Henri said with gratitude. "We're forever in your debt."

"Well, I haven't done anything yet," Marcos said with a smile. "It's getting late now, but I'll go up to the Kastra tomorrow and speak to him. I know he's a good man, and some cash won't hurt. How many are we talking about?"

"There are six of us. Allegra, Andreas, and me, Avram, Myriam, and Daisyka."

"How much can you afford?"

"We can pay with gold coins, but our money has to last as long as possible. We need to pay for our food, too. This person will have to buy our food because we won't be able to go out very often. Could you offer him one *lira** for two weeks of rent and food?"

Kastra: A district on the north side of Thessaloniki, referring to the Byzantine castle there.

Lira: An English gold coin; the Greeks called these *lira* like the pre-euro Italian currency.

"I will do that," Marcos said, stubbing his cigarette out in the ashtray. "I'll see him tomorrow and then meet you here around the same time. If this man won't help, we'll find someone else."

Marcos held out his hand and Henri reached across the table to shake it. "Thank you, Marcos."

"I'm glad to do it." Marcos said, standing up to go. "I'll see you tomorrow."

He slipped into his coat and looked down, smiling at Henri. "No matter what, I will make sure you and your family are safe." In a moment, Marcos had stepped through the door and was gone.

"Safe," Henri thought. "What is it like to feel safe?" He sat there for the length of a cigarette, trying to remember.

* * *

Early the next morning Marcos Hombitis climbed the long hill up toward the walled castle at the crest of the *Kastra* district. He walked past the pastel-colored buildings with their metal and canvas awnings, some with long drapes of green ivy hanging down from the balconies, still wet with the morning's rain.

Several people walked quickly past him, keeping to themselves, the morning breeze blowing up from the port far below. A widow in black was carrying a bag with a few vegetables, walking slowly up the steep street. Going downhill, an elderly man with a cane carefully chose his steps on the slick pavement. Marcos caught the face of a woman staring down at him from a second story window, quickly vanishing. A heavy motorcycle rumbled from a street below, and a brown and white dog came around the corner and trotted down the hill. There were no signs of any German soldiers.

Marcos passed an alley and saw a small group of children playing. The sounds reminded him of Nicolas and Calandra. Last night Anna had greeted him from the top of the stairs, her eyes smiling. A greeting, a quick kiss, and then his arms were full of his squealing children, wrestling on the floor before dinner. "How fortunate I am," he thought. Then he remembered the ghetto, and he seethed with anger.

Marcos climbed ever higher on the ascending street and as he crested, he stopped to admire the beautiful view of the Bay of Thermaicos* below. The uphill breeze had turned light and cooled his face. The maze of tan-beige buildings and tiled roofs stretched in all directions, bordered by the blue water blending with sky far out to sea. A single seagull begged for food nearby.

He took a full deep breath and continued, the street winding around the side of the Byzantine castle. The hill soon fell away and he descended toward the rural side of

---

Bay of Thermaicos: The name of Thessaloniki's bay.

Thessaloniki where buildings were less densely packed and small fields revealed themselves under the morning fog.

A few minutes later and Marcos was at the front door of a large two-story farmhouse at the edge of a pear orchard. He knocked and waited.

"Who is it?" said a woman's voice.

"Marcos Hombitis, Customs," he said. "I am here to see Leonidas Paraschos on port business."

"Oh!" said the woman, and the door opened. "I'm his wife," said an elderly woman. "Is he expecting you?" Marcos was surprised at how much older she was than he expected, as Paraschos was in his early 50s.

"Yes. Is he home?" asked Marcos.

"He's upstairs. I'll get him for you. Do you mind waiting here?"

"No, not at all." The woman closed the door and Marcos walked along the veranda, enjoying the peaceful yard. A moment later, the door opened and Paraschos stepped out to greet him.

"Marcos! Good to see you."

"Good to see you, too, Leonidas."

Paraschos invited Marcos inside and before long they had finished some paperwork and were enjoying a cup of ersatz coffee by the window. Marcos lowered his voice and leaned closer to his host.

"Leonidas, I have some other business to discuss. I know you have no sympathy for the Germans and wish, as I do, that they would all go to hell."

Paraschos smiled and nodded. "I get along with them," he said, "but not because I want to."

Marcos nodded. "I know a family that's in trouble and they need certain arrangements...I thought you might be able to help, or know someone who can."

Paraschos's face grew serious. He held Marcos's eyes with his own, and then looked out the window at his pear trees. "Is this family Jewish?" he asked.

"Yes. Six people, including two elders and a young child. They will pay for rent and food."

Paraschos thought a moment, weighing his answer. "Am I willing to put my life at risk, and my wife's?" he thought. He'd heard of people being executed for helping Jews. He didn't know if the rumors were true, and he didn't want to find out.

"I can't help them myself," Paraschos said, "but I may know someone who can. My neighbor. I heard he sheltered some British soldiers trying to escape to the

Middle East. Maybe he can help."

Marcos nodded, understanding Paraschos had limits. "Who is he, and how do I find him?"

"His name is Linos. Linos Pachis. He's on the other side of my orchard. He has a small house and needs the money. His wife works at the women's prison as a cook. They have two children, a boy and a girl. You should talk to him, Marcos."

"Thank you. I'll go there now." Marcos stood up and Paraschos saw him to the door.

"Please give my regards to your wife. Thank you for keeping this quiet."

"Of course," said Paraschos. "Good luck to you, and your friends."

Paraschos watched Marcos go. It was the right thing to do, deflecting trouble from his door. This business with the Jews...it could not end well. He then thought about going into town to spend the evening with his mistress and their daughter.

Chapter 27
Farewell

March 4, 1943

The Baron Hirsch district, located next to Thessaloniki's railway station, is fenced off with barbed wire and wooden boards, and residents are forbidden to leave.

Avram waited with Henri in the crowded noisy taverna. Discourse was animated and opinions ranged from suspicion of Rabbi Koretz as a foreigner imported from Berlin, to relief that everyone would soon have a better life in the New Israel. Food shortages, inflationary prices, the execution of Jews trying to escape Thessaloniki, partisan activity, and arguments about the structure of the Jewish government were all loudly discussed, debated, and deplored.

Avram shook his head slowly; he had seen too much. "How could people be so easily fooled?" he wondered.

Henri read his father's thoughts. "They are afraid, Babá, so they believe anything that promises relief."

Avram looked at his son and nodded. He lit up another cigarette, shook out the match and let it fall in the ashtray. "We're running out of time. The deportation orders could come any day. We don't want to be in the ghetto when the orders are given. It'll be too late by then."

"We'll go as soon as possible. By the way, I visited Mamá's family today," said Henri.

"How are they?" asked Avram.

"Reconciled. They believe there is nothing they can do. I spoke to *Yaya mou*.* She was sitting on the ground with her back against the wall enjoying the sun. She asked me what I would do."

"The poor woman is in her nineties..."

"I said, 'Yaya, I want you to know we are not going to go. We are going into hiding,' and she said, 'God be with you...'" And then Henri began to cry.

"It will be a miracle if she survives the trip," Avram murmured.

"She said a blessing for you and Mamá, Allegra, and Andriko."

Avram thought of his wife's mother and how frail she had become. She was too infirm to go into hiding, and there was nothing he could do for her. She was already leaning on Death's shoulder. "May God be merciful to her," replied Avram softly.

Yaya mou: An endearing term meaning "my grandmother."

The taverna was busy with men entering and leaving, and Henri spotted Marcos, coming in and making his way through the crowd.

"Welcome!" said Henri. As Marcos unbuttoned his coat and sat down, Henri smelled the winter air on his coat.

Henri motioned to a waiter. "Can I buy you a drink?" asked Henri.

"Yes, I'd like a *retsina*," replied Marcos, lighting a cigarette. Marcos looked at his friends and his face grew serious. "I think I may have a place."

Henri and Avram exchanged quick glances, then looked at Marcos.

"My friend owns a pear orchard. He ships fruit through the port, and I know he's an honorable man. He told me he has a neighbor who took people in before."

The waiter suddenly appeared at the table. "A *retsina*, *parakaló*,* and two more coffees," Henri told the waiter. The waiter nodded and left.

"I went to meet him. His name is Pachis. He has a little three-room house and would rent one of the rooms. He has a wife, two teenage children, and his mother. It's not a big room, but the six of you can make it work."

Parakaló: Please.

"How much does he want?" asked Henri.

"He wants payment every Thursday on market day. One *lira* will pay for the week."

Henri glanced at Avram. Avram nodded. "That's for both rent and food?"

"Yes. The house is on the edge of my friend's pear orchard. There are a few other houses nearby, but it's a quiet street. I didn't see any Germans up there, and hardly anyone walking by."

"I like that it's quiet. And the price is right," said Avram.

"What did you find out about the other people Pachis hid?" Henri asked.

"He's hidden British soldiers trying to get to the Middle East. They stayed a few days until they could escape south."

"It's risky, but what isn't? What do you think, Babá?"

"I trust Marcos. If you think we'll be safe, we should do it."

The waiter walked up to their table with their drinks, took the money and left.

"How soon can we move?" said Henri, relieved they had refuge.

"I'll go back tomorrow and pay him a *lira* to secure the deal. If this works out, you can move this Sunday, in three days. Does that sound all right?"

"Yes," agreed Avram. "What do you think?" he asked Henri.

"That's good," Henri said. "It will give us time to see Allegra's family before we go, and I know Daisyka will want to see her family, too."

Henri reached into his pocket. "Here's a coin for Pachis," he said, passing it unnoticed into Marcos's big hand.

"All right, then," Marcos said, reaching for his glass with the other hand. "Unless I hear otherwise, I'll meet you at your apartment this Sunday. It's best we travel at night."

"I agree," said Henri. "It gets dark around 8...let's plan to leave around half past."

"Sounds good," Marcos affirmed. "Don't bring much. Just a single suitcase, one for you and Allegra, and one for you and Myriam. We don't want to attract attention. Pack lightly, a few things for a day or two. After you're settled, I'll bring more."

"How will we get there?" Avram asked.

"The best way will be to walk out. We'll break into three groups. Henri, Allegra and Daisyka will travel together, and you and Myriam will be a pair; Andreas can be with me. This way, if any of you are caught, at least Andreas will have his life. After we leave the ghetto, we'll walk to the Saint Sophia station and take a trolley part of the way up the hill to the Kastra."

"A trolley?" asked Henri. "Isn't that dangerous?"

"Only if we act suspicious. Remove your yellow stars, or wear other coats. We'll get off the trolley at St. Sophie where the hill starts and walk the rest of the way. We should arrive by 10 or so."

The three men looked at each other, and there was silent assent. "All right," Henri said. "That's our plan."

"Tell Andreas we are playing a game, and that he is to be quiet, and is not to call out to you. We'll pretend I'm his *theíos*, and we are going to a magical place high above the city. Let him know there will be a special treat if he plays the game well."

Marcos finished his *retsina* and stood to go. "I'll see you on Sunday around eight o'clock. Wear dark clothing, and explain to Andreas that we're playing a game."

"Thank you, Marcos," said Avram. "You're our guardian angel."

"Mother," said Allegra, "you really must listen to me."

"It will be all right, Allegra, you'll see. We'll be fine. Your father has looked into this matter. Rabbi Koretz met with him personally and your father was reassured." Allegra's mother, Doudoun, poured some more tea into the delicate china teacups.

"I have a very bad feeling about this, Mother. You and Babá know the Nazis hate the Jews, so it doesn't make any sense to believe what the rabbi is saying. He's only telling everyone what the Nazis are telling him to say."

Allegra's sister Rosa spoke up. "The Rabbi wouldn't lie," said Rosa. "He is the leader of our community."

"But how can you possibly think the Nazis are sending Jews to a nice place in Poland?" Allegra felt a scream rising inside her.

"Girls," said Doudoun, "please don't argue. Allegra, we're not going to hide someplace…we're going to stay here and follow the Rabbi's orders. He knows what's best for us. I think you and Henri should stay here, too. I can't believe you're going to go hide in somebody's house somewhere. How will that be good for Andreas?"

"All right, Mother." Allegra's voice became soft, knowing there was no point arguing. "Our minds are made up, too. We'll be leaving in a few days, and I'll try to come back for visits if I can."

"Of course you can," replied Doudoun, looking at her daughter with raised eyebrows. "Why couldn't you?"

"Things won't stay like they are. But I will come if I can."

"Good!" said Rosa. "Then we can have more afternoon teas with you!"

"Yes," said Doudoun. "That would be very nice."

"Mamá, if Babá changes his mind, I can have our friend help you."

"Thank you, Dear. That won't be necessary. Give me a hug before you go."

Allegra hugged her mother, and then Rosa. Putting on her coat with the yellow star, she looked at them both through swelling tears, anguish in her heart, wondering if she would ever see them again.

✳ ✳ ✳

Henri's face was glum as he walked along the street beside Daisyka. He was carrying a large suitcase, and Daisyka had a smaller one. The morning was cold and they walked briskly, in step with each other. Daisyka's mother was in the Singrou ghetto, and since Jews were not allowed to use public transportation, they had to walk the whole way. Henri hadn't said more than a few words. With a heavy heart, it was impossible to be cheerful.

Henri noticed the eyes of the passersby looking at their

yellow Stars of David, avoiding eye contact, skirting them as though they were diseased. Daisyka noticed it too, but held her head up and walked straight ahead without looking at the people walking by.

As they approached a big intersection with lots of people, horses and carts, Henri saw two German soldiers walking toward them. They were without weapons, walking along the streets of Thessaloniki, visible reminders of the occupation.

The soldiers' eyes were on Daisyka, and both men had broad smiles. *"Schau mal eine huebsche Juedin!"** said one.

"Ja," said the other, *"Was für eine Verschwendung!"**

Henri knew what they had said and it made his face red with anger. Daisyka didn't speak German, but had her own thoughts about what they'd said. If she felt any discomfort, Henri could not see it.

"Don't let them bother you," Henri said.

"I don't," replied Daisyka. "They are rude and poorly bred. Their mothers would be ashamed of them."

Arriving at the Singrou ghetto, Henri didn't know where his aunt and cousins lived. Daisyka guided them, stopping at a simple two-story building. She rang the

---

Schau mal eine huebsche Juedin!: Look at the pretty Jew!
Was für eine Verschwendung!: What a waste!

bell. In a moment Daisyka's younger sister was hugging her and then all three walked up the short flight of stairs. A brief visit, drinking tea with his aunt and cousins, and it was time to leave.

"I'll see you to the door," said Daisyka. She led him down the stairs and at the bottom she turned to him. "Thank you, Henri, for taking such good care of me."

"Allegra and I also want you to know how much we appreciate your loving care of Andreas. You have been a huge and wonderful help to us."

"You're welcome," she said. "And thank you for offering to take me with you when you leave this Sunday."

"I wish I could change your mind."

"My mother will need me. When it's our turn to travel to the New Israel, I want to be there to take care of her."

"We'll always love you, Daisyka," Henri said, feeling his throat tighten.

Daisyka smiled. "I will always love all of you," she said.

Henri reached for her and gave her a big hug.

"Goodbye!" she said, and Henri stepped through the door and into the cool, sunny afternoon. Once on the sidewalk, he turned to wave. Daisyka was just closing the door, her beautiful long hair the last he ever saw of her.

Chapter 28
Escape

March 11, 1943

The Jewish Community has issued a statement that Jews should remain calm, but two days later the 104 officials of the Jewish Community are arrested and informed they are now hostages, being held to guarantee the population's obedience to anti-Jewish orders. Rabbi Koretz volunteers himself as a guarantor and the 104 officials are released. Three days later new orders forbid the sale or purchase of Jewish property of any kind.

They had been ready for hours. One little light brown suitcase was by the door. Andreas was asleep in his bed in the corner, dressed in his pants and shirt, ready to go when awakened. Henri could feel the knot in his stomach getting tighter as time slowly passed. Allegra appeared calm on the outside but her eyes too frequently left her book to watch the door and their sleeping child.

"Should I make some tea?" Allegra whispered.

"No," replied Henri. "It's almost time, and besides, we don't want to have to look for a bathroom."

Allegra smiled. He was right, of course, but she wanted to be busy and take her mind off her fears.

There was a slight knock on their door. Allegra looked at Henri. "Who is it?" he said in a low voice.

"Marcos," and Henri admitted their friend.

"Come in," Henri whispered. Marcos came in and nodded toward Allegra, noticing the sleeping child and suitcase.

"You're ready to go? Are Avram and Myriam ready?" Henri nodded.

"Good, then we should go. Where is Daisyka?"

"She's not coming. She decided to stay with her mother." Henri saw his momentary disappointment and then his usual strength and resolve.

Marcos looked at Allegra. "I think the most danger we will face tonight will be from Andreas."

"What do you mean?" Allegra asked, taking a short breath.

"We agreed he should come with me so if you are caught, he will have his freedom. Is he prepared to play the game we talked about...being quiet and not paying attention to you?"

"I think so," Allegra replied. "He's old enough..." Marcos looked at the sleeping child and knew their fate rested with him.

Allegra walked toward Andreas's bed. "I'll wake him. I'll remind him it's time to play our game."

"Good," said Marcos.

"I'll get Avram," said Henri.

In a few moments Andreas had roused and the six of them were ready to go. Everyone put on their dark coats with the yellow stars, lightly attached with only a few stitches of thread to keep them in place.

"Remember," whispered Marcos, as they were about to open the apartment's door, "stay in three separate groups. We'll gather at the trolley stop on Martiou Street. When you're out of the ghetto, tear off the stars and put them in your pocket. We'll get off at Saint Sophie as planned. Whatever happens, just stay calm. We'll be all right."

He looked at each of them, and made his face relax with a little smile to reassure them. "They look ready," he thought.

Marcos reached down and picked up Andreas. "Come, Andreas," he said. Andreas allowed himself to be picked up by the massive arms. "Are you ready to play the game?" asked Marcos.

"Yes," said Andreas in his tiny boy's voice.

"Good! This will be fun!" said Marcos in his warm

father's voice. "Andreas and I will go first. We'll get a head start!" and with that, Marcos stepped into the empty hallway. In a moment he and Andreas were on the street, the night illumined only by an occasional lamppost and muffled light from the buildings along their way.

His eyes and ears were alert for any threatening sight or sound. A few people were walking along the dark street, singly or in pairs, and several horses were pulling carts even at this late hour. Otherwise the streets were empty. Marcos turned briefly to see if the two other pairs were following, and they were.

"Andreas, this is fun, isn't it?" he asked in a playful voice, keeping Andreas in the game.

"Yes," said the little boy as Marcos walked steadily but without haste.

"We will have some fun soon," Marcos added. "We're going to get on a trolley." Andreas didn't say anything, his sleepy eyes on the street ahead.

The light breeze picked up a little. "Are you warm enough?" Marcos asked, as he kept walking.

"Yes." Marcos could tell Andreas was becoming drowsy, glad the young child was quiet. Nothing...nothing... could go wrong tonight.

Another block, and a block after that, walking in the

crystal night air, just the sound of footsteps passing from the danger behind to the danger ahead. Marcos and Andreas reached the edge of the ghetto. There was no one to challenge them, and Marcos crossed the street, leaving the ghetto behind.

"Isn't this fun?" Marcos asked. There was no reply, and Marcos kept walking, carrying the sleeping child in his arms. As he approached the trolley stop, he slowed down, not wanting to get there too soon; they all had to be on the same trolley.

Marcos saw the others about half a block behind, and thought he could hear a trolley in the distance. It looked like their timing was good. A couple in their 40s, dressed against the cold in heavy coats, was waiting, their breath showing in the cold night air. Nearby was a single man, tall and thin, smoking a cigarette, lost in his thoughts, staring off into the dimly lit street.

In a moment all three pairs of fugitives were standing at the stop, spread out, waiting for the trolley. Andreas was still sleeping, but began to stir as the trolley approached and the noise of its wheels grew louder. "It's all right," Marcos said softly. "Go back to sleep." Andreas snuggled into his arms.

Suddenly the noisy, bright trolley was rolling toward them, coming to a screeching stop. Andreas woke again, and Marcos quieted him. He stepped onto the trolley, paid the fare, and took a seat at the back. Almost empty, there were just a few passengers; it was a chilly Sunday evening and most people were already home.

Allegra and Henri boarded. It was all Allegra could do to not look at Andreas; if she looked at him, he might call out. She sat in one of the seats in the front, Henri beside her. Myriam and Avram boarded next, before the single man who was taking a final draw on his cigarette. The doors closed and the trolley swayed along its tracks, slowly rolling through the early night.

The trolley stopped a few times, receiving and releasing one or two passengers. Uneventful, it was a quiet trip through the familiar lower streets of Thessaloniki. Marcos pulled the lanyard to get off. The trolley slowed, and he carried the sleeping Andreas off the coach and back into the chilly night. He watched as the trolley continued slowly on its course, stopping a block later to let off two pairs of passengers carrying small suitcases. Marcos watched, waiting with the sleeping boy, and when they were about 40 meters away he led them up the hill toward the Kastra.

It was a long slow climb up the hilly street, Marcos pacing himself to keep a distance, yet not so fast that he would tire the older couple. Andreas stayed asleep in his arms as they walked past dark or dimly lit apartments.

The breeze followed the three silent groups as they ascended, the lights of the city far below, ending abruptly at the edge of the dark sea. A few leaves raced along at their feet, agitated by the swirls of air flowing through alleys and at the cross streets. One by one the pairs crested, three singular shadows moving unnoticed through the quiet night.

Marcos slowed as he neared Pachis's house, waiting for the others. The first was Allegra and Henri; Allegra took the sleeping Andreas from Marcos, happy to have him in her arms again. In a moment Myriam and Avram joined them. Marcos led the group down the dark street along the orchard's edge to a small house sitting by itself among a scatter of houses and small open yards.

A knock on the door and a thin narrow face greeted them quietly. Quickly the six travelers entered. Allegra saw it was a small room in a poor house with a dirt floor. The walls were wood and plaster and a simple hearth in the wall served as the stove; there was an old table, a few chairs, and hanging on the wall was a small statue of Jesus on the cross. A candle in its wall sconce lit the room, its light flickering gently as the drafts subsided.

"This is Pachis," said Marcos, indicating a thin-faced man in his 30s, "his wife Nantia, their children and grandmother." Nantia was a thin woman, her hair in a scarf drawn tightly about her head; two teenage children, a boy and a girl, stood at the edge of the shadows. The grandmother, stooped and dressed in black, nodded her welcome.

"This is Henri and Avram, their wives Allegra and Myriam, and little Andreas," Marcos said. Henri nodded toward Pachis and they shook hands.

"Welcome, welcome," said Pachis. "It isn't much, but we can shelter you. Your room is over here," and he walked to a room with a curtain as its door.

"We have some blankets you can use," Pachis said, indicating a small pile of old wool blankets.

"Thank you," said Henri. "You are very kind."

"It is nothing," said Pachis, offering a small smile. "Get settled tonight and tomorrow we will talk."

"That's good," said Henri, and he slipped a coin into Pachis's hand. Pachis smiled more broadly and excused himself from their room.

"Good night," said Marcos. "You'll be safe here, for a while at least."

"Thank you, Marcos," Allegra said. "We are grateful."

"I'm glad to help." Turning to go, he said softly, "I'll return tomorrow with a few of the things you said you wanted. It may take a few trips, but I'll get them here. Get some sleep," and he stepped through the open doorway, drawing the drape across the opening.

Quickly setting up a sleeping area, soon everyone had settled down. Henri took his place beside Allegra and his son, and though he was very tired and drained, he stayed awake, still edgy. Eventually the sounds of slumber lulled him to sleep as the night yielded to the dawn of their first day in hiding.

Chapter 29
The First Days

April 7, 1943; 27 Days in Hiding

Seven trains have left for Auschwitz-Birkenau. Another will leave today. As the Jews depart Thessaloniki on the cattle cars, the inhabitants of other ghettos are ordered to take the empty rooms in the Baron Hirsch ghetto near the train station, waiting their turn.

It was early April and the days were cool, the nights frosty. As Henri and Allegra became more comfortable with the quiet street, they allowed Andreas outside to play in the fresh air. There were a few children living nearby, and it wasn't long before Andreas was enjoying the company of companions. Henri's insistence that Ladino should never be spoken near him now rewarded his foresight.

Pachis advised everyone to stay close to the house and if a neighbor asked, they were to say they were cousins, refugees from the north, and their name was Toufexides. Allegra and Myriam did the family's wash every few days, and a neighbor or two introduced themselves. Allegra would do all the talking, explaining that her mother-in-law was a mute... because if Myriam ever responded, the sing-song Ladino accent of her Greek would quickly give them all away.

On market days Henri gave Pachis money to buy food and Pachis returned with the beans, flour, and vegetables Allegra and Myriam would cook. They were frugal and resourceful because they couldn't know how long their money would have to last.

Marcos visited two or three times a week, always at night. He quickly brought the few remaining essentials from their apartment in the ghetto. Everything else they had brought from Tsimiski Street was left behind. They had traded it all for their freedom.

Pachis and his family, were friendly but reserved. They were a very poor family and did not eat as well as their guests, and this worried Henri. It occurred to him more than once that their host's fidelity could easily be swayed. Nantia worked as an assistant cook in the women's section of the prison, Yedi Koule, the "Fortress of Seven Towers," just a few streets up the hill and sometimes they could hear the women prisoners singing. Allegra had seen Nantia come home and pull scavenged food from her coat, gratefully received by the waiting mother who prepared whatever delicacy had been smuggled home.

Pachis often came home late at night after frequenting the tavernas and spending more of his wife's money than he should. This also worried Henri, because it wouldn't take much for Pachis to confide in a drinking partner, getting them denounced and shot.

Yet, they had no choice...no choice. Pachis was not a good man, even though he had a reputation for bravery for hiding the British airmen. "He must have been rewarded for his troubles with a wristwatch or other valuable," mused Henri.

"He didn't do it because he was a patriot..."

There were only two men they could count on. Their heroes were Marcos and Nicos, and without these two brave men, they would likely be in the Baron Hirsch ghetto awaiting deportation.

Whenever Marcos came to visit, he always brought a few essentials such as extra food, a recent newspaper, a sweet for Andreas. The most important gift Marcos brought was news about the more than 50,000 Jews in the three ghettos, and news from their family. Allegra's family was still in the ghetto, waiting for transport to the New Israel. Her father, mother, and two sisters were in one ghetto, and her cousin, Joseph, who had been denounced and thrown in jail for a short while, was living in another ghetto with his family. Marcos, of course, knew the whole family because of their years of business with customs and the port, and he visited the Carasso families once a week, offering assistance and being a messenger between the different family groups.

"What news do you have about my family?" asked Allegra. "Are they still in Thessaloniki?"

Marcos looked at her and nodded his head. "Yes, I saw your mother and father yesterday, and they and your sisters are well. I also saw your cousin Joseph, and he told me he wants to take his family into hiding."

"That's great news!" said Allegra with excitement. "Have they found a place?"

"No. They asked me to speak with Pachis and see if he knows someone. Joseph said he wants to hide here in the Kastra like you. He thinks it's safer, and I agree," said Marcos.

"Yes, yes," added Henri. "Out here on the edge of town is a very good place. I can speak with Pachis in the morning. He may know someone who can help."

"If you find someone, let me know and I'll get the information to Joseph. But it has to be soon. I don't think there's much time left. The trains are emptying the ghettos. Each train carries between two and three thousand people, I was told. The eighth train left today, and the ninth train is in three days, April 10."

The five adults were sitting on the blankets in a circle on the floor, their faces dark and sad. Allegra felt ill, her stomach turning, thinking about the thousands of Jews boarding the trains for Poland. She shook her head. Henri put his arm on her shoulder to comfort her.

"Because there are so many people, the Germans are using cattle cars to carry the Jews out of town. I haven't seen it, but I've heard that people are being packed in with standing room only, like animals."

Allegra gasped, seeing now the horror of her first dream. "Children, too?" she asked.

"Everybody," replied Marcos, "children, adults and the elderly. From what I can figure, about half the people have been transported so far. There are sometimes two trains per week."

The next day Henri spoke with Pachis. "Yes, I think I may know someone who could help. I'll talk to him today. How many people are there?"

"Eight. Five adults and three children."

"That's a big group. It may be hard to find a place for all of them, but I will try," and Pachis left the house to talk to his friend. He returned with good news.

"I have a friend who lives a few streets away. His name is Kiros. For a group that size, and for the food he has to buy, he wants two *lira* per week. If Joseph agrees, then Marcos is to bring the group to my house two nights from today. Kiros will meet them and take them to his house."

"All right," said Henri. "I'll see Marcos tonight and tell him. We should know tomorrow night if this plan will work."

"That's good," replied Pachis. "I'll let Kiros know."

Marcos returned the next night confirming Joseph's acceptance. He would lead Joseph and his three children, his wife Vida, Joseph's mother, a dear friend of Allegra named Jilop, and Jilop's brother.

The slim crescent moon obliged, and two nights later,

well after ten o'clock, Marcos ushered the eight refugees to Pachis's house. Henri and Allegra took them all into the small room where they sat on the floor, waiting for Kiros to come for them. It was a chilly night, and warm tea was welcome. They spoke in muffled voices but before they could finish their tea, Kiros arrived and a moment later they were gone.

Gone, only to return in three short days.

Joseph walked the two blocks in disbelief, and he was frightened, his guts turning. "This wasn't supposed to happen!" he thought. "We just moved out of the ghetto! Now we have to move again? We made a bargain!" Everything was shifting, going in the wrong direction.

He was careful to walk casually, though he wanted to run. "I must see Allegra!" he thought. There was a roaring in his head he could not stop. "I'm a Carasso! How could this be happening to me?" He cursed under his breath, looking ahead, careful not to draw attention.

He and Vida were shocked when, just an hour ago, Kiros told them they had to move out for a week or even longer. "Unexpected news? Maybe it's part of his plan?" Joseph thought wildly. Kiros's wife had a brother, an officer in the Greek army.

"You have to go tonight!" Kiros had said. "You can't be seen here. He might report you!"

"What do you mean, go tonight? Where will we go? We don't have any place to go!"

"Go see Pachis," Kiros said. "You can stay there a few days, with your cousin. I bet they have room for you."

"They already have five people there, and with us that would make 13."

"Well, 13 is a good number for Jews," Kiros said with a half smile.

Joseph held his anger, but he was boiling inside. "What about all our clothes and things?"

"Take what you need and leave the rest. I'll store everything until you come back, but I'm just not sure when."

Joseph told Vida what Kiros had said, saw the shocked look on her face, and then grabbed his coat to see Allegra. "If we can't stay with her," Joseph thought, "we'll have to move back to the ghetto!" That was the last thing he wanted to do.

In the late twilight Joseph reached his cousin's hiding place and knocked on the door. The woman, Nantia, answered. She recognized him and let him in.

"I need to see Allegra."

"Yes, of course." Nantia called out quietly for Allegra.

In a moment, Allegra had pushed aside the doorway's drapery and saw her cousin's panicked look.

"Joseph! What is it?"

"We have to move. Kiros said his brother-in-law is coming in the morning and we have to get out for a few days. We're hoping we can stay with you."

Henri heard the exchange and joined them. "This is terrible," he said, "but we'll figure something out."

Nantia heard what Joseph said and saw the opportunity. "Yes," she said, "you can stay here for a few days. As you see, this is a small house. You and your family will have to stay in the same room with your cousin. Will that work?"

"Yes! Thank you!" said Joseph.

"That means there will be 13 of us in the room," said Henri. "Can you bring just a few things?"

"Yes. Kiros said we should leave our belongings. He'll store them until his brother-in-law leaves."

"Good," said Nantia. "If you'll pay us for a few days' rent, I know Pachis will agree."

"Here," said Joseph, and he gave Nantia some money. "I'll go and bring everyone. We'll be back within the hour," and he left.

"Thank you, Nantia," said Allegra appreciatively.

Nantia smiled. "We are glad to help," she said, and returned to her place by the hearth.

Henri and Allegra began to make room for the family and friends on their way. Thirteen people would have to fit in a room that was crowded with two.

* * *

Eight silent figures walked through the dark streets of the Kastra, fugitives afraid for their lives. Vida led the first group with the children, and Jilop and his friend were close behind. Joseph and Yalina, his aging mother, slowly followed them all.

Again, a soft knock on the door and one by one each group slipped inside. Allegra and Henri helped them into the tiny sleeping room where they sat on the floor. Vida tried to control her anxiety, but couldn't hold a smile. The children were also agitated, and Vida, Allegra and Jilop hugged and comforted them.

The last group to arrive was Joseph and his mother. Yalina was in her late 80s, and very frightened. The stress of moving quickly in the night exhausted her. "Please, I must sit down."

"Can you bring that chair?" asked Joseph. "And a little water?" Yalina, pale, sat down and took a small sip with trembling hands.

After a few moments, Yalina smiled a little and nodded her appreciation. Joseph helped her to the bedroom's floor to rest. Allegra and Henri got everyone ready for the night, and soon the sound of long slow breaths filled the room.

Joseph went to check his mother. "Oh!"

"What is it?" asked Vida.

"I think she's dead!" Disbelieving, Joseph put his ear to his mother's mouth. Then he took her arm to feel for a pulse. "There's no pulse!" he cried.

Yalina was motionless, mouth open, eyes closed. Allegra took the other arm of her *theía* to feel for a pulse, but the arm was cold and lifeless, and just then, "I think I felt something!" said Allegra.

Joseph renewed his own efforts. "I think you're right," he said. "But it's very light...and she is so cold!"

"Let's warm her up," offered Vida. "Rub her. Cover her with more blankets. Each of us take an arm or leg!" They did as she asked, rubbing Yalina with their hands, working frantically to restore the old woman.

"What if she dies?" thought Henri. "Where can we bury her? Maybe the orchard across the street..." but he kept his thoughts to himself as he rubbed her leg. The old

---

Theía: Aunt.

woman felt like a sheet of ice.

They massaged Yalina for a long time, occasionally hearing a soft moan, and eventually she grew warmer and her pulse returned, though slight. With the crisis over, they took turns watching Yalina through the night, praying she would live to see the dawn. The dark night passed slowly.

Allegra and Vida woke early. "I think she'll be all right now," said Allegra.

"That was so scary!" said Vida. "I thought we'd lost her."

They started cooking beans and vegetables, and heating water for tea. Nantia had already left for her shift at the women's prison. Pachis wasn't around; he hadn't been seen in a few days. Allegra wondered if he even knew a large group had moved in.

When the food was heated and the tea prepared, Allegra summoned everyone to fill their bowls with the warm meal. Yalina was still asleep and everyone ate quietly or whispered.

Then they heard a knock on the door.

They froze. There was a second knock, louder this time. Then a man's voice called, "Hello?" In a moment came a third knock, and then the door handle was tried. The unlocked door swung open as someone stepped into the next room.

Chapter 30
Discovered!

April 14, 1943; 35 Days in Hiding

Ten trains have left for Auschwitz-Birkenau.

"Hello! Is anybody here?" said the voice.

Everyone stayed silent, hoping the intruder would leave without looking further. Allegra regretted not pulling the drape across the doorway of the room...

Frozen in place, watching the open doorway, they heard the person step into the middle of the room. It was a Greek policeman in uniform! When he saw all 13 of them sitting on the floor staring in horror, he also froze in surprise.

Seeing their fear, he quickly reassured them. "Don't be afraid! I'm not going to harm you. I'm from Crete. My name is Yannis Kerakis. Let's talk. I want to talk with you." The policeman sat down with them in the crowded room.

"I'm not looking for you," he said. "And I'm not going to report you." Yannis smiled warmly and looked at each of them in a friendly manner. "I will keep your secret."

Everyone relaxed, but just a little.

"I am looking for Linos Pachis, who I think is the owner of this house. Have you seen him?"

Henri answered, "No, we've not seen him for days."

"But this is his house?"

"Yes, that's right."

"All right, then," said the officer. "I was sent here to find him. How long have you known him?"

"Only a few days," replied Henri.

"I understand," said Yannis. "You must be careful of him. He is not a good person. I came today to find him because he may be stealing from an old woman, and I want to talk with him about this. You should beware of him."

"What is this stealing business with the woman?" asked Joseph.

"I believe he is the caretaker of a woman living near here. We have a police report accusing him of taking her money."

Joseph shook his head and scowled. He and his family were jumping from one catastrophe to the next. Vida put her arm around her husband.

"My advice," said Yannis, "is you should be wary of him. He may try to harm you in some way."

"Thank you, Yannis. You're very kind," said Allegra. "We'll consider what you said, but for now we have no other place to go."

"Yes, I know this is a frightening time. I'll keep my eyes and ears open at the station; if I hear anything that could cause you trouble, I'll come and tell you right away." The policeman spoke with respect and sympathy. "Also, I'll make sure I'm the only policeman who comes here. This is my assigned area, so you'll be safe for the time being."

When Yannis left, Joseph expressed his outrage and indignation. "I can't believe it! All these people are traitors! They aren't true Greeks...they would sell us for a handful of beans! Here in the *Kastra*, if we're caught, we'll all be shot! I wouldn't trust anybody! We were promised a safe place...and we're not even here three days! There is no place to go!"

"We'll be all right here," said Vida, trying to calm her husband, "until we move back to Kiros's house."

"We're not moving back!" Joseph said angrily, his face red with fury. "We're going back to the ghetto! I'd rather be around the damned Germans! At least there we have a chance to stay alive."

"What?" said Allegra. "You're moving back to the ghetto?"

"Yes!" Joseph said with a hiss. "We're safer there. We're taking a huge risk up here. At least if we go back to the ghetto, the only thing that will happen is we'll be deported."

"You can't be serious!" said Allegra, raising her voice. "Do you really think the trains are taking people to a Jewish community in Poland?"

"It's our only chance. If we stay here, we'll be murdered. I prefer to take our chances in the ghetto." Joseph looked around the room for approval. "This was a mistake," he said. "You should come with us. You'll be safer there."

"We're not going back," said Henri. "We'll take our chances here."

"That's foolish, Henri," said Joseph. "You can't trust anyone. You heard the policeman. They'll sell you out, and you and Allegra and all of you will be shot. Come with us."

"No," said Allegra. "Henri is right. We'll stay here, and you should stay with us. The ghetto is a bad idea. We don't believe the propaganda. Since when did Germans want anything good for Jews?"

"Even if there isn't a New Israel," replied Joseph, "it has to be better than this. Maybe it's only another ghetto in Poland, but at least we won't be living in fear, never knowing if one of our so-called friends will sell us."

Joseph's group decided to return that night. They'd leave as they'd come, in several groups moving through the shadows. It would be difficult with Yalina's poor health, but that couldn't be helped.

Joseph returned to collect the belongings they'd left the night before, but Kiros laughed at him, telling Joseph to go or he would report him. This enraged Joseph more, confirming that their fate was better with the Germans than their own countrymen. That night they slipped through the door, returning to the ghetto to await their call to the New Israel. Allegra was distraught, knowing she would never see them again.

Leonidas Paraschos stepped off his front porch and walked toward his tool shed. "Today is beautiful," he thought, "and such a good day to prune branches." A section of his pear orchard on the south side needed attention now, before the spring got much older. "It's your turn today," he thought, selecting a pair of pruning shears.

Walking through his orchard, enjoying the fragrance of the moist earth, the ground gave slightly underfoot; blossoms were just beginning to yield their sweet scent. The late morning sun was heating the earth, and the shadows played delicately, a mosaic of light and dark as a breath of air played with the leaves and young branches.

"Who is that?" he thought, seeing a young man sitting in his orchard, in the sunshine. "What is that fellow doing?" This was unusual...no one ever had sat in his orchard before. The young man, maybe in his early thirties, was sunning himself and reading a newspaper. He looked up as Paraschos got closer, and seemed slightly surprised.

"Good morning," the man said to him.

"Good morning," Paraschos said in reply.

"It's a lovely day, isn't it?"

"Yes, it is. I see you are enjoying the sunlight."

"I am. A day of sunshine is always welcome."

"Do you live around here?" asked Paraschos.

"Yes, I'm a cousin of Pachis."

"Oh! I know you. You're not his cousin."

"What do you mean?" The young man looked nervous.

"You're Marcos's friend."

"You know Marcos?"

"Yes, he came and asked if I knew a place for...you know."

"Oh! So you're the one!" Henri stood up. "Please let me introduce myself. I'm Henri Algava. Thank you for helping me and my family."

"I'm Leonidas Paraschos. I'm glad to do it. It's working out?"

"Yes, we're making do."

"Good. I've known Pachis for years. I don't know him very well, but I thought he could help. I'm glad."

"You have helped immensely. We're in your debt."

"I need to get some work done, but you're welcome here any time. If anyone asks, I'll tell them you're a nephew and you have TB. Your doctor says you must have plenty of fresh air. That should keep everyone away!"

"Yes, I think so!"

Marcos had good news.

"I saw your mother and father today," he said to Allegra. "They've changed their mind and want to leave the ghetto."

Allegra felt her heart lift! "Oh!" she cried, "When? Where?"

"I don't know. They haven't made plans yet, but the deportations have frightened them."

Henri nodded his head. There was no shaking his distrust of the Germans. "I hope it's not too late," he said. "They should get out right away."

Allegra looked at Henri. "I want to go see my mother," she said.

"It's too dangerous!" said Henri.

"I know it's dangerous, but I want to see her. Maybe I can convince them to get out quickly while they can."

Henri heard the urgency in her voice. "It's not a good idea, Allegra," he said, "but if you really need to go, I'll come with you."

"No, Henri," she replied. "I don't want us both to risk our lives. I'll go alone."

Marcos looked at her and said, "If you're going to go, you should go tomorrow night. The moon is a slender crescent and the sky will be dark. I can visit them tomorrow during the day and let them know you're coming."

"I'm going tomorrow night," said Allegra. Henri could see there was no point arguing.

* * *

Allegra looked out the small window. It was after nine o'clock and the sky was very dark. Putting on her overcoat, she whispered, "I'll be all right. Don't worry about me. I'll be home late."

"I'll be waiting for you," said Henri.

Allegra stood over Andreas, knelt down, and gave her young son a kiss above his ear. She could smell the sweet fragrance of his skin.

She stepped through the hanging drape and in a moment was by the front door. With a final look at Henri, she slipped into the night. It was cool but not icy, and Allegra stayed in the shadows, walking quickly under the dark trees on the moonless side of the street. In a few moments she was at the old Byzantine castle, then heading downhill on the quiet streets. A scattering of city lights winked and breathed as she silently descended. Some light fog lingered, making her passage even more furtive. The windows in the buildings were mostly dark, the inhabitants in bed; an occasional streetlight was all that exposed her downward path.

With much of the hill now behind, she neared the ghetto where her mother, father, and sisters were waiting for her. Slowing to a determined gait, down one street, over two, and to the third house on the left, she knocked lightly on the unlit door.

Allegra heard a bolt slide open, and she slipped inside. The door quickly shut behind her, and she was being hugged by her mother Doudoun.

"Oh, my angel!" her mother said, happy to hold her once more. Tears ran down both their cheeks.

"Mamá!" cried Allegra. They held each other for a few moments and then Doudoun led her by the hand as they walked down the hall into a small living room with a sofa, a few chairs, and a menorah on the side table.

Her father, Mordechai, greeted her, and they hugged. "Allegra! I'm so glad you came," he said, "but it is too dangerous! I wish you hadn't."

"I know, Babá," said Allegra, "but I had to. Marcos says you're thinking about leaving the ghetto. Is it true?"

"Yes. In fact, we have packed a few things and are ready to go immediately. We were going to take a ship to Palestine. Do you remember Jacob Abravanel?"

"Of course," replied Allegra. A good friend of the family, Jacob had supplied many of the dyes her father used at the factory.

"He was making arrangements, but they fell through. Instead, we think the best choice now is to do what you and Henri have done," Mordechai said. "We found a family willing to hide us. They live on Filipou Street, not far from the big church. I'll give you the address. We're going tomorrow night. Marcos will help us get there; he is such a very brave man."

"Yes, he is. He has been a great friend," Allegra agreed. "I am so relieved, Babá," Allegra cried, tears welling in her eyes. "Don't delay! Go as soon as you can. There isn't much time left."

"Oh, my dear!" said Doudoun. "We'll be safe," her eyes looked quickly at Mordechai, "you'll see."

"And did you hear?" her father asked. "Pepo is getting married. He met a very nice woman. He'll be living apart from us, also in hiding, with his bride and her parents."

"Tell him, please, I wish them great joy," said Allegra. In the midst of this madness, her brother had found a wife!

Hugging goodbye, Allegra was again in the dark night, walking up the long hill to the *Kastra*, and then inside their tiny haven. Myriam and Avram were lightly snoring on their pallet and little Andriko was asleep in his bed of blankets. Allegra slipped in beside her husband with a prayer of thanks. More dangers lay ahead, but tonight...tonight she felt the most at peace in months.

* * *

The two Greek men in the taverna spoke in whispers, sipping their coffees, exchanging suppressed smiles under the brim of their caps.

"Do what I did," said Kiros, leaning forward over the table at the taverna. "It was easy and there is nothing they can do. Are they going to complain to the police? No!"

"I need to make up a story like yours," Pachis said.

Kiros smiled. "It can be anything. You can even tell them you also have a cousin or brother-in-law in the army."

"That's good," Pachis said, swirling the ouzo in his glass. "It's an amusing game," he thought, "scaring the Jews and taking all their things. Too bad there aren't many left."

"How will you get them out of your house?" said Kiros.

"I'll send one of my neighbor's boys with a message that the Germans are looking for me. That should be enough to get them out!" Pachis was pleased with his treachery.

"Yes! That will do it." Kiros tapped his glass against Pachis's. "Then you can keep all their food and all their clothes, and sell that stuff like I did."

"I owe it to you, my friend."

"And you can start thanking me by buying the next round!"

Chapter 31
A Brush with the Gestapo

May 27, 1943; 78 Days in Hiding

Sixteen trains have left for Auschwitz-Birkenau.

The trains were steadily emptying the Jews from the ghettos. Nicos didn't know much about this, except he'd heard that the remaining Jews were being mistreated, and collaborators, especially the Jewish Hasson brothers,* had started a terror campaign in the ghettos. There were rumors of beatings, rapes and murders that made Avram and Henri sick with helplessness and rage.

Starved for news about the war, Henri and Avram were astonished to hear that the Greek People's Liberation Army had liberated Karditsa from the Nazis and declared it the capital of Free Greece. There was also good news from North Africa, with Rommel on the defensive...but the war's end still looked a long way off. Hitler was dominant in Europe, even if his armies were struggling with the Russians. The Americans seemed to be moving very slowly, possibly distracted by their war in Asia. It might be several years before the Germans were forced out of Greece...if ever.

The Jewish Hasson brothers: The Nazis used Jews to police the Jewish community, appointing Vital Hasson as the head of the Jewish police. He and his brother were gangsters, known for their brutality. See the Carasso testimony in Appendix A.

Henri needed to visit Nicos Efcarpides. He was running low on money, and Nicos was keeping most of Henri's gold and cash. Nicos was also protecting Avram's funds, and Avram said he needed to go, too.

They left early in the morning, at dawn, blending in with Greeks going to work, catching the trolley to Liberty Square where Nicos lived with his wife, Sousanna. As far as Henri knew, Nicos had never confided in anyone else that he had married a prostitute. The story was brief; Nicos had met Sousanna and somehow transformed her. She dedicated her life to him and now was his deeply loving partner. This was another astonishing facet of Nicos, an amazingly kind and generous man.

Arriving at their friend's apartment where Henri and Allegra had witnessed the humiliation of the city's Jews from the balcony almost a year ago, Henri and Avram walked past a typing school on the ground floor, then up two flights and knocked on Nicos's door. Sousanna welcomed them, and brought coffee and fruit, hummus, bread, and olives, and discreetly left the room so the men could talk.

"And now I think you're up to date with the news," said Nicos, telling them what he'd heard on his hidden radio.

"Good to hear that Hitler is being punished by the Russians," said Avram.

"I wish the Americans were involved. Between the two, Hitler will have his hands full," added Nicos. "Have you heard anything about the Carassos?" he asked, changing the subject.

"Our latest news is that Joseph Carasso and his family were deported. Marcos said their train left last week." Henri wondered if they were in Poland by now.

"God keep them safe," Nicos prayed.

"Amen," said Henri.

"We need to go soon," said Avram. "Thank you for this visit and the delicious food. One of the reasons we came was to get some of our money, and..."

"Of course," Nicos interjected. "Your money is well hidden. How much do you need?" Nicos excused himself, returning with their requests. Expressing their gratitude and saying goodbye, Henri and Avram went down the stairs.

"Wait!" said Henri. "Look!" A Gestapo sedan was parked in front of the entrance. As they watched, two Gestapo officers got out and began walking toward the front doors.

"In here," Henri said, almost in a panic. They quickly stepped through the typing school's doors and took a seat at the back of the room. Through the windows of the door, Henri saw the Gestapo officers walk by and heard them climb the stairs.

The typing instructor let his students continue working and approached the two seated men. "Hello, can I help you?"

"It's my father," replied Henri. "He became suddenly fatigued. Would you mind if we rested for just a moment?" Avram pretended to look exhausted.

"Can I get you some water?" asked the concerned instructor.

"No," said Avram, "thank you. I'll be all right." A moment later Henri and Avram slipped out of the school and through the doors onto the street, mixing with the pedestrian traffic. The fright of being so close to discovery stayed with them until they were high up the hill in the *Kastra*.

"Too close," said Henri. "That was crazy. We never should have done that."

"I'm never doing it again," said Avram.

Nicos and Sousanna, however, paid the price for their benevolence.

* * *

There was a sharp knock on the door. Sousanna was too slow, and the knock repeated, louder. "It must be Henri and Avram," she thought. "Maybe they left something..."

so she was unpleasantly surprised when she saw two Gestapo officers standing in her doorway.

"Mrs. Efcarpides?" asked the first officer. He was tall and thin with a long rectangular face.

"Yes..." replied Sousanna, ineffectively masking her surprise. Unprepared and knowing two Jews had just left her apartment, she felt her face betraying her.

"I am *Kriminalkommissar** Weisser, and this is *Kriminalobersekretär** Schinkel. May we come in?"

There was no way to refuse, so she opened the door wider and said, "Yes, please do."

The officers stepped inside, their eyes scanning the apartment.

Weisser turned to look at Sousanna, and said in a gentle voice, "They are here. Where are you keeping them?"

Nicos walked into the room. Hearing the sound of male voices, he also expected to see Henri and Avram; rounding the corner with a smile, he was surprised to find two Gestapo officers in his home. Almost blurting out a greeting to his Jewish friends, Nicos quickly

---

Kriminalkommissar: A Senior or First Lieutenant in the Gestapo.

Kriminalobersekretär: A Second Lieutenant in the Gestapo.

recovered and prepared for the worst.

"Mr. Efcarpides?" Weisser did not wait for him to reply. "We know you have two Jews in this apartment. One old Jew and a younger one. Please bring them out."

Nicos looked at Weisser. "You are mistaken. There are no Jews here."

Weisser studied Nicos for a moment. "Yes, they are here; an old man and his son. They were here today. We know this."

"I don't know what you are talking about," replied Nicos calmly.

"If you don't bring them out, we will search your apartment and find them ourselves," Weisser said menacingly.

"You may look if you insist, but you will find no one. There are no Jews here."

"If we find the Jews, we will arrest you and your wife. She is an attractive woman, and I understand her experience with entertaining men is prolific..." Weisser threatened.

Nicos's face turned red with anger but he held himself in check as he replied, "Look around the apartment. You will find nothing. You have no reason to be insulting."

"Perhaps not. We shall see. Please sit here on the sofa

while we inspect your apartment," and the two officers began their search.

Schinkel disappeared into the other rooms, looking in closets and under beds. He checked for false walls and ceilings, moved carpets to check the floor...but found nothing. Schinkel then began to look inside desk drawers and dressers.

Weisser stayed in the living room where Nicos and Sousanna were seated, also looking inside furnishings. He opened an armoire.

"What is this?" asked Weisser, finding a stack of folded cloth Henri had given Nicos when he'd closed the fabric store a year ago.

"It's just cloth," replied Nicos. "The cloth will make nice suits some day."

"How many suits do you need? Why would you have so much cloth? This belongs, no doubt, to the Jews. One of the Jews who visited you today was in the textile business. We have records at Gestapo headquarters. We also know how much you helped him during his trial. Why would you help Jews, Mr. Efcarpides?"

Schinkel entered the room, carrying a drawer. He put the drawer down on the table in front of Nicos and Sousanna. "Why do you have so much money in this drawer?" He turned to Weisser and said, "I found this in a bedroom dresser."

"This is money from the Jews, isn't it?" said Weisser. "The Jews are paying you to hide and supply them, isn't that true?"

"No, it is not true. I always keep money in the apartment. It's wise to have some extra cash, for emergencies," answered Nicos.

"It's not wise to harbor Jews, Mr. Efcarpides. If we find you doing that, we'll have you shot. Do you understand?"

Nicos nodded his head, feeling his fury. Though his lips were tight and his eyes had narrowed, outwardly he kept calm. He could see the pleasure in the faces of the two Gestapo officers.

"We know you have a brother in Thessaloniki. We're going to pay him a visit, in case he is harboring the Jews for you."

Nicos forced a smile. "You will find no one at my brother's home, either. Neither of us is hiding Jews."

"We'll see, Mr. Efcarpides. You should think about being helpful to yourself and your lovely wife by cutting all ties with these Jews. You're on a dangerous path. Good afternoon, Mr. Efcarpides, Madam..." and both Weisser and Schinkel departed. Nicos closed the door after them.

Nicos took a deep breath, the first since the Nazis had entered his apartment. Sousanna was quickly in his arms and they hugged for a long moment.

"That was frightening," Sousanna said.

"They are evil scary bastards," said Nicos. "I need to call my brother right away and warn him."

"You also need to get word to Henri and Avram," counseled Sousanna.

"Yes," agreed Nicos. "This was much too risky. I'll send a message not to come again, not for a long while. They must stay indoors."

That wasn't the only news Marcos would bring. Something even more tragic was happening.

Chapter 32
Run!

June 2, 1943; 83 Days in Hiding

Seventeen trains have left for Auschwitz-Birkenau. Few Jews remain. The last two trains will leave in August, and one of them will carry Chief Rabbi Koretz and his associates.

Marcos walked up the hill to the *Kastra*, carrying a small bag of supplies for Henri's family. The night was cold, and the lights sparkled in the city below just as the starlight sparkled in the sky above.

He paused at a street corner and stood still, listening to the night. Though it was June, the nights had not grown warmer and he felt the cool air on his face. Looking down the street, thousands of buildings carpeted the hills of his beloved Thessaloniki. He could see church domes and towers, and the great dark expanse of the sea. Thinking of his wife and children and the danger he'd put them in, he knew he had no choice. It was not in his character to betray his friends or abandon them, but instead to resist this huge dark evil that had captured his homeland, his city, and threatened the people he loved.

Marcos knew he risked being murdered and his wife and children deported or worse, but he couldn't understand how men could turn against men, women and children of their own country who needed help against the Nazis. These same people would think nothing of feeding a hungry dog, yet would quickly condemn a family of Jews for a few gold pieces. How different was their betrayal from what Judas did?

He thought of the Massacre of Smyrna* a generation ago, Greek blood pouring down the streets, murder, rape and pillage by the tormenting Turks, thousands of corpses consumed by the flames of the torched city. How could his own countrymen forget the fear and horror of genocide but tolerate Nazi persecution? The muscles of his clenched jaw jumped with anger.

"How do I tell Allegra the news," he thought, "her whole family captured by the Gestapo?" Safe for two short months, they'd been overheard speaking Ladino. Reported by the neighbors, German soldiers arrived with the Hasson brothers. They broke down the door and discovered the family in hiding. The neighbors were rewarded with their blood money, and now all the Carassos were under guard, waiting for the next train.

Marcos did not want any harm to come to his family, but neither was it a choice to let his friends perish. He shouldered the bag of supplies, turned from the view of his city and its people, and walked through the darkness toward the tiny house where his friends were waiting.

Massacre of Smyrna: The massacre of Greeks in Smyrna, Turkey in 1922.

Allegra was overcome. Captured! Her mother and father, her three brothers, three sisters, Pepo's new wife and her parents...all taken, captured by the Nazis! Allegra's mind was tormented. "They sold my family!"

For the longest time she sat in shock. "They are never coming back," was her constant thought, her heart breaking. Henri held her when her sobbing was fiercest. A day passed, and another, before Allegra found composure.

They were alone in the tiny house. Andreas was a little tyrant, demanding to go outside to play. Myriam, still in her slippers and robe, was helping Allegra rinse the breakfast pot in the wash tub and putting away the food. Henri and Avram were rolling up the bedding for the day.

Pachis was on a week-long trip to buy wheat and vegetables from a farmer he knew in Imathia, and Henri had given him two *lira* to procure food. Nantia had already left for the women's prison, and the old woman had taken her two grandchildren to the market.

There was a sudden loud knock on the door. Everyone froze. Who would be knocking so early in the day?

"Who is it?" Henri asked.

"Manos," said a boy's voice. He was the neighbor's boy.

"What is it, Manos?" asked Henri from behind the closed door.

"I have a message for Pachis," the boy called.

Avram was looking out a corner of the window and saw the boy; he nodded to Henri. Henri opened the door slightly.

"A message for Pachis? He isn't here."

"Well, if you see him, tell him he should hide. German soldiers are looking for him at the *Portara*."*

"Looking for him?" croaked Henri.

"Yes!" Manos continued. "Soldiers are asking for him there. I was sent to warn him. The soldiers will probably come here next! They want to arrest him!" Manos looked around the street. "I think they'll be here soon!" and the boy left, running down the street to his family's house past the open yard.

The news was stunning! "The Germans! Coming here!" Henri's mind was in a riot.

Portara: A "gate" or opening in the Byzantine walls that used to surround the city.

"Everyone!" Henri cried in a muted but commanding voice. "Get out of the house! Go through the window, to the orchard!"

Dressed as they were, they ran to the large, low window facing the orchard.

Allegra unlatched it, stepping through. Henri handed Andreas to her, and she rushed into the orchard holding her son. Avram went next so he could help Myriam, and Henri was last, running after the others into the shadowy orchard of leafy trees.

They ran, Myriam in her slippers, past several ranks of trees and stopped, out of breath, about 50 meters from the road. Dropping down and hiding, they watched the house, waiting for the soldiers to arrive.

An hour went by, but nothing happened. The morning became warmer and their fear relaxed and now seemed foolish. Another hour passed, and Andreas became thirsty and dissatisfied playing with sticks and stones. In the third hour Myriam had enough.

"I need to get some things," she said. "I'm going back to the house."

No one could stop her; she wanted her shoes and some clothes; wearing only her robe and slippers had become too much to bear.

"I'll bring back some water for Andriko," she said. With

that, she stood up and walked back to the house. She disappeared around the corner and was out of sight for about 10 minutes, reappearing with a small pile of belongings.

"Pachis was supposed to be on that trip to the farmer, but he's in there. They are all in there," she said.

"What do you mean?" asked Avram.

"He's back, and so are Nantia and the others. They're eating our food and using our olive oil." She gave a container of water to Allegra for Andreas's thirst.

They remembered what Yannis the policeman had said. Avram stood up. "I'm going to go." He walked through the orchard and disappeared into the house. A few minutes later he came out empty-handed and when he rejoined the group, he told them that Pachis had been pleasant enough, but wouldn't let Avram take anything.

"But it's our property!" exclaimed Henri.

"I know, but he said you should go talk to him. He said, 'Let Henri come. I want to talk to him. I'll give you anything you want.' I wasn't going to argue with him, so I came to tell you."

Henri went back to the house and found Pachis sitting by the hearth.

"Hello, Henri!" Pachis greeted him. "Come in."

"So what are you doing? You are throwing us out?" asked Henri, the anger clearly in his voice.

"It is time for you to go," Pachis said, slowly carving a stick with his knife.

"But we have nowhere to go," Henri said.

"You will find some place. You Jews are very clever."

"Then I want the money back I gave you for the food, and I want to take our things."

"You can take your things, but I want six *lira*. You pay me six *lira* and you can take it all."

"I don't want to pay you for what is mine!"

"It's not yours. This is my house, so it's mine. If you want it, pay me. If you don't want to pay me six *lira*, you can choose a few things and I will tell you how much you will pay."

"You're a bastard and a thief!" said Henri, wanting to fight, but knowing better.

"And you are a Jew," said Pachis. "You Jews have lots of money. Pay me, or go."

"I'm not paying you anything!"

"Then you better leave my house now or I will denounce

you and your filthy Jewish family! You lived here for three months, eating and sleeping and sunning yourself in the orchard while my family had to hide you and lie for you and shop for you! And what did we get? A little bit of money for our trouble? The Germans are right! You are all ugly, filthy, greedy Jews! Get out of my house and never come back!"

Henri left seething, but in one piece. Back in the orchard, he said, "We lost everything. He wants me to pay for what is ours. He is a liar and a thief."

"Better to lose a few things than our lives," Allegra said.

"I know, but what shall we do now? We can't sleep here."

"Let's go see Paraschos," she said. "He is Marcos's friend. He'll know what we should do."

They all stood up and headed to the farmhouse where Paraschos lived with his aged wife. Paraschos was friendly. Maybe he would have an answer.

* * *

"So many people," Paraschos said. "Where are you going to sleep now?"

"We don't have anywhere to go tonight."

"Well, you shouldn't return to that house anymore. Pachis faked the scare. No Germans came to the *Portara*,

I can tell you. I was at the café, and I didn't see any soldiers or Gestapo looking for him."

"It was a fake," Henri said. "He wanted to steal from us."

Paraschos shook his head in disgust. "I'm sorry. I thought he was a brave man. Now I see he's a nasty bastard."

"We're in trouble. Unless we find a place, we're going to have to sleep outside tonight."

"Do you know anyone who can help you?"

"We have some friends in town, but we can't get a message to them. Marcos is the only one who knows where we are, and he's not going to visit for another day or two..."

"I'll see what I can do, but what will you do tonight?"

"Can we sleep in your orchard?" Henri's face was ashen. They had no food, no clothes, no shelter, no blankets, and with a young child and two elders, even one night in the open was unthinkable.

"No, no, that won't do. All right, look. My only idea, my only suggestion, is that I tell you the truth. But do not tell anybody, is that understood?"

"Yes, of course," agreed Henri.

"Don't say a word." Paraschos sighed. "I have a mistress, and we have a daughter. They live at a place I keep in town. Not too far away. It's just below the castle, a few blocks below. It's easy walking distance from here."

Henri began to feel relief surging through his body. "Thank God!" Henri thought, anticipating what Paraschos was about to say.

"I will talk to her. I'll put you in this house at least for a couple of nights, and in the meantime we'll discuss the matter with Marcos to see where we can find some other place for you."

"Thank you, Leonidas. You are saving our lives."

"I am glad to help. But this is just for a couple of nights, all right?"

"Yes, of course. I understand. Marcos will help us find another place."

"All right, then. Stay in the orchard for now. Don't go back to Pachis again. He's a real bastard. Go deeper into the orchard so you can't be seen, and I'll come for you in a few hours, after I speak with Tressa."

The day passed slowly, Henri and Allegra on edge, listening for every sound, worried about Pachis denouncing them, worried what would become of them that night. Myriam had grabbed some food they had hidden in their clothes, and they had a meager meal, making sure Andreas was satisfied and wouldn't cry.

Paraschos returned close to dusk, walking through the trees as the early evening chill began to rise and the shadows lengthen. "I have good news," he said. "I spoke with Tressa and she welcomes you to our house. We'll wait until it's dark. In the meantime, here is some food and warm clothing." There was nothing more to do but wait, wait in the darkening gloom with their thoughts, fears, and hopes.

After nightfall Paraschos came back. "It's time to go," and he led them out of the orchard toward the castle, down the hill a half dozen blocks to a quiet, dark street, and into the lower floor of a small apartment building. "It's good to get indoors," thought Allegra, glad to have her son out of the gathering cold. After introductions everyone quickly settled down and went to sleep at the end of this frightening, exhausting day.

A day passed, and another. Marcos was alerted, and Aleko at the taverna, but no new hiding locations were available. Speaking with Nicos was out of the question; he was being watched by the Gestapo. A third day passed, and a fourth. Tressa, at first only troubled, now grew extremely nervous.

"You said you would stay only a day or two, and it's now four days!"

"We can't find anything...our friends are looking."

"I don't care! It's a crime to give shelter to Jews! My child, my mother, me, we are all in grave danger! I didn't mind helping for a night or two, but if we're found out, we'll all be shot! I am afraid for my life!"

"I promise we'll move as soon as possible," Henri said glumly, worried that Tressa would report them.

In the morning they were stunned to find Tressa gone. She had run away with her daughter and mother, their rooms in disarray.

"Oh, my God," Allegra said. "Look what we've done. We've frightened this poor woman out of her home."

A fifth day, and a sixth went by. Paraschos came by and was shocked to learn his mistress had run away. "Oh, she'll be back, but you must leave right away. Is there nowhere you can go?"

On the eighth day Avram and Henri found new sanctuary. Aleko's friend had an apartment where Avram and Myriam could stay, while Henri found lodging with his old friend, Marika Karakitsou from Albania.

Chapter 33
Marika's

Henri knew Marika before the war when she'd helped with his imports. Delightful and eccentric, Marika's personality and playfulness made her an attractive character. Marika spoke many languages including Turkish.

"Don't worry; you can all stay in my house. My house is your house, and I don't care what happens to me. If the Germans catch me, I don't care. You come here. But I have to tell you I have a friend who visits. Now don't get scared, because it will be all right. He is a Gestapo officer I have known for years."

Henri felt a chill run up his spine. His voice rose an octave as he said, "Gestapo?" He looked at Allegra and her face was white. She was staring at Marika with disbelief. Marika raised her eyebrows as if to say, "...but what can I do?"

"We practice speaking Turkish. He finds it relaxing to spend a few hours here and we talk about the old days, and family news, of course." Marika was pulling at a cloth napkin in her hands. "So I think it would be best if you, Henri, stayed in the bedroom when he visits. I don't think it's a good idea you should be seen while he's here."

259

"What about me?" asked Allegra.

"Oh, with you there is no problem, dear. I'll tell Josef that you are a cousin of mine, you and Andriko both, from Albania. I can explain that your husband was killed in the fighting. I'll make up some excuse about why you're staying with me. It will not be a concern."

"I don't mind hiding in the bedroom," offered Henri, "as long as Allegra can keep Andriko out of the room."

"It will be all right. If you just stay in the bedroom and Andriko plays out here, nothing will happen. If I stop seeing him all of a sudden, he'll become suspicious...and you need a place to stay and have nowhere else to go." Marika breathed out a slow sigh. "We will just have to make the best of it."

"Dear God," thought Henri, "Gestapo!" He felt sick to his stomach. Allegra looked no better. Only Andriko was unaffected, on the floor playing with his toy trucks and a few wooden blocks.

They moved in. Decorated with Old World charm, the big apartment had five rooms in the downtown area, on Agapinou Street, not far from their old apartment on Tsimiski. Framed family photographs, bookcases filled with books in several languages, and a cherry wood dining room table with elegant upholstered chairs reminded Allegra of the home she'd once had.

A vase of fragrant flowers and comfortable chairs in the

parlor welcomed conversation in the pleasant summer evenings, lacy curtains framing the large windows above the busy, noisy street below.

"Hello, I am Nikos Ekindjoglou," greeted Marika's other tenant, extending his hand.

"Very nice to meet you," said Henri shaking the offered hand. "I am Aristides Toufexides. This is my wife, Anghela, and our son Andriko."

"Marika told me you were coming," said Nikos. In a lowered voice he said, "I know your secret, and it is safe with me." Nikos was a large man but not overweight, with silver-black hair brushed back from his broad forehead and a precisely trimmed mustache under his modest but pointed nose.

"I told you about Nikos," chirped Marika. "He is the manager of the Thessaloniki branch of the Bank of Greece." Allegra sensed their attraction and saw that Marika held a torch for him.

"I am delighted you've come to share the apartment. You'll find the accommodations entirely satisfying!" Nikos said.

"It is our great pleasure, and relief, to join you here. I'm grateful to Marika for her compassion and friendship, and to you for your kindness and courage."

In the evenings, Henri and Nikos enjoyed their

conversations. Nikos brought home the daily newspaper and they tried to distinguish between the news and the propaganda. Even though the Germans were being pushed back by the Russians, and the Americans and British had invaded Sicily, Nikos was pessimistic about the war. He felt the Americans were distracted by the war in the Pacific and had not yet pressed their shoulder to the war in Europe.

"It will be a long war, Aristides," he said to Henri. "The Germans are tenacious, and it will be a long while until they are undone. But don't worry! You and your family will be safe here. Marika and I know how to keep a secret," and the first several weeks in their new refuge passed easily.

"So it's working out for you and Myriam?" Henri asked his father.

"Yes, quite well." Avram stubbed his cigarette out in the ashtray, and sipped the last of his coffee. He caught Aleko's eye and Aleko smiled, rising to get a refill. "Do you remember her, Henri? Marika Pavlidou."

"Not so much. I vaguely remember her from the days when you owned the Café of Mirrors."

"Those were good days, Henri," Avram said, reminiscing. "Marika often came to the café with her girlfriends and their paramours. They loved the food and the music. Do

262

you remember how much fun we had?"

"Yes, those were happy days."

"Marika married Thanos and then the Spanish Civil War began. He never came back and her heart never healed. She's a communist, you know. She was always brave and in love with life."

Henri looked at his father and saw the younger man within the older body, and he felt like he would weep. "I know, Babá. Those days will come again."

"I hope so, *pedí mou.*"

"And now she's opened her home to you and Mamá."

"She is very kind. It's lucky we're in the *Kamara.** It feels like home there, near the Arch."*

Kamara: A district in Thessaloniki inhabited by Greeks with ties to the Jewish community, named after a Roman monument that looks like a round chamber (*kamara*), decorated with scenes in marble celebrating the Victory of Galerius, the Roman Emperor from 305–311 A.D.

Arch of Galerius: An arch commissioned by the Roman Emperor Galerius commemorating his victory over the Persians in 298 A.D.

Chapter 34
Under the Bed

June 28, 1943; 110 Days in Hiding

"Jupp!"* said Marika, greeting Josef Weisser, Gestapo *Kriminalkommissar*, at the door. Come in! It's always so good to see you," she said in Turkish.

"Hello, Marika. I hope these will delight you," he replied in Turkish, giving her a bouquet of fresh lilies.

"They're lovely. Thank you!"

Weisser stepped inside and took off his hat, following Marika into the parlor.

"I'll just be a moment, Jupp," Marika called from the kitchen. "I want to put them in water right away."

"Yes, of course. I'm in no hurry...we have all afternoon." Weisser stood at the window, looking down at the busy street below.

"I received a letter from cousin Dazem a few days ago, and she's better, thank you. In fact, I have some news to share. My cousin Anghela and her son Andriko have

---

Jupp: A Bavarian nickname for Josef.

come to stay with me for a while. They arrived last week from Albania."

"My dear, please sit down," said Marika, returning with a vase of flowers for her table, placing them in the center just so.

"Thank you," said Weisser, taking a seat on one of the comfortable parlor chairs. "It's been two weeks...so sorry I could not visit last week. How have you been?"

"Quite well," said Marika. "The weather has been perfect and I enjoy the late evenings so much! One of my silly little pleasures is going out to dinner at one of the local cafés and dining under starlight! It's so romantic, don't you think?"

"Yes, I remember how much you enjoy that. I'm glad you can treat yourself. Most of life's little pleasures can sustain the human spirit. Have you heard from your Aunt Besmira? You said she was ailing. I don't remember hearing of Anghela before," said Weisser.

"Oh, yes, I thought you knew of them. Anghela is the daughter of my Aunt Samira and Uncle Bakull, from Sarandë. Can I get you some coffee? A special friend of mine," and Marika winked at him, "brought me a gift of delicious beans!"

Marika got up to prepare the coffee, calling over her shoulder, "You'll adore Andriko...he's such a sweet little boy."

"How old is he?"

"Just three. He'll remind you of Jürgen."

"Oh? I'd like to meet them. Are they here now?"

"Yes, but they're taking a nap. I think they'll come out soon...it's about time for them to rise."

Marika and Weisser continued their conversation over coffee and some *loukoumades** Marika had bought for his visit. They heard a door open down the hall, and the sound of a child's running feet.

"Andriko!" called Marika. In a moment Andreas had rounded the corner and run into the parlor. Seeing the unknown man, his broad smile changed to shyness as he ran to Marika's open arms and buried his face against her.

"My Andriko," she cooed in Greek, encapsulating his head with her embrace, hugging him in her arms and rocking him gently. "Did you have a good nap?" and the young boy nodded his head without moving his face.

"Jupp," said Marika, "this is my wonderful friend and second cousin, Andriko."

"What a handsome big boy," said Weisser admiringly,

Loukoumades: A pastry of fried dough soaked in sugar or honey with cinnamon.

thinking of his own son. "I am very glad to meet you, Andriko."

"Andriko, this is my friend, Josef Weisser. He came all the way from Germany to visit with me. Would you like to say hello?" Andriko shook his head, still not taking his face from Marika's lap. Weisser laughed lightly, amused.

"Andriko," he said, "I have a son as old as you. Are you five years old?"

"No," said Andriko, moving his face a little.

"No?" said Weisser with surprise. "How old are you?"

"I'm three," came the reply.

"Three? Three years old? *Mein Gott,** what a big boy you are!" said Weisser with mock surprise.

"Yes," said Andriko. "I am a very big boy!" Both Marika and Josef chuckled.

Allegra came into the room and said, "Yes, he is a very big boy!"

"Ah, Anghela," said Marika. "Come meet my friend."

Weisser greeted Allegra, standing formally for the

Mein Gott: My God.

introduction. "Anghela, may I introduce Lieutenant Josef Weisser. Josef, this is my cousin, Anghela Toufexides, from Sarandë."

"I am delighted to meet you, Mrs. Toufexides," Weisser said. "You have a most charming son."

"And I am just as delighted to meet you," said Allegra, playing her part. "Thank you for your kind comments about Andriko."

"He's a lovely boy," continued the Gestapo lieutenant. "I have a son just like him. Of course, I miss him and all my children greatly. I have not seen them since Christmas, so I truly enjoy occasions like these."

The conversation continued, and eventually Andriko released his hold on Marika, playing at their feet on the carpet. Allegra prevented her loathing to interfere, and as Andriko became familiar with Weisser's presence, he became increasingly curious. Allegra knew to expect it, but it was still a great shock when the Gestapo lieutenant sat Andreas on his lap.

Astonished, Allegra watched as the lieutenant of the Secret State Police held her son, spoke with a father's loving voice, laughed and made little jokes, and Andriko, for his part, endeared himself to this dangerous Nazi who just weeks earlier had almost captured his father and grandfather...his father, who at this moment was under the bed in the other room.

* * *

Under the bed, uncomfortable behind the fabric skirt, Henri lay quietly, unable to move or turn for two hours as his wife and young son visited with Marika and her Gestapo friend.

"This is crazy," thought Henri. To keep his mind off how close death was...in the next room...he turned his thoughts to happier times, remembering that perfect day when he carried Andriko on a walk along the harbor and they had dinner at a café near the White Tower. Allegra told him how much she loved him. "Those were good days," he thought. "Will they come again?"

He prayed for all the brave souls helping his family. From the deepest part of his soul, Henri prayed they would survive and live again in a safe world. "May the day come soon!" prayed Henri as the door suddenly opened.

Henri listened, instantly alert...and felt relief as he heard Allegra softly say, "You can come out now, Henri. He's gone."

Henri stiffly pushed himself out from under the bed. "Everything's all right?"

"Yes," she replied. "He doesn't know a thing."

"Where is Andriko?"

"With Marika. We were smart to tell him you'd be going out. We'll tell him you're back."

Henri stood up and stretched with a small groan. "Oh, that feels good..." and silently added, "Thank you, God, for keeping the Angel of Death from us once more..."

Chapter 35
A Dangerous Slip

October 4, 1943; 208 Days in Hiding

*Dr. Max Merten, the representative of the military governor
of northern Greece, had a mistress who was married to
a Greek Jew. Because of this, Merten allowed the Jewish
partner of an interfaith marriage to stay in Thessaloniki and
avoid deportation. There were 18 couples in this category.*

Three months passed, with a dozen more visits by Senior
Lieutenant Weisser. Allegra and Henri worried that
Andriko might slip and mention his father...and though
this never happened, Andriko did give them away...but
not to Weisser.

Nila was Marika's friend from Izmir, and they enjoyed
a weekly afternoon of tea and gossip as Henri waited
under the bed; Nila knew Henri before the war, and
knew he was Jewish. The risk was too great to take.

Nila knew Marika had a crush on Nikos. "You are so
fortunate," said Nila, "the manager of the bank staying
with you. How very convenient!"

"Oh, no, Nila," replied Marika with a laugh. "It's not
like that at all. Nikos is a good tenant, and we are just
friends." Though the attraction was platonic, Marika

privately wished it was more.

"You can't fool me, Marika. I can see how much you like him."

"Oh, he is handsome, and I do like him, but we have separate lives."

"I know you, Marika. I can tell you would not say no if he said yes!"

"That's silly!" Marika demurred unconvincingly.

One day Nila told Marika her suspicions. "I think something's not right. Nikos is fooling you. I think they are both fooling you. Beware," she confided. "Nikos brought his girlfriend here, and his own son. Look at the child. He has the same eyes, the same face, the same..." insisted Nila. "Look how he talks to Anghela, how he talks to the boy. They are fooling you. I believe Anghela is Nikos's mistress and Andriko is their child!"

Marika knew this was foolishness, though she admitted her jealousy of Nikos's warm relationship with Allegra. "How nice it would be to receive his romantic attentions," she often thought dreamily.

Even though Marika dismissed Nila's insinuations, the onslaught made Marika nervous. "She's very suspicious. Has anyone else noticed? Maybe Allegra and Andriko are drawing too much attention...I must be more careful."

An incident occurred one warm afternoon in early autumn. Marika, Allegra, and Andriko were on the terrace having tea. Marika's terrace was shared with her apartment neighbors, Alena and Solomon. Everyone knew Solomon was Jewish, and he was tolerated by the authorities because he was married to a Christian. When Alena appeared on the terrace, Marika invited her to join them.

The three women were enjoying each other's company as Andriko played with his trucks and blocks. The sounds of the street below were light and almost melodic as everyone forgot about the German occupation, caught up in the relaxed mood of the early afternoon. This was abruptly shattered.

"I'm going to make a nice stew tonight," said Alena. "I bought some fresh vegetables from Modiano Market on Mitropoleos Street."

"That reminds me," said Marika. "I've been thinking about our dinner tonight. We'll be having lentils with eggplant, tomatoes and cucumbers. Does that sound good, Anghela?"

Andriko looked up from his play. "Mamá, do you remember when your name was Allegra?"

Allegra immediately saw recognition in Alena's eyes and Alena saw it in Marika's. No one spoke. A long moment passed, and Allegra replied, "Oh, yes, Andriko. My middle name. I haven't used it in so long. I'm surprised you still remember it."

The afternoon tea quickly came to an awkward end. This was now the second incident that heightened Marika's fears.

A few days later another incident occurred. Henri was in Marika's kitchen storing a bag of wheat high on a shelf when he fell and broke his wrist. Seeing a doctor was risky, but fortunately Henri went to Dr. Matarasso, who was Jewish and married to a Christian French woman. Matarasso set Henri's wrist and wrapped it in a cast. Several night visits were necessary to make sure the wrist was healing properly, and with no identification papers, the risk was great. This incident also added to Marika's alarm.

Nikos returned one day with disturbing news. "Henri, Allegra, I have to return the valise with all your paper money. The Germans are opening the vaults with Sephardic names. Your money is not safe there anymore."

"I understand," said Henri. "Yes, bring the money here. We'll think of some place to hide it."

"I think you should exchange it all, Henri," said Allegra. "*Drachmas* are no good. If anything happens, it's just paper. You should change the money into *lira*. I don't trust the Greek currency. *Lira* are better."

"I disagree. We'd be exchanging too many *drachmas* for so few *lira*. I think it's a bad trade. What makes you think the British money will be any good when the war is over?"

"All right, if that's what you think, then do half and half. Exchange half the *drachmas* for *lira*. That way we'll at least have two chances."

"I don't know. Let me think about it. I can exchange our *drachmas* for the older *drachmas*. After the war they should be as good as gold. The old *drachmas* will be restored."

"Henri, at least make half and half. If you lose from one, you will make it up with the other."

"People treasure the old *drachmas*. Let me think about it and I'll decide." The next day Henri asked Nikos to bring back the money in pre-war *drachmas* only, and he hid the valise in their bedroom.

A week later, Marika returned with terrible news. "Nikos has been arrested!"

"Arrested? Why? What happened?" Allegra cried, startled.

"I'm not really sure. All I know is the Gestapo arrested Nikos because he refused to give them the money they demanded!"

"If he's been arrested," Allegra asked, "will the Gestapo come here to search his room?"

"They would have been here by now," replied Marika, "but I definitely think it's time you found another place to live. It's not safe anymore, for any of us."

That night Henri visited Avram and his mother in the *Kamara* and told them he and Allegra needed a new place, and soon.

"I'll ask some friends in the morning," Avram said. "If you have to, you can stay here with us for a few days."

Nikos was released the next day, looking worn and weary. "It was quite unpleasant," he said, sipping a cup of coffee. "In my experience, the German people are generally not bad, though I have an extremely different opinion of the Nazi Party and their secret police."

"I'm so glad you've returned to us safely," Marika said in a soft voice.

Nikos told his story and how angry the Nazis had been. "They wouldn't believe me when I told them that almost everyone has emptied their accounts because of the poor economy, which the occupation created. Really, there's almost nothing left in the bank!"

"It's their fault!" Marika said angrily. "They're the ones who have been robbing our people of everything we need to feed ourselves and stay alive!"

Nikos finished his coffee and set his cup upon its saucer gently. "Being interrogated by the Gestapo is quite uncomfortable, as you know, Henri," Nikos remarked. "I think it's an excellent idea, as Marika suggests, that you find another place to live as soon as possible."

That night Henri, Allegra and Andriko left Marika Karakitsou's apartment and walked the dozen blocks to Marika Pavlidou's home to join Avram and Maria in the *Kamara*. It was almost the end of October 1943. The night sky was covered with thick wintry clouds, visible only by the meager reflection of the sleeping city's lights. The brilliant moon had fled, its waning powers at lowest ebb, unaware of the three travelers slipping through night's shroud.

Chapter 36
The Café of Mirrors

October 31, 1943; 235 Days in Hiding

The invasion by the Italians was three years ago, on October 28, 1940.

Allegra woke first. She got up softly from their makeshift bed. Avram and Myriam were asleep on the other side of the small room. "It's a relief to be out of Marika's apartment," thought Allegra, "even if we're crowding into one room again."

Allegra pulled her robe tight and stretched her back, lifting her arms far above her head. After a long moment, she released her taut muscles and felt much better. That's when she saw herself in the vanity mirror.

"What?" she thought. "That can't be!" She stepped closer to the mirror. In the half light of the early morning Allegra saw a large section of hair above her forehead had turned white overnight. Allegra pulled on it to make sure it was really her hair, and looking at her reflection she saw herself again for the first time.

* * *

Avram stepped into Aleko's taverna and took his

customary seat in the back. Aleko acknowledged him and when he was done pouring drinks, he came to Avram's table with a cup of ersatz coffee and *koulourakia*.*

"Did they get in all right?" asked Aleko.

"Yes, they're with us now. Have you heard of a place they can stay?"

"Not for sure, but Stefanos will be in later this morning, after court. He said he might have something."

"That's good. Moving around isn't easy."

"I can imagine. However, I agree with Henri. You and Myriam should also move."

"Yes, once Henri and Allegra are settled we'll look for a new place."

"Staying with a communist...it's just a matter of time until the Gestapo comes for her. When they do, you don't want to be there."

Aleko left to serve some customers, and Avram took a sip of the bitter coffee. Pulling out his pack, he lit a cigarette. Letting the smoke out through his nose he

---

Koulourakia: Greek cookies with egg glaze and a light vanilla flavor.

remembered the night, 20 years ago, when he had been arrested...for the second time.

> Avram owned a magnificent café...and it
> was full of mirrors all around. In the summer,
> people would be outside, enjoying their drinks
> and food in the café's big garden with over
> 100 marble tables and all the chairs. It was
> a wonderful place to come on the weekends
> when the spring had released its flowers, or
> in the summer when the weather was warm
> and bright, or in the early part of the autumn
> before the breezes became too cold and the
> leaves had turned their colors dry brown.

> The café's name was Aynalar, which in
> Turkish means "Mirrors." The mirrors came
> from Venice and had blue velvet frames; they
> were huge, from ceiling to floor, reflecting
> all the happy moments, all the laughter, the
> music, the waiters in white shirts and dark
> pants, the people in their festive clothing, and
> all the dizzying forms of light that danced
> across their surface, changing with the
> various hues of the setting sun, and capturing
> the nightly birth of candlelight on the dozens
> of linened tables laden with delicious foods,
> sparkling wines and glasses of bubbling beer.

> Tremendous amounts of food were prepared...
> stacks of bread by the dozens, and cases of
> beer, big mounds of salads and hors d'oeuvres,

and lovely pastries and desserts to tempt the palate.

Saturdays and Sundays were the big nights, and people would come to Aynalar to start their weekend's evening, either before attending a show...or to enjoy the relaxed and happy moments after their entertainment was over. Of course, some people would come just for the delightful ambience, have their food and drinks, and talk for hours, enjoying the live music and the special moments, dining outside under the fabulous sky with its millions of stars. Few buildings were more than two or three stories high in the Vardar district, so on a clear night, which was often the way it was in the summertime, the pleasant laughter of Avram's guests was a mirrored reflection of the sparkling light from the stars above.

Except on the weekends. That was when it rained, dampening Avram's business! Sometimes it only rained a little, so the tables and chairs were dried off in anticipation of adventurous guests. Avram always hired an orchestra to play on the weekends, and they played mostly Turkish music. The Sephardic Jews were very fond of this type of music, with the long and short-necked lutes, the clarinet-type wind instruments, and the light percussion that captured the ephemeral

resonance of laughter and sadness. The sweet
music made people want to dance, or reflect
sorrowfully on the bitterness of life.
Henri used to work with Avram at the
café. Sometimes the guests would sing the
popular songs along with the orchestra; in
those days everybody knew the words and
almost everybody at all the tables would sing
together. The guests were Greeks and Turks,
but mostly Jews. Sometimes the orchestra
would also play other popular songs, and the
guests would join in, singing in Ladino. More
prevalent than Greek among the Jews, Ladino
was spoken in the streets and cafés.

The family joke was that Saturday morning
was always a beautiful day until around
four o'clock in the afternoon when the sky
suddenly became covered with clouds, and by
five o'clock there was a beautiful rainstorm
without fail…and that was the end of
business for the day! Only on weekends; the
rain never came on weekdays.

When it rained, Avram would tell the
musicians, "Sing for me." Avram sat at his
own table and the musicians would play and
sing, just for him. Avram would pour a small
glass of ouzo, and Henri sat with him, and
they enjoyed the music as the rain fell on the
tables outside.

Avram eventually made some changes
and decided to forego the music from the
orchestra, installing a phonograph instead,
the one with the big horn that directed the
music out from the box. This was a big hit
with his customers because now Avram
could buy all the newest and most popular
records and play them at his Café of Mirrors.
Every week, Avram and Henri would go to
the record store to buy the newest releases. It
was a Jewish store, Abravanel & Benveniste,
and they were representatives of Odeon, one
of the leading brands of records in Europe.
The customers were always anxious to hear
the new releases, so this was very good for
business.

One evening the café was absolutely full,
and everybody was having a wonderful time.
The guests were particularly exuberant, and
the music was drowned out, except in the
direction the big horn faced. One of the guests
walked over to the gramophone, upset that he
was missing the music he had come to hear, so
he faced the horn toward his table. A moment
later another guest from a different corner of
the garden also went to the gramophone and
changed the horn's direction...

This, of course, only created more rancor, and
since many of these guests had already had

*several drinks, their fury grew quickly into a
giant melee!*

*At least 100 people were fighting each other!
The whole place was at war! Tables were
overturned, plates and glasses smashed on
the ground, women shrieking, men throwing
punches, waiters running away, flowers and
bushes crushed underfoot, and the police were
called!*

*So who do you think was taken to the police
station? Avram!*

*Henri rushed to the station and spoke to
the officer in charge. Henri asked, "Why do
you have my father here?" The policeman
explained about the huge turmoil at the café,
that the skirmish had disrupted the peace,
and violent behavior would not be tolerated.
Henri explained what had happened, and
eventually Avram was released.*

Avram shook his head from side to side, remembering.
He had such a terrific loss that night. So many of the
beautiful marble tables had been broken, and all the
plates and glasses...and on top of that, nobody had paid
for their dinner or drinks! Well, what was to be done?

Avram smiled and took a last puff of the cigarette before
stubbing it out. "When a man lives, he has stories to tell,"
he thought to himself. Looking up, his smile broadened

because Stefanos was entering the taverna.

"Avram," Stefanos said in a hushed voice so no one could hear his name. "Good to see you!"

"And you. Come, sit down."

Stefanos pulled out the chair and sat down. "There is room at my place. Sultana and I agreed. We can make some room by moving the children around. Henri, Allegra and Andreas are welcome to stay with us."

"That's great news, Stefanos! Thank you. Henri will be relieved."

"As I imagine you will, also," quipped Stefanos.

"Yes, things are a bit tight at Marika's. When can they move?"

"Tonight is good, any time after dark. Do they need help carrying anything?"

"No, they have very little."

"All right, then," said Stefanos, "find out if they are going to move tonight. I'll meet you back here after work so you can let me know." With that, Stefanos stood up and left the taverna, tipping his hat to Aleko on his way out.

Aleko looked at Avram from across the room. Avram nodded and Aleko smiled.

Chapter 37
New Neighbors

November 10, 1943; 245 Days in Hiding

Stefanos and Sultana had four children. Galen, the older boy, and Fotis their second; Theo was their third, and Mairula, their daughter. A very nice family with modest means, sincere and religious, Stefanos was a clerk at the Court of First Instance,* and he was away at work all day. Theo was very bright and became Andriko's best friend, teaching him this prayer to say at bedtime:

> I played, I sang,
> I danced and jumped,
> I said lots of words,
> And always I had at my side
> My Angel
> Who led me
> To do good things,
> And now when night is coming
> And darkness is spreading,
> I beg you, my little God,
> Send to me again,
> Near my pillow
> My good Angel,

Court of First Instance: The Court of First Instance hears civil disputes.

And keep my Daddy and Mommy,
And Maria and Andres*
Away from any evil.
Amen.

"You won't be able to stay here during the day," said Stefano.

"The neighbors visit all day," explained Sultana. "Because we live on this dead-end street, everybody is friends with everybody else, almost, and they'll get suspicious if they see you here all day every day."

"What do you think I should do?" asked Henri.

"It's best if you left early in the morning and stayed away until dinner, like the other men."

Henri was looking out the window. "Sure," he said. "I can pretend I'm going to work."

"We can tell everybody you work at the Bank of Greece. You were transferred here from Athens..." suggested Allegra.

"Great idea! I can wear one of my suits, and if I had a briefcase, I'd look the part."

"I have an extra briefcase you can have," said Stefano.

―――――――――

Maria and Andres: The names Myriam and Avram used in hiding.

"Well, that's it, then," concluded Sultana.

Just then Henri saw something outside the window. "Oh my God," he said. "Does he live here?"

Stefano looked out the window. "You mean Gianakos? Yes, he lives here. He's in the third house up the street."

"I know him," said Henri. "He works at the Chamber of Commerce. If he sees me, he could report me."

"We'll have to be extra careful," said Allegra.

"He and his wife are friendly, but they keep to themselves. You should definitely keep your eye out for him, but I know they won't be dropping in unexpectedly like the others," said Sultana.

"Another thing to worry about," thought Henri.

At that moment, Andriko and Theo came running through the house with the two older boys in pursuit. Laughing and shouting, they fell in a heap by the sofa. Suddenly there was a loud thumping from upstairs and the muffled sound of somebody yelling.

"Oh, that woman!" complained Sultana. "She is such a witch!" Henri and Allegra looked at each other, and then at Sultana.

"It's Karalis, our upstairs neighbor," Sultana said. "She hates me and she's always trying to hurt us. She thinks I insulted her, but I didn't. I've tried to talk to her about it, but she won't listen. She has it in for me and harasses me every chance she gets. I've tried everything, including prayer, but she won't stop."

"What was that thumping?" asked Allegra.

"That was her broom!" Stefano said. "She's banging on the floor with her broom handle to tell the boys to be quiet."

"Oh," Allegra said thoughtfully, remembering that her family had been sold to the Nazis by neighbors. Henri looked at her and knew what she was thinking.

"Allegra's family was denounced by angry neighbors," Henri said softly. "Your feud with her could be very dangerous for us."

Sultana looked at Stefano, and then at her guests. "I understand. I'll avoid her as much as possible, which I do anyway. If you'll help me keep the boys in line, I think we can keep her subdued."

"Our new life," thought Allegra, "living deceptively..."

"...through the compassion and kindness of friends," thought Henri.

They should have expected that Andriko would bring their next torment.

* * *

"What has gotten into that boy?" said Allegra with exasperation. Andriko had just run screaming through the house with Theo close behind, disappearing into the yard.

"I told Theo not to chase him!" Sultana growled, and she followed them outdoors. Allegra could hear her reprimands.

Allegra shook her head, quite displeased. Andreas was growing up and acting like a little madman. It would not have been all right to behave this way if they had their own apartment, and it certainly was not all right when their lives depended on not drawing attention and stirring up trouble.

"I'm grateful, Sultana," said Allegra when her friend returned.

"Oh, it's nothing, believe me. I have three boys!"

"Well, we are in your debt." Sultana was cleaning up the downstairs room. "What can I do to help? Can I do the dusting or shake out the carpets?"

"No! I don't want you to do any housekeeping. That's my job...besides, I'd rather do all the cleaning myself."

"Sultana, I have to do something to contribute. What can I do? Can I do some sewing for you?"

"Ah! Now that would be helpful. I've got a few things... If you really wouldn't mind..."

"Yes! Please! I'm happy to do it. I'll need your needles and thread, though."

Sultana was back in a moment with a pile of clothes, and Allegra began to sort and select threads. Just then she heard Andreas outside, the loudest of the pack.

"What is he doing?" She quickly got up in a mood mixed with fear and anger. From the back door, she saw Andriko throwing fistfuls of dirt and stones at the other children and several neighborhood dogs.

"Andreas!" she yelled. "Stop that!" She immediately stepped off the back porch and grabbed her errant child, giving him a light smack on the *opísthia*,* shaking his clenched hand to free a fistful of dirt.

The other children were taunting him, but Andreas kept laughing, unmindful. "You're coming inside with me!" Allegra said and she scooped him up into her arms and headed across the yard to the back door. Seized by his mother and pulled from his play, Andreas began to kick wildly, the heels of his shoes bruising Allegra's hip. "Stop that!" Allegra commanded again, but this only incensed Andreas to kick more violently and scream louder.

Opísthia: The "tush," buttocks.

"Oh, my God, what am I going to do with you?" Allegra asked, trying to control the 40 pounds of boisterous boy who now was going completely wild with his legs, arms, and shrieks.

Eleni Karalis, the upstairs neighbor, came out to see what was causing the chaos. "That boy needs to see the priest...he has the Devil in him," she scolded and made the sign of the cross. "Take him to church, take him to church because sometimes children are possessed!"

This was exactly what Allegra had wanted to avoid, the unwelcome attention of neighbors, especially Karalis who had a vendetta against Sultana.

"You're right," said Allegra, "that's exactly what we need to do." Arguing would only create more tension with this dangerous neighbor. "I'm taking Andreas to the priest!"

"Good!" responded Karalis. "And maybe you can have the priest take the Devil out of Sultana!" and she went back inside her apartment and slammed the door.

"Oh, Lord!" thought Allegra as she brought Andreas inside and thumped him on his rump again. "Your father is going to have to teach you a lesson!" she said loudly to Andreas who was now crying and fallen like a lump to the floor. "And I'm taking you to the priest!" she said, surprised at her words. It then occurred to her this was actually a great idea. Seeing the priest would further conceal their identity...and eliminate the suspicions of their neighbors. "I'll talk to Henri tonight," she thought, "and if he agrees, I'll tell Sultana our plans."

Allegra picked her unwilling son up from the floor. "How odd!" she thought, "We're going to go to church!"

✳ ✳ ✳

Father Nikolai was seated, dressed in black robes. "Andreas, why do you behave like that?" Andreas was silent, his eyes on the floor, shoulders shrunken. Allegra felt her mother's heart going out to her son, but knew better than to interfere.

"Andreas, look at me." Andreas squirmed in his seat but did not look up.

"Andreas, do you want to be a good boy?" asked the priest. Andreas nodded his head.

"Then you must listen to your mother and father, and obey them. Will you do that, Andreas?" Andreas nodded his head again. Father Nikolai cleared his throat. "All right," he said, "I am expecting to hear only good things about you from now on."

Father Nikolai looked at Allegra. "*Kyría* Toufexides, I want you to say 'The Lord's Prayer' with Andreas five times a day until he has memorized it." Father Nikolai had years of experience teaching boys who had become the playground of the devil.

"Yes, Father," Allegra said, smiling to show her gratitude.

"I also want you and Andreas to attend services here at *Saint Ypatios** every Monday morning so your entire week will be blessed."

"We will, Father. Thank you."

"And now that you are part of our community, I want you, Andreas, and *Kýrios* Toufexides to attend Sunday services. I think this will set Andreas on a strong path. Christmas services aren't too far away, and by then Andreas will be familiar with our prayers and ceremonies."

"Thank you, Father," Allegra said, seeing how this would quickly build her reputation as a good Greek Orthodox woman. Henri would never come.

Allegra led her silent son out of the church into the warm sunlight. "Mamá, what is Christmas?"

✳ ✳ ✳

Christmas 1943 was spent quietly and in reverence with the Chrissafis family. Sultana spread a white tablecloth on the dinner table to symbolize purity, with some straw to remind the family of the manger's simplicity. White candles adorned the table, and the food, quite basic this year, was rich with the communion of affection and prayer. The two families, one Christian and one Jewish,

---

Saint Ypatios: A Byzantine church near the *Kamara* district.

shared what they had and feasted, celebrating their wish for peace and love for all of God's children.

Soon after the holiday Avram and Myriam moved out of Marika's apartment, ending the threat of living with a communist. Costas Papapavlou and his wife Evghenia welcomed them, longtime friends since the days when Costas was a waiter at Avram's Café of Mirrors. They also lived in the *Kamara* near Aleko's taverna, just three blocks from where Henri, Allegra and Andreas were living with the Chrissafis. Myriam was to continue pretending she was a deaf mute so her Ladino accent wouldn't betray them, and except for the Papapavlous and Chrissafis, no one else was to know. At least, that was the plan.

"I know," said Henri shaking his head, "I know."

"Oh, Henri, what are we going to do?" Allegra looked at him, and then at the cloth she was twisting with her fingers.

"We'll be all right," was all Henri could say. "I'll see Nicos. I know he'll help."

Allegra looked at the suitcase full of useless paper money. She sighed. "Something will work out," she thought. She turned her head so Henri wouldn't see how upset and scared she was.

"You were right," he said. "I should have converted half of it into *lira*. All of it, actually."

"I have some rings and bracelets," said Allegra. "We can use that to pay Stefanos for our room and board, at least for a while."

In a few days Henri met with Nicos, and Nicos told Henri to stop selling their jewelry. "I'll lend you money," he said. "We'll calculate in *lira*. I'll give you the value and you can buy what you need, and as much as you need... with no interest. You can repay me after the war."

His friend's character, courage and compassion overwhelmed Henri.

Sultana heard their predicament, and she also had a solution. "You're so good with a needle and thread, Allegra. I know you could earn money sewing and making clothing. I'll ask around. I have some friends who might be interested." A few days later and Allegra's hours were full. One of her customers was a family that came into possession of a Jewish pasta factory and Allegra was paid with macaroni and *lira*.

✳ ✳ ✳

One day Allegra was doing laundry in the backyard. It was a chilly winter afternoon and Allegra felt her hands getting raw and chapped. As the white vapor of her breath made small clouds, Allegra scrubbed a pile of clothes in the big tub. One of the neighbors, Barbara, was also outside. She had finished her laundry and was brushing the caked mud from her shoes.

"Such a cold day," Allegra said to her neighbor. "My hands are freezing!"

"I know," replied Barbara. "My hands feel frostbitten. I can't wait to get inside and warm up."

"At least you're done. I still have to scrub this pile. I wish Andriko was more careful with his clothes."

"It's in a boy's nature!" laughed Barbara. "It's easier when they're babies. Boys love to take dirt baths," she chuckled.

"You mean I have another 10 years of this?" joked Allegra.

"More likely 20," and the two women laughed.

Suddenly, from around the corner of the fence that edged the yard, Myriam appeared. Happy to see her daughter-in-law, Myriam's smile dropped when she saw Barbara.

"Who is this?" asked Barbara, looking at the old woman as though she might be some beggar, disdain clearly in her voice.

"Oh! Hello, Mother," Allegra called out as Myriam approached. Half turning to Barbara, Allegra said, "This is Maria, my mother-in-law. She's a deaf mute." Allegra gave Myriam a warm hug and Myriam responded with a smile, but in silence, keeping her tongue still.

To Barbara, Allegra said, "She lives a few blocks from here. I was visiting yesterday and invited her to help me with the laundry."

"A deaf mute?" Barbara had softened a little, but was still judging. "Pleased to meet you, Maria," Barbara offered. Myriam simply smiled.

"She's been this way since she was a baby, but she is a dear soul, and it's thanks to her I have my Aristides."

"Poor thing. Well, she must have gone to a Jewish doctor. I heard Jewish doctors squeeze the heads of newborns to shape them, and sometimes babies lose their hearing and speech." Barbara had finished brushing her shoes. "I'm glad the Jews were deported. They're greedy and treacherous, and I hope they got what they deserved," she said, and was gone.

On the first day of each month Father Nikolai visited all the Christian houses in the neighborhood, blessing every room. Sultana and Allegra followed the priest from room to room, and when the priest had finished, the two women kissed his cross. Allegra took Andreas to church every Sunday, and on Monday they attended the liturgy and prayed for a good week with everyone else.

One morning Allegra awoke suddenly, startled. "Henri, I had another dream..." Allegra's voice was subdued in the semi-dark room.

Henri turned to face her. "A dream?" He was sleepy, but began waking. He knew to pay attention.

"Yes. I was walking up a flight of stairs..."

"Stairs. Like at Tsimiski Street?"

"No, no... The stairs were much higher. I kept walking up the stairs. They seemed to go up forever."

"Endless?" said Henri.

"Yes, it felt like that. I was so tired, and I kept going up and up..."

Henri was more awake, listening.

"The stairs went up, far beyond what I could see. I kept climbing higher and higher...and I never saw the last step. I kept climbing until I woke."

"What does it mean?" asked Henri.

"I think it only means one thing."

"What?"

"We have a long way to go..."

Chapter 38
Rabies

March 15, 1944; 371 Days in Hiding

One afternoon in March, before the last breath of winter was expended, Barbara was in the backyard as Andreas stepped out the back door of the apartment. He looked at her...and she looked at him. Incapable of anything but suspicion and cynicism, Barbara asked, "And where are you going, Andreas?" in her usual sour tone.

Without a thought or even a glance, Andreas shouted, "None of your business!" as he jumped off the back stairs and skipped down the street on his way to Avram's and Maria's with a basket of food.

Later that day Andreas and his comrades were playing outside. Exuberantly spirited, Andreas enjoyed the many opportunities to tease his comrades. Several dogs from the neighborhood were willing participants, and today a new dog joined them. Some of the boys recognized him; he was brown with floppy ears and a long white tail. No one knew his name, but he was welcomed into the noisy din.

Andreas was pretending to be a pirate captain fighting the Turkish fleet, and when he charged the enemy with a loud battle cry, the dog cowered. Andreas ran up to tag him and the frightened dog bit him on the cheek.

Suddenly the game was over; Andreas was crying and holding his face. The dog ran and all the boys gathered to see the wound. Theo and some of the boys brought Andreas to the back door.

"Andriko was bitten!" shouted Theo. "Look, he's bleeding!" Andreas was in tears, unable to speak.

"Oh, my God!" shouted Allegra. "My baby!"

"We need to go to the hospital right away," said Sultana.

"I can't! I don't have papers!" said Allegra.

"Don't worry about that. I'll take him. I'll tell the doctor he's a relative..."

"Thank you!" cried Allegra. "I don't know what I'd do without you! Let me wash off the blood."

"I'll get some water on the stove."

Andreas was coming out of his shock, crying with pain and fear.

Sultana heated the water and the two women washed the wound. "We better go," said Sultana.

"Sultana and I are taking you to the hospital. Sultana will take you inside to see the doctor. Do whatever Sultana tells you."

Andreas looked up at his mother, and nodded. The wound was swelling. "My face hurts, Mamá."

"I know, Honey, you'll be fine. Sultana and the doctor will take good care of you."

Sultana looked at Allegra, pale and edgy. "He'll be all right," she said. "We'll be there soon."

The doctor examined Andreas. He also lived in the *Kamara*, not far from the Chrissafis, and when he asked Andreas to explain what the dog looked like, he recognized it. "I know that dog," the doctor said, "and I also happen to know he doesn't have rabies. You're a lucky young man, Andreas."

"You're completely sure, Doctor?" asked Sultana.

"Yes, but it's a good idea to have the shots anyway. At his age he can have them on his thigh and they won't be as painful. I can give him the first shot today. He'll need 10 shots, so you must come every day. It's better not to take any chances."

It was a lesson for Andreas, whose days of fighting Turkish armadas manned by sharp-toothed canines had passed.

✳ ✳ ✳

Avram was at a table in the back of the taverna, hat pulled low, over his eyes. His glass of *retsina* was almost empty, the ashtray filled with *Papastratos* butts and ashes.

"A long day," he thought, "but better here than playing solitaire on the floor at Costas's house." Avram tried to ignore the table with the drunken German soldiers, but it was difficult. "Like not wanting to watch a dangerous snake," he thought wryly.

Four uniformed soldiers sat at a table close to the front, and had been here for nearly two hours. They had not paid him any attention because he was just another old Greek doing what every old Greek did, which was smoking, being surly, and drinking quietly with friends.

Avram overheard some of their talk, and though his German wasn't very good, every once in a while he heard them grumbling, and the word *Juden* endlessly repeated. "*Juden…Juden…die verdammten Juden…*"* Avram wondered why the Germans were so obsessed. There were no more Jews in Thessaloniki. As far as he knew, everyone had been deported a year ago, and yet these Germans were still talking about how their lives had been scarred by the damn *Juden*.

Aleko came up to his table. "Andres," careful to use his alias, "how are you doing back here?"

"Fine, thanks. Maybe you can bring another *retsina*."

Die verdammten Juden: The damned Jews.

"Did you hear the soldiers talking? They're very unhappy...the war is not going so well," Aleko said with a subtle smile.

"What's the news?"

"The Red Army is at the Romanian border, and Berlin is being bombed day and night."

"I love good news," Avram said softly. He winked at Aleko; Aleko grinned.

"I've been thinking about your grandson. He's a brave little fellow, getting those rabies shots."

Avram looked up from under the brim of his hat. "Andriko is a special little boy, a real bravo. Allegra said she was watching the other day when he was bringing some food over. One of the neighbors called out and asked, 'Andreas! Where are you going?' You know what he said?"

"What?"

"None of your business!" The two men laughed softly as the table with the soldiers suddenly got louder.

"I better get back over there," said Aleko. "Business is good the worse it gets."

Chapter 39
Burning the Jew

April 9, 1944; 396 Days in Hiding

Andreas stood in the long procession, dressed in dark pants and a new white shirt. Standing in front of him in the boys' line was Theo, also in dark pants and a new white shirt. Theo's sister, Mairoula, was in the girls' line, wearing a white dress and white shoes, her hair adorned with a pink ribbon.

It was early evening, and Andreas was tired of holding the tall white candle, tired of standing, and tired of waiting for the priests. "When do we start?" he asked Theo again, in a more whiny voice this time.

Theo half-turned, distracted by some older boys. "I don't know. Stop asking me."

Andreas looked down the street at the big church, its courtyard and steps illuminated. The *Agios Ypatios** towered impressively over the gathering of children and adults, its three cupolas and crosses gleaming. The main door was closed, and the long double line of children waited in the half-light until the black-robed priests and their assistants were ready.

Agios Ypatios: The oldest church in the city, demolished and then replaced in 1956 with a new church, *Panagia Dexia*.

Suddenly Andreas saw a flurry of activity at the head of the line as the assistants began lighting the candles. They moved quickly down the two rows of children, and in a moment an assistant was lighting Andreas's candle. "Hold your candle straight," the man said, "like this," showing Andreas how to hold it with two hands, one above the other. "Keep it straight or the wax will burn you," he added, then touched his candle's flame to Andreas's wick, and Andreas's candle bloomed with light. "*Christos anesti!*"* the man said, moving to the next child.

Andreas smiled with pleasure, now that his candle was lit. He tilted the candle a little; the light grew brighter and a big drop of wax fell onto Andreas's hand. "Ow!" he yelled, and brushed off the hot wax. He held the candle more reverently, and then the double line of children began moving forward.

"Go!" Andreas said to Theo, and Theo again half turned, saying angrily, "I can't!" But in a moment the line was moving sufficiently forward. Andreas's eyes glowed with the light of his candle, and he had the feeling of being part of something big and important. Andreas looked for his parents, and saw them smiling and waving, seeing him in his new white shirt, holding the bright white candle. He knew he was not supposed to call out so instead he took one hand off the candle and waved back, and then his focus quickly returned to the back of Theo's

---

Christos anesti!: Christ is risen!

306

head and the front of the church that grew bigger and bigger until he was mounting the marble steps and walking through the main doors, consumed by the vast interior of the magnificent church.

Once inside, adults took the children's candles, blew out their flames and stacked the candles on side tables. The two lines of children proceeded to the pews and took their places.

The inside of *Agios Ypatios* was exquisite. Enclosing a voluminous space, the walls and ceilings were covered with beautiful murals of the Mother of God with angels and saints. A large image of the Son of God adorned the ceiling of the central dome, and the marble columns and floor were gorgeous, seemingly made of liquid light.

When everyone had filed into the church, the doors closed and the service began. Standing up, sitting down, standing up...eventually the beauty of the glorious building began to wear thin. Besides, Andreas had been told there would be a huge bonfire, and he wanted to see that. The long ceremony finally over, the monitors guided the children out of the church and into the cool night.

Waiting for their children, Allegra and Sultana found them quickly. Henri had already left.

"Well, did you like that?" Allegra asked her son.

"Yes, Mamá," Andreas said. "When is the big fire?"

"Soon," she replied. Though not looking forward to it, this would be another example of being a good Orthodox Christian family. Even so, she didn't want Andreas to witness the burning of the effigy of Judas; the idea of burning an effigy seemed medieval and repressed.

"The whole world is at war!" she reflected. "Aren't we all brothers and sisters? Isn't this the message of Christ? Haven't we had enough? Dear God, when will we stop?"

Obligated and unwilling, Allegra led Andreas up the church steps for a good view of the bonfire. Sultana and her children joined them. "How odd it's also the first night of Passover,"* Allegra thought.

In a corner of the large square the men had built a giant pyre of wood two meters high and a dozen meters around. From the center of this pyre rose a tall, heavy wooden gallows. A rope with a noose hung from the gallows beam, and hanging from the rope was a life-sized mannequin clothed in pants and a coat.

Allegra gasped. Expecting to see only a straw dummy, she was stunned to see the Judas wearing a coat with a yellow Jewish star. On the mannequin's head was a *yarmulke*,* and suspended from the mannequin's neck

———————

Passover: An important Jewish holiday celebrating the passing-over of the Angel of Death just before the exodus from Egypt.

Yarmulke: A simple Jewish cap worn on the head as a symbol of humility before God.

was a sign that said "**Ιουδας**"* in bold red letters. She stopped herself from blurting out in shock, and then felt violently ill, wanting to vomit.

The crowd was excited, eager for the show to begin. Suddenly all the church bells began to ring, sounding the doom of Christ's betrayer. The bells were loud, strident, creating a huge upswell in the crowd's anticipation, the sharp claps of metal vibrating in everyone's chests and ears.

The full-bodied mannequin seemed to almost float in mid-air, suspended high above the giant pyre of wood, hanging by its neck...it looked real, its arms and legs splayed out, twisting gently in a light current of air.

A church assistant ran up to the pyre with a torch and there was a sudden giant burst of yellow flame! Soaked in flammable liquids, the tall stack of wood quickly became engulfed as large bursts of orange-rimmed flames leaped into the sky, reaching for the straw and wooden body of the Jew.

The crowd erupted with cheers and the entire plaza shook with their shouts. The loud church bells were relentless, inspiring the flames to reach higher until at last the eager blaze caught the foot of the hanging monster and encased the creature in a suit of fire. Wild

---

Ιουδας: Judas was traditionally burned in effigy, but the difference this time is that the straw dummy has a yellow Jewish star on its coat.

with excitement, the flames danced on the body of the burning Jew with the exhortations of the crowd, the entire pyre engulfed in the ravishing fire, the straw body completely ignited and rapidly incinerating, a blazing focus for the crowd's malice and hate!

In moments, having reached its fiery zenith, the burning carcass of wooden bones was all that remained of the villain. The cries and jeers of the crowd continued as the burning corpse of wood swung idly in the air above the smoky pyre…and then the rope holding the wood and straw cadaver burned through, dropping the remains of the skeleton onto the burning pile, sending a final sudden burst of sparks jumping upward from the mound of scorching timber.

The church bells slowed and ceased; the crowd of men, women, and children began to disperse. The funeral pyre collapsed and smoldered as the dark smoke rose and wafted away.

Andreas was pleased…this had been a great show!

Allegra was exhausted. She and Sultana walked their children home through the dimly lit streets, their boys up ahead, happily leading the way.

Holding her daughter's hand, Sultana walked beside her friend. "I'm so sorry," was all she said.

Chapter 40
Three Near Misses

May 18, 1944; 435 Days in Hiding

Myriam was alone in the backyard, Avram was in the house, and the Papapavlous were at the market shopping for food and charcoal. It was a lovely day in May, and Myriam was by the fence admiring the new purple blossoms of wild gladiolus, their petals delicate and curvaceous. Observing the delightful flowers, Myriam was distracted by their beauty until she heard someone entering the yard behind her.

Turning, she saw the water meter man, and their eyes met. Seeing what she was doing, he smiled and said, "Lovely flowers!"

Myriam replied, "Spring is such a wonderful time of year!"

The man immediately stopped, his mouth open in surprise. Myriam realized she had betrayed herself.

"Oh, my God..." Myriam said softly, frightened. Worse, she recognized the man from a few years ago. He had been the policeman in their old neighborhood.

"Wait a minute...I think I know you," he said. He looked

at her more closely. "Didn't you used to live in the *Vardar*?"

"Yes." There was no point denying it. "I am the wife of Avram."

"That's right! I remember you. Avram Algava, with *Aynalar*, the café! I used to stop by there all the time. It was a wonderful café," he reminisced. "I remember the night Avram was arrested."

Myriam was holding her hands and squeezing her fingers in distress. "What am I going to do?"

The man suddenly realized how frightened she was. "Do? Do nothing. Do you think I am going to denounce you?"

"Yes, I'm afraid."

"Don't worry. I will never say a word, not even to my wife."

"Thank you," said Myriam, her lips trembling.

"As a matter of fact, I can help. Let Avram know that Pippo Trakas came by today. He'll remember me. I was at the café a lot. I'm going to give you my address, and if Avram wishes, he can visit. He's an old friend! I can help with rations, or whatever you need. Will you do that?"

Myriam looked at him with gratitude and gave a slight

but nervous smile. "Thank you. You have a kind heart."

The man quickly wrote his address and gave it to Myriam. "Don't worry," he said. "I will help as much as I can." He read the meter...and was gone.

In the busy outdoor market, a thin chiffon scarf covered Allegra's face, protecting her from the summer sun. Many women wore the gossamer material at this time of year, looking through the cloth, but not being seen.

Hundreds of people moved among the different stalls buying beans, lentils and chickpeas, arguing with the vendors about their inflated prices. Some wild berries, oranges and apples were displayed on the tables, along with meager amounts of root vegetables, garlic and zucchini. There was no meat or fish, and the price of olive oil was out of reach.

Allegra walked among the stalls selecting food for dinner; distracted by the commotion and lost in thought, she was startled to realize she was found out. Lifting her scarf to shoo away a tiny fly, Allegra was recognized by the man who sold spices from his cart on Tsimiski Street. He was frozen, mouth partly open in surprise.

Without hesitation Allegra put a finger to her lips, signaling to keep her secret, and the man recovered quickly, nodding briefly, turning away. Allegra stepped into the crowd, but was surprised to see her neighbors,

Napoleon and Kaity, the ones on their dead-end street with a hidden radio. They had a surprised look on their faces, too; then, smiling and waving, they resumed their shopping.

"Oh, no," she thought, a sinking feeling in her stomach. "What if I've given us away?"

* * *

Allegra, Henri and Andreas climbed the stairs above the stable at *Arslan Han*, the Lion's Shelter, and knocked gently on the door of Baba Yorgo's room.

"Come in," said the mystic in his high-pitched voice. The room was dark, a heavy curtain drawn across its only window. Candles lit the room with their gentle glow, and the fragrant scent of incense curled from several sticks on the altar of religious statues, flower petals and crystals.

"Dear Lady and Sir, welcome, welcome again! Yes, please come in. And this is your son. I have been expecting all of you."

Allegra smiled; she knew Baba Yorgo would say that. Henri wasn't sure what to think, but he had plenty of respect for Allegra's premonitions, and he was receptive to the Hindu's intuitions. Andreas was quiet, taking everything in.

"It is good to see you, too, Baba Yorgo," Allegra said.

"This is our son, Andreas."

Baba Yorgo reached for Andreas's palm. The boy gave it freely and after a moment of study, "This," the mystic said, "is the lucky one."

Allegra and Henri looked at Andreas. They smiled. Andreas smiled, too, not sure what the adults were talking about.

"Baba Yorgo, we are here for a reading." Allegra and Henri sat on the floor near the Hindu.

"Yes, of course. Show me your palm." Baba Yorgo took Allegra's hand and studied the lines. "Do you have a question?" he asked.

"When are we going to be liberated? We have been hiding from the Germans for over a year and it's been very difficult." Allegra felt tears gathering. "I want to know how much longer."

"Do not worry about it. You will get through. I see this very clearly. You are safe and nothing bad will happen to any of you, so just do what you're doing. It is enough."

"But Baba Yorgo, how much longer?"

"Soon."

"But how soon? How many more months? Can you see that in my palm?"

"I can see it, yes. Three months. Three months and you will be safe. Is this what you wanted to know?"

"Three months? That means August!" Allegra's face lit up, happy to hear this news. "And we will all survive? Andreas, Henri's parents, both of us? We will all survive?"

Baba Yorgo curled up Allegra's fingers, returning her hand. "Yes, yes. All will survive. You will all see the soldiers go. Be at peace, my child. Is there anything else you wish to know?"

"Yes, Baba Yorgo, I brought some photographs. Can you look at these and tell me if these people will also survive?"

"I can do that. Let me see them," said Baba Yorgo. He took the dozen pictures, spread them on the carpet and looked at each one. "This man, he will come back." It was a picture of Larry Nachmias.

"Look, Henri, it's your cousin Larry," Allegra said softly.

When Baba Yorgo saw a picture of Allegra's brother Pepo, the mystic said, "This one will come back. I don't see anybody else," he said.

"What is happening to them?" Allegra asked, afraid to know.

"I don't know. They are suffering. I cannot tell you. The

316

only thing I can tell you is that I see this man alive, and I see this man alive, and that's all I can say."

Allegra pointed to a photograph with her brother, Salomon. "And him?"

"I don't know. I don't see anything."

Allegra then pointed to a photograph of her mother.

"Oh, she's sick. She has pain in her legs. That is all I can tell."

Allegra winced. It was better not to ask any more questions. She had learned what she needed.

"Thank you, Baba Yorgo. You are very kind. May I come again?" Allegra asked.

"Yes, yes. I will see you all again, I know it. You are always welcome. Remember what I say. It will not be easy, but you will survive. Three months…you will be free."

Allegra and Henri bowed and left. Henri carried Andreas down the flight of stairs amid the sweet fragrance of fresh hay mixed with the bite of manure. Stepping from the gloom into the blinding light of the street, Henri shaded his eyes and suddenly realized they were in serious trouble.

The street was completely blocked on both ends by

German soldiers conducting a control, asking everyone for identity cards. Allegra, Henri and Andreas would be immediately arrested.

"Get back into the stable," whispered Henri, half pulling Allegra into the shadows. Allegra stifled her surprise. "How will we get out of here?" she whispered.

"I don't know." Henri was furious they had taken this terrible risk. Peering from the stable door, he saw Gestapo and soldiers filtering people through the checkpoint with their *ausweise*.* "This could be the end," he thought.

"Dear God, please help us!" prayed Allegra.

Boots on the cobblestone street came close, the footsteps stopping just outside the stable's wall. Near the edge of the open door, two German soldiers were talking, lighting up cigarettes. One of the horses in the stable shifted her weight and snickered. Andreas looked surprised and was about to say something, but Henry motioned him to be silent.

One of the soldiers stepped to the open door and looked in. *"Pferde!"** he said to his companion, but not accustomed to the stable's darkness he never noticed the three Jews in the shadows.

Ausweise: Identity papers (singular: *ausweis*).
Pferde: Horses.

"*Lass uns gehen*,"* said the other soldier, and they strolled away leaving Allegra and Henri trembling. An hour later the German troops and Gestapo departed; Allegra, Henri and Andreas slipped out of the stable and walked home with a mixture of horror and relief.

"That was a crazy thing to do," scolded Henri. "We were lucky today."

Lass uns gehen: Let's go.

Chapter 41
Ausweis

May 24, 1944; 441 Days in Hiding

Henri met Marcos a block from the police station.

"Good to see you, Marcos," Henri said gratefully.

"Glad to do it, my friend," Marcos replied. "Let's get your identity papers and ration cards."

They walked into the midtown station and Henri brought the application to the officer behind the desk.

The policeman looked at them. "So, what do you want?" he asked gruffly.

"I lost my family's identity cards," replied Henri. "This is my application for replacements."

The tall policeman looked at the application and then at Henri. "You are Aristides Toufexides?"

"Yes, I am."

The policeman studied Henri's face. "You claim you're from Athens, and recently moved to Thessaloniki?"

"Yes, that's right."

"Why don't you have your identity and ration cards?"

"My wife and I went to the movies last Sunday and I lost my wallet."

"Losing your *ausweis* is a big problem. Do you have other papers?"

"No," Henri replied. "I don't."

"What is your job?"

"I'm an electrician," Henri replied.

"Well, you must belong to the union, right?"

"Yes."

"All right. Bring me a union card with your photograph. When I see the card, we'll issue new papers for you and your wife."

"Thank you. I'll be back soon," said Henri.

"*Kýrios* Toufexides," the officer called after him, "next time come with your wife and child, and bring two witnesses, not one."

"Thank you. I will," Henri said with confidence he did not feel, and then he and Marcos were back on the busy street. "Kosmas is in the union," Henri said. "I'll get in touch with him right away. Can you come again?" Henri asked.

"Yes, of course," said Marcos. "Count on me." He shook Henri's hand and disappeared into the afternoon crowd.

✳ ✳ ✳

The photographer's shop was a small storefront, unexpectedly dark. The bell above the door announced their arrival and a thin man in a jacket and bowtie came from the back to greet them.

"Hello," he said. He sized them up. "What can I do for you?"

"We lost our identity cards and need a photograph."

"I can take your photographs now. Would that be convenient?"

"Yes," answered Allegra. "We were hoping you would."

"Excellent. Please follow me." In the back were several cameras and an assortment of flash bulbs. A camera on a tripod was ready for use.

"Would the lady like to be first?" asked the photographer.

"Yes, please," replied Henri.

"Please take a seat," indicating a chair.

Allegra sat down and faced the camera. She reached for the simple silver chain around her neck and adjusted the large cross so it clearly showed just below her neck.

"I'm ready," said Allegra.

Henri was with Avram in the back of Aleko's taverna when Kosmas entered and came to their table.

"Good to see you, Henri, Avram," he said. "Doing all right?"

"Yes, we're all right," smiled Henri, "and we'll be even better if you can help us."

"What do you need?" asked Kosmas with a questioning brow.

"I need identity and ration cards for me and Allegra. The police will issue them if you can help me get a union card."

"Absolutely! All I need are photographs."

Henri pulled the two photos out of his shirt pocket and gave them to his friend.

"That was easy!" laughed Kosmas. "Yes, perfect. I know

the president. There'll be no problem getting you a union card. What about you, Avram?"

"I can't get one," replied Avram. "My accent."

Kosmas nodded, remembering. "I can have your union card by tomorrow night. Let's meet here at the same time."

"Thank you, Kosmas."

"Happy to help. Have a good night. Give my regards to Allegra and Myriam," and Kosmas was gone.

"I'm so grateful for our friends," Henri said, "risking their lives..."

Avram nodded. "Each one a hero."

✳ ✳ ✳

"Aristides Toufexides?" asked the police officer.

"Yes," replied Henri.

"This is your wife, Anghela Toufexides, and your son, Andreas Toufexides?"

"Yes, that's right."

"Who is this person?" the policeman asked indicating Marcos.

"He came as a witness."

"And you?" the officer asked Yannis, the policeman who had discovered them hiding so long ago in the *Kastra*.

"I am also here to bear witness about this family."

"Very well," said the officer, turning to Henri. "Show me your union card."

"Here it is," said Henri.

"I also need a photograph of your wife."

"All right, this is good." The policeman looked at Andreas and then at Henri. "This must be your son?" Henri nodded. "I want to speak with him," he said.

Henri's pulse quickened. "Yes, of course," he said, trying not to show his anxiety. Henri looked at Andreas standing near his mother and forced a smile. "Andreas, the policeman wants to ask you a question."

Andreas looked at his father; something wasn't right. Andreas became subdued.

The policeman walked up to Andreas. Kneeling on one knee the policeman asked, "What is your name?"

Andreas looked at the policeman, then at his mother.

"Look at me," said the policeman. "What is your name?"

"Andreas."

"Andreas, what is your last name?"

Looking into the policeman's eyes, Andreas said, "Toufexides."

"What does your father do?"

"He is an electrician," replied Andreas. Henri breathed a silent sigh; the coaching was working!

"What is your mother's name?" asked the officer.

"Anghela."

"Very well, then," the officer said, standing up, walking to his desk. Allegra motioned to Andreas and he took her hand, feeling the reassuring squeeze.

Looking at both Marcos and Yannis, the officer asked, "You verify that this is *Kýrios* and *Kyría* Toufexides and their son Andreas?" Both assented.

The officer nodded and pounded a few documents with his rubber stamp. He motioned Henri forward. "*Kýrios* Toufexides, here are the *ausweise* for you and your wife. Do not lose them."

Chapter 42
D-Day

June 6, 1944; 454 Days in Hiding

"Did you hear? The Allies have invaded France!"

No one was supposed to know, but everyone did. One of their neighbors, Napoleon and his wife Kaity, had a radio. Forbidden, but they had one, and American, British, and Canadian forces had landed in France!

Henri got on the phone and called Nicos. "Nicos, is it true?"

"Yes, Henri, it's true! It's the most fantastic news ever!"

"Can I see you? I want to talk to you," said Henri.

"Sure. Let's meet on the edge of town, in *Evosmos*.* There is a little taverna on Kiprou Street, at the corner of Kimis. Meet me there in two hours."

Two hours later Henri and Nicos were sitting at a little table quietly discussing the wonderful news.

"Henri, the period of waiting is almost done. I'm convinced that within the next two or three months this

---

Evosmos: A suburb of Thessaloniki.

thing will be over and you and your family will be free."

Free! The word sounded almost magical to Henri. "What was it like to be free again?" Henri thought.

"Do you think it will be as soon as that?" asked Henri. "Two or three months?" He suddenly realized that Baba Yorgo was right.

"I do, because the Soviets are making enormous gains, and with the Allies pushing up from Italy and the new beachhead in France, Hitler is being squeezed on all sides. He's going to have to pull out of here."

"I hope you're right, Nicos. We've been in hiding for almost 450 days. You can't imagine what it's been like."

"I know. But the war will end soon. Just keep low and be patient. It won't be long now, I promise you."

Henri wanted to believe this good news. It was all he could think about. Maybe they would survive after all. Maybe Andriko would have a decent life, maybe he and Allegra would walk along the street and not be afraid. Maybe the hated Germans and their Nazis would be crushed in battle by the Americans and Russians. Maybe all the Jews that had been deported would now return home.

"Patience," Nicos counseled. "It's not over yet. Anything can still happen." This was good advice, considering what was going to happen next.

Chapter 43
A Baby on the Way

August 8, 1944; 517 Days in Hiding

"What do you mean, you're pregnant? How did that happen?"

"What do you mean, 'How did that happen?' How do you think it happened?"

"Allegra, dearest, we can't have a baby now!"

"Why not? We're safe here."

"We're in hiding...it's another mouth to feed...what if we're discovered? What happens to the baby then?"

"We're having this baby."

"No, we're not. I want you to get an abortion."

"I will not. Never."

"I'll make the arrangements today. I'll contact Dr. Platis. You have to go. Today."

* * *

Allegra felt the turmoil in her stomach as she waited in the doctor's office. "This is not right!" she thought, wishing she hadn't come. "Maybe I should just leave," she considered, her anger toward Henri increasing.

"I'm going to go," she decided and just then the doctor came out and greeted her. Dr. Platis knew Allegra before the occupation.

"*Kyría* Toufexides," he said, greeting her by her fictitious name.

"Hello, Dr. Platis," said Allegra.

"Please come in," he said, leading Allegra into his private office. "Let's have a little talk."

Allegra sat in the patient's chair.

"So you want an abortion," Dr. Platis said.

"No, I don't. Henri and I have been fighting about it. He wants the abortion. I do not."

"So why are you here?"

"Because maybe he's right. Having a baby now, when we are hiding from the Nazis...I don't know."

"This is your decision, Allegra."

"I know." Allegra gave a big sigh, her lips trembling. "I don't know what to do, Doctor."

"You don't have to decide today. Go home and think about it. If you wish, I can induce termination with an injection. I do this for my patients with TB."

Allegra nodded, unable to speak with a tight throat. Confused and uncertain what she should do, she left the office.

✳ ✳ ✳

A day went by, and another, and a third and a fourth, and Henri and Allegra were miserable.

"I'm keeping our baby."

"It doesn't make any sense to have a baby now. It's hard enough to feed the five of us with our two ration cards and borrowing from Nicos. How do we feed another mouth? We are already in a lot of trouble. We don't need more!"

"I don't care what you say, Henri. This is our baby. We'll find a way."

"Allegra, we're in a war! German soldiers are patrolling the streets...we're Jewish! There's a food shortage. What if you need a doctor, or the baby does? Can't you see this is the wrong time?"

"This is the right time. It doesn't matter what you say. God wants this baby."

"Allegra..." They argued, and argued for days...and Henri wore her down.

"Maybe he's right," Allegra thought. "What if things don't work out? Baba Yorgo said we'd survive, but he didn't say anything about another child. What if I put Andriko and Henri in danger? And Stefanos, Sultana, and their children? I can't let that happen," and Allegra became morose. Resisting the thought, neither could she endanger Andriko and her benefactors. She sobbed, alone with her heartache, knowing what she had to do.

* * *

"I don't know, Henri," Allegra said. "Nothing happened. It's been two days and I've not discharged. It's a sign we're meant to have this baby."

"Maybe you need a second injection."

"No! You talked me into it the first time, but I'm not doing it again."

"Allegra, that's crazy!"

"I don't care what you say. I'm going to keep our baby. I'm not going back to the doctor."

"Allegra, you're going to go."

"No, I am not! No matter what! Kill me! I'm not going!"

Allegra ran out of the room in tears, into the arms of Sultana.

"It's all right, Allegra," Sultana said softly. "Don't worry. Don't worry. You'll have your baby here, in this house. Don't you worry, Dear."

* * *

"Don't do that, Henri," said Nicos. "Don't make Allegra get an abortion."

"But how can we have a baby? We're in hiding! We have no money, we're always under the threat of discovery…"

"Henri, don't worry about it. Have the baby."

"Don't worry about it? How can I not worry? How are we going to have a child while we're in hiding? We have to see doctors; we might need special food or medicines! What if something goes wrong? What would happen to the baby if we're found out?"

"Don't you worry. I'll declare the child as mine. Don't worry about any of this. I have plenty of money for all of us. I assure you, when the child is born, you will be free. I know it! You will be free."

"You've been telling me this story for a long time," Henri replied.

Nicos looked at him firmly, and smiled. "No, times are different now. The Germans are losing. Everyone can see it. It won't be much longer. Keep your baby, Henri. I promise you I will take care of your baby."

Henri burst into tears, and his friend held him as he shook.

Chapter 44
The Candy Store

September 28, 1944; 568 Days in Hiding

"Babá, I want some candy," Andreas said, seeing the chocolates and colored varieties of sweets in the window.

It was mid-afternoon on a warm September day, and Henri and Andreas were on one of their usual walks through the less-trafficked neighborhoods of Thessaloniki. Venturing close to a commercial area, Andreas spotted the chocolates and alluring confections. Henri recognized the shop as a popular store once owned by Jews.

"Andriko *mou*," said Henri, noticing his son's keen interest, "have you been a good boy?"

"Yes, Babá," Andreas said hesitantly, considering whether such was actually the case.

"I think so, too," Henri said with a warm smile. "You deserve a treat."

"Thank you, Babá," Andreas said, his eyes on the impending treasure.

Henri opened the door, the doorbell announcing their entrance. As soon as they were inside, Henri knew it was a mistake…a horrible mistake.

Turning to greet his customers, Stavros Venepopoulos recognized Henri. "*Kýrios* Algava, what are you doing here?" he said in astonishment. "I thought all the Jews were deported," he blurted.

"Hello, *Kýrios* Venepopoulos," said Henri, trying to keep his voice calm. "No, not everyone. I was not deported, as you can see." Henri noticed the rich-looking overcoat Venepopoulos was wearing, out of place on the poor valet who had once brushed Henri's coat and swept hair from the floor of Samuel's barbershop.

"No? You were not deported? How did you escape?"

"I didn't escape," replied Henri. "I was given special permission to stay." Henri knew they had to get out as fast as possible. Turning to Andreas, Henri pointed to a chocolate confection and said, "Andreas, how about that one?" but Andreas was ambivalent.

"I never heard of any Jews being given special permission," Venepopoulos said, his tone changing from surprise to suspicion.

"Oh, yes," replied Henri. "We are living in *Sindos** now, helping the Germans with document organization."

Sindos: A suburb of Thessaloniki.

Henri looked at Andreas and saw it would take his son too long to choose. What had begun as a pleasant distraction had now become desperate.

"Please wrap that one for us," said Henri pointing to a sweet. "My God!" thought Henri, "he might call for the police!"

"But Babá..." Andreas began, and Henri silenced him with a look.

"Thank you, *Kýrios* Venepopoulos," said Henri, as chocolate and money exchanged hands. "Good day," he said, the doorbell chiming their exit.

The minute they were a few steps down the street, Henri grabbed Andreas in his arms and started running, running, running... When they were at least a kilometer away, Henri finally slowed down and then stopped, out of breath.

Crossing the street in front of them was a brown terrier. The dog went where it pleased, sniffing, stopping, wandering along without concern.

Henri suddenly burst into tears, sobbing uncontrollably as he held Andreas.

"Why are you crying, Babá?" the young boy asked, looking at his father's wet face.

"Because that dog is free and I am not..."

A few days later Henri opened a note from Marcos with Nicos's handwriting.

"In Samuel's. V there. Did not believe you. Swears will find you. Be careful."

Chapter 45
Night's End

October 22, 1944; 592 Days in Hiding

"Liberation is soon," Aleko whispered to the table of seated men. "Athens and Piraeus have been liberated and the Germans are pulling back along the entire mainland. The Peloponnese is almost free, and more islands are coming under British control. It won't be much longer now."

Avram allowed himself a restrained smile, and lit another cigarette. He drew a deep breath, feeling the smoky satisfaction. This had been a long time coming. "But we are still in danger," Avram said. "We should stay indoors and away from trouble."

"I'm glad we're in the *Kamara*," said Henri. "I heard the *ΕΛΑΣ** are openly patrolling the *Kastra* with rifles and pistols."

"I'd rather be up there. I think they're safer," replied Avram.

ΕΛΑΣ: Ellinikós Laïkós Apeleftherotikós Stratós (ELAS), The Greek People's Liberation Army. *ELAS* was the major Greek military resistance organization of the left-wing *Ethniko Apeleftherotiko Metopo (EAM)*, The National Liberation Front.

"Probably," added Marcos. "The Communists will protect us. The Nazi pigs are still in charge down here."

"How much longer do you think it will take?" asked Avram.

"There's no way of telling, but it must be soon," said Marcos. "The Russians are coming in quickly from the East. If the Germans don't hurry, they could be cut off."

"I'd like that," said Avram.

"We all would," said Aleko. "I'm looking forward to the last time I have to serve those bastards. They're rude and arrogant. I'm buying all of you a round once the last chamber pot is gone."

"I'm buying the second round!" said Avram.

"I'll get the third..." exclaimed Henri softly.

A few days later Henri saw a crowd of people in the street near a warehouse used by the German army. A man walking toward him was carrying a few German army coats and sweaters.

"Excuse me," Henri said. "What's going on?"

"The Germans are selling supplies. If you have cash or something worth trading, you might get some good things." Henri walked up to the crowd. Men were gesturing and speaking with a soldier who was passing goods through the open window.

As Henri watched, the soldier was taking *lira* and wristwatches for socks, gloves, flour and sugar, coats, and a variety of supplies. The action was fast and Henri moved up. The soldier was putting out the next armful of goods.

"*Alexíptoto!*"* he said in Greek.

"Here," called out Henri. "How much?"

"What have you got?" asked the soldier.

Henri offered him a handful of coins. "*Kalós,*"* the soldier said.

The soldier took the money and gave Henri the parachute pack. "Allegra will love this," Henry thought. "She can turn it into a dress or something spectacular." In a few minutes he had purchased a wrench kit, a number of screwdrivers, and three heavy sweaters. The turtlenecks would come in handy for winter. He couldn't

---

Alexíptoto: Parachute.

Kalós: Good.

wait to see Allegra's face when he showed her all the silk.

"This will make up a little, maybe, for arguing about our baby," he thought.

Chapter 46
October 30, 1944

600 Days in Hiding

EAM* partisans infiltrated the city's streets as the Germans withdrew on foot, mules transporting their supplies. Three and a half years ago the Nazi invaders had proudly entered Thessaloniki on motorcycles, troop trucks, and invincible panzers; now they were depleted and would have to fight their way back to Germany through the murderous Yugoslav partisans, and possibly engage the advancing Red Army that was crushing them along the entire front.

It was a very long and anxious day. Henri, Allegra, and Andreas were warned to stay indoors, away from windows. The streets were empty. Occasionally they heard shouting, and once Henri saw partisans running down the street. Rifle fire was just a block away. The children played quietly on the floor in front of their parents, everyone waiting for news.

Allegra was thinking about the baby growing within her and how their new child could be the first Jew born in a free Thessaloniki. Henri was wondering how he'd make

---

EAM: Ethniko Apeleftherotiko Metopo (EAM), The National Liberation Front. EAM was the main movement of the Greek Resistance during the Nazi occupation.

a living with a new business. Andreas was unhappy having to stay indoors all day, but he understood something important was happening and did his best to play quietly.

Snipers harassed the retreating Germans who were blowing up the docks and setting the remaining supplies on fire.

"They came on tanks and are leaving on donkeys," mused Henri.

By nightfall the Nazis were gone.

Gone!

All gone!

The feeling of freedom quickly grew into ecstasy. The whole city came out from behind their shuttered doors and windows, and the taverns filled with celebration. Church bells in every part of the city were ringing and people were in the streets singing and dancing and drinking, and laughing and crying. Emotions flowed as freely as the *retsina* and ouzo. Everyone was happy beyond the greatest happiness they could ever remember, and the shouting and the faces of joy and relief were everywhere.

Free!

The very essence of being Greek is Freedom, and here was Freedom once more. Free of evil, free of murder, free of oppression, free of thievery and injustice, and free of the jackbooted soldiers that mocked the proud Greek men, ridiculed their women, and dismissed them as inferior.

Now it was the Germans and their Nazis that were ridiculed and disdained...the Greeks were triumphant! They had played the sullen game with their oppressors, had endured them, fought them with the Resistance, cheated them at every chance, scorned them in the dark nights behind silent walls that masked the hatred and fury of the righteous Greeks.

Now there was a great celebration and the shadows that held these feelings were released with exultation. In the morning an accounting would be made for those who had been foolish enough to sell their ancestry for German coin and comfort, and the retribution would be quick, and deadly and complete. But that was for the morning.

Tonight was a night for festivity and joy and the remembrance of a freedom that had been denied for more than three agonizing years. This misery was washed with laughter and tears of joy and with the surprise of...for just a moment...unrestrained indulgent pleasure at being alive and Free!

∗ ∗ ∗

"The city is free!" exclaimed Henri, "We're free!"

"Thank God!" Allegra said. She could say no more. The feeling was new, and even though expected, the sudden presence of freedom was electrifying and numbing at the same time.

Henri gathered Allegra into his arms and hugged her. "I feel like dancing!" he said.

"Yes! Let's do that! Get Andriko. Sultana, let's all go together!" Sultana and Stefanos dressed their children in coats, and they headed for Aleko's taverna as the church bells rang.

Avram and Myriam were already there, in the middle of the crowded taverna, its walls bursting with jubilation. "Henri!" shouted Avram, seeing his son across the room, and he worked his way through the singing and dancing people. "Henri! We made it!" He hugged Henri, and then Allegra and Andriko, and then Myriam was there... "Let's dance!" And everyone, Sultana, Stefanos, their children, and all their friends, everyone, danced and sang, exuberant with joy and relief. Marcos arrived with his wife and children and everyone who knew the story saluted him and raised their glasses, grateful such a hero was among them.

Aleko honored his pledge and bought drinks for them all, and then Avram fulfilled his vow as well. And when

346

everyone had toasted and downed the second round, Henri bought the third, and the tavern reverberated with cheers.

"We have to get back," Henri shouted to his father and mother. "Allegra needs her rest with the baby coming, and Andriko needs to get to bed."

"Yes, Henri. Go. I'll see you tomorrow, but not until late, very late!"

"All right, Babá! Have fun. Good night, Mamá!" and he kissed his mother good night as they left.

Returning to the dead end street where the Chrissafis family lived, many of the neighbors were still visiting. Kaity and Napoleon, Barbara, the sour neighbor, and others came into Sultana's kitchen to share their excitement.

"We knew all along you were Jews," Kaity said to Allegra and Henri.

Henri looked surprised, but Allegra nodded. "I thought so," she said.

"You always dressed Andriko so well, and the way you talked, we knew you didn't belong to this neighborhood."

"Bless you for not saying anything," said Henri.

"We knew for sure when we saw you in the market that day, and every day we prayed for your deliverance. We never told you because we didn't want you to be afraid." Allegra gave Kaity a long warm hug, and Henri shook hands and hugged Napoleon.

"You're not Greek Orthodox?" Barbara asked, unable to believe what she just heard.

"We are Jews, Barbara," said Allegra, remembering her many insulting remarks. "We've been in hiding since the deportations almost two years ago. We owe our lives to the courage and compassion of Sultana and Stefanos, and many other Greeks who risked their lives for ours."

Barbara looked astonished, and then embarrassed, unable to hold Allegra's gaze. She soon slipped away.

The other neighbors congratulated Henri and Allegra, some with surprise, some with a warm smile, glad their new friends, living among them for the past 12 months, had been protected.

It was late after all, and time to withdraw for the night. Everyone left, anticipating the arrival of the British, a secure civil order, and desperately needed supplies of food, medicine, and crates of all the normal things that had been absent for so long.

That night, as Henri got into bed, achingly tired, thankful that Andreas was safe, and feeling his wife's growing belly under his warm hand, Henri drifted to sleep with two thoughts. "Thank you, God, for saving us and protecting us," he thought. And then, as sleep subdued him, Henri's final thought was imagining the pleasure of enjoying a cup of real Greek coffee.

Chapter 47
The Greek Typewriter

October 31, 1944; Day 1

Henri walked rapidly along Tsimiski Street until he arrived at Aristoteles Square; at the waterfront he turned right and walked to the entrance of the Mediterranean Hotel. It was the biggest and most luxurious hotel in Thessaloniki; now occupied by British soldiers, just yesterday it had been the residence of the Nazis.

Henri walked up to a table in the foyer. First Lieutenant Karakoulas was seated there.

"Hello," said Henri in English. "I am Henri Algava. I am a Greek citizen and I've lived in Thessaloniki all my life. As you can see, I am fluent in English and I think I may be able to help in some significant way. I would like to see your commanding officer."

The lieutenant looked at Henri and smiled. "Yes, we may be able to use your services. My name is Lieutenant Karakoulas. I am a Cypriot Greek and the aide-de-camp to Major Smethurst. I'll see if the major can see you now."

A moment later the lieutenant led Henri into a suite where Major Smethurst was seated behind a desk. Henri explained his circumstances. "I have lived in

Thessaloniki since birth. I'm also Jewish and have been in hiding from the Nazis for almost two years. I have a family, and we are completely destitute. My wife is pregnant with our second child. I am willing to help the British Army in any way I can. Perhaps I could act as a provisioner of foods or other commodities to the British Army here in Thessaloniki."

"I understand your situation, Mr. Algava," said the major, "and I wish I could be helpful. We do not need a supplier because we don't need any supplies from Thessaloniki."

"Well, certainly you must have a use for a man with my abilities. I'm fluent in English, and might be a good liaison for you with the population."

"We are an advance force for the distribution of foods and essential commodities. We're not really a military unit. In a sense, we are a military unit performing civilian duties...a military government, if you will."

"All right, I understand." Henri couldn't hide how disappointed he was.

"I'm really very sorry, Mr. Algava. Of course, what I recommend is that you and your family take advantage of the food supplies we are bringing in, and as the economy is reestablished, I believe you will find opportunities for employment."

Henri thanked the major and excused himself. Walking

through the foyer, the Cypriot lieutenant called out to him. "*Kýrios* Algava, wait a moment!"

Henri felt a surge of hope.

"*Kýrios* Algava, would you take a job as an interpreter?"

"Certainly."

"But this job requires a Greek typewriter, which we don't have. If you provide a Greek typewriter, you have the job."

"Lieutenant, I accept!"

"All right, then, you start tomorrow."

"That's great news! I'll bring the typewriter tomorrow." Henri felt his heart lift...but where would he find a Greek typewriter? A few minutes later he was knocking on the door of his friend, Nicos Efcarpides, and was suddenly embraced by Nicos and Sousanna.

"I told you, Henri!" Nicos said, jubilation in his voice. "I told you you'd make it through! Come over here. Sousanna and I are enjoying some champagne to celebrate our liberation. I've kept this bottle for a day like today!"

Before Henri could say a word, a glass of champagne was in his hand and they were toasting each other as the bubbles went to his head. "How delightful," he thought, "to be with these dear friends after such a dark journey."

"Nicos, I was just at the Mediterranean Hotel and I met with the new commanding officer, Major Smethurst. I need to get back on my feet and they offered me a job as an interpreter. The job is mine...if I can find a Greek typewriter. Do you know where I can get one?"

"Henri, my friend, take my typewriter."

"What about you?"

"Don't you worry. Take the typewriter and get the job!"

"How did it go today?" asked Allegra.

"Good, a good day," replied Henri. "Major Smethurst said two more supply ships are coming this week. We'll be able to handle more ships once the docks are repaired. The Germans did a thorough job destroying them."

"God, what they did. Now we all have to suffer another shortage. They were so cruel."

"It's been going on for centuries."

"Well, it's time it stopped," Allegra said angrily. "How many more centuries must we endure?"

"Do you remember what Baba Yorgo asked you?"

"No. What?"

"What is it you want to do? Do you think you can save the world?"

"Yes, I remember. Maybe I can't save the world, Henri, but I want to. Don't you? Isn't that what we should all be doing? The only way is with kindness and compassion for each other."

"The only way."

"We have to rise above our own suffering."

"Be brave and take a stand for what we know is right."

"We'll take that trip to New York, Henri, the trip we never took. We'll go to America, and live there."

"Leave Thessaloniki?"

"Yes. America is a big country, a great country, a place where we can make a new life, where we can build a better world. If we want, we can always come back, but I don't think we ever will."

I Archi*

I Archi: The Beginning.

The Carasso Family in 1932:
Only two survived.

Left to right, standing: Allegra, 17;
Pepo, 15; the only two survivors.

Middle row: Rosa, 7; Doudoun;
Solomon, 11; Mordechai; Mathilde, 13.

Front row: Marika, 5; Alberto, 9.

Epilogue

Of the 56,000 Jews living in Thessaloniki, only three families are known to have survived in hiding in the city: the Algava family, the Assael family, and the Pardo family, each with five family members, a total of 15 people. A few individuals survived as well, married to Orthodox Greeks or hidden by friends. After the war, about 1,900 Jews had returned to the city, fewer than 1,000 survived the concentration camps. Thessaloniki's Jewish population today is estimated at 900.

Allegra and Henri Algava: Baba Yorgo was right; Henri and Allegra lived in a big country when they moved to the United States in 1946. They spent most of their many remaining years in New York City. Allegra was a loving mother to her two children, took care of the household, was a companion to Myriam, and volunteered in the community. Henri started several new businesses in the U.S. and Argentina, and when Henri began an association with Niehaus & Dütting, a German textile company, Allegra managed that business relationship.

Henri always wanted Andreas to write the story of their survival; he often intended to do this himself, but was too busy with business. Andreas began the process over 35 years ago by interviewing Allegra and Henri, transcribing the conversations that recorded the facts of the family's story, and now finally publishing this book nearly 74 years after Greece was liberated. Allegra and Henri moved to Israel in January 2005; Allegra was 95 years old when she passed away soon after, in October

2005, while Henri passed away in July 2008 at the age of 97 after relishing a long life with the love of his life, a witness to his children's and grandchildren's peaceful and productive lives.

Andreas Algava: Andreas fulfilled his father's desire by writing this book. Moving to the U.S. with his mother, father, and baby sister, he grew up in New York City. Andreas joined the U.S. Army after college and was stationed in France and Fort Knox, Kentucky. Andreas enjoyed a distinguished engineering career and, now retired, lives in Providence, Rhode Island near his two daughters, Alisa and Carin, Carin's husband Michael, and his two grandchildren, Drew and Sabria.

Allegra's Family: Almost all of Allegra's immediate family perished in Auschwitz; her mother, Doudoun; father, Mordechai; her sisters Mathilde, Rosa, and Marika. Her brothers, Salomon and Alberto, both died of typhus in the Warsaw concentration camp where they were sent with other Greeks, Pepo included, as a workforce to clear the remains of the Warsaw Ghetto after its destruction by the Nazis. Only Allegra's brother, Pepo, survived Auschwitz. Seven of the eight family members sent to Auschwitz perished.

In Auschwitz, Pepo was a kapo, an SS-appointed leader, probably because he spoke fluent German. Pepo helped all the Jewish prisoners he could, stealing food for them and nursing them when they were ill. There is a story that one day he stole some baked potatoes to give to others, and the potatoes were so hot, he burned his legs smuggling them into the barracks in his pockets. Pepo's first wife died in the camp...but miraculously he met a Hungarian woman there named Eva. When the camp was liberated, Pepo and Eva married, later returning to Thessaloniki where they lived happily with their sons Mordechai (Maky) and Maurice, and their daughter Daisy. At the time of this printing, Eva is 95 and still lives in Thessaloniki. Maurice, one of her sons, helped with the facts of this book.

Baba Yorgo predicted that Pepo would survive the war and return, which he did. Pepo gave evidence in court denouncing the Hasson brothers who had perpetrated horrendous crimes against the Jews in the ghettos and concentration camp, and Pepo's evidence led to the execution of Vital Hasson. Years later Pepo was invited to attend a gathering in his honor in New York City, hosted by the many Jews and their descendants who owed their lives to him. The official trial testimony of Pepo's experience follows in Appendix A. A story from Eva's experience in Auschwitz appears in Appendix B.

Alberto Capon, Allegra's and Pepo's cousin, was the first to return from Auschwitz, and he told the remaining family that Larry Nachmias, Henri's cousin, had survived.

Henri's Family: Only one member of Henri's family survived Auschwitz, and that was Larry Nachmias, as predicted by Baba Yorgo. Larry was assigned to the stables to milk the cows, and stayed alive by drinking some of the milk he collected.

Avram: Avram left Thessaloniki in 1947, escorting his two grandchildren to the waiting arms of Allegra and Henri. Avram lived with his children, grandchildren, and Myriam until he passed away in 1957.

Myriam: After the war, Myriam lived in Thessaloniki at the Tsimiski apartment, waiting to join her husband, Avram, in the United States. Upon moving to New York in 1948, she lived with Henri and Allegra until her death in 1967, enjoying her life as a grandmother.

Daisyka: Daisyka was never seen again.

Aaron: Aaron was Henri's cousin, and after his return to Thessaloniki with Henri, his story remains unknown.

Jacko: Jacko was one of the children who escaped the ghetto with his parents, Joseph and Vida, when the family went into hiding at Kiros's house in the Kastra. After returning to the ghetto with his parents and family, Jacko and his friend Sami did not board the deportation trains as his family did, escaping instead into the mountains where they fought as *EAM* guerrillas. Jacko became the aide and main courier of Aris Velouchiotis, the most important leader of the Greek People's Liberation Army (ELAS), the major Greek resistance organization. Jacko survived the war and returned to work and manage the Carasso dye factory. None of Jacko's family survived the camps.

Marcos Hombitis: Marcos was about 50 years old at the start of this story. He later had problems with his eyes; over the years he became completely paralyzed, eventually passing away. His son became an officer in the Greek Air Force, and a pilot for Olympic Airways.

Henri wrote, "Our dear friend Marcos has been dead for many years now, but we will never forget his kindness, his courage and all the good things he did for us during our period of forced captivity. Marcos was the one who took the big chances, testifying to our identity, carrying messages, walking for an hour twice and even three times a week up the hill to the Kastra in all kinds of weather to check on us and bring news and supplies. Marcos never said no."

Nicos Efcarpides: After the war Henri paid back all the money he had borrowed from Nicos. They stayed good friends from afar. Years later, Nicos died of a heart attack while swimming.

Stefanos and Sultana Chrissafis, and Costas and Evghenia Papapavlou: The families stayed in touch after Henri and Allegra moved to the United States. Henri and Allegra often sent packages and money to help out.

Marika Karakitsou: Marika was immediately arrested by the *EAM* after the Germans evacuated Thessaloniki, accusing her of being a Nazi collaborator because of her friendship with the Gestapo *Kriminalkommissar* Jupp. When Henri and Allegra heard Marika had been arrested, they went to the police station where Marika was held and told the authorities how she had helped them survive. Marika was released.

Linos Pachis: Pachis was arrested by the Germans for criminal behavior a few months after the family had been chased out of his house. Had the Algavas stayed, they would have been discovered and deported to Auschwitz...or immediately executed.

93 Tsimiski Street: After the occupation, Henri and Allegra had to go to court to reclaim the property they had been forced to surrender. The family that occupied their apartment did not want to return it, but the court ruled in the Algavas' favor.

The Carasso dye factory: The few surviving members of Allegra's family had to prove their pre-war ownership. When Allegra and Avram first went to the factory to assess its condition, a Romanian claimed the factory as his; they caught this man in the act of loading the heavy machinery belts onto a cart, and just managed to stop him from selling the equipment for quick cash.

Two other families survived in hiding: Aside from the five members of the Algava family, the Pardo family and the Assael family also escaped deportation to the death camps.

Numbering five people, Haim Pardo, his wife Eugenie Beraha-Pardo, and their three daughters, Lily age 13, Rose age 10, and Denise age 4, all survived the war hidden in the home of the Dr. Karakotsos's family on Tsimiski Street in the heart of the city.

The Assael family also had five members: Marc and Ida Assael, their son Fred, and two daughters, Lulu and Janine. Their saviors were Manolis Koniordos, a family friend who was in love with Lulu, and Maria Voudouroglou and her son Anton. Maria opened her house to the Assael family without knowing them and without the payment of money; Maria did this because she knew Manolis, and her hate for the Germans was intense. Unlike the Algavas, the Assaels never had to leave their hiding place.

Single Jews and Jewish families also managed to survive in the mountains and villages or fighting with the partisans. Only these three Jewish families are known to have been hidden from the Nazis, each surviving in Thessaloniki together as a family.

Baba Yorgo: After the occupation, Henri and Allegra returned for another session. Allegra asked Baba Yorgo why he had told them they only had to wait a little longer...when they had so much longer than he'd said. "If I had told you it was going to be longer, you would have become despairing, and you would say you would never make it."

No more information is known about any of the other people in this story; their paths have led them from view...

Andreas Algava
Providence, Rhode Island
January 2018

Appendices

Appendix A

The Trial Testimony of Pepo Carasso

Introduction: After the war, Pepo Carasso, Allegra Carasso's younger brother and Andreas's uncle, was asked to testify against one of the Hasson brothers for his alleged war crimes during the occupation. The following testimony is from this document:* *"The Hasson Trial" (July 2, 1946), Accession #2003.4, 12–14, United States Holocaust Memorial Museum Archive (Washington, D.C.).*

Karasso* Testimony Note:

THE TRIAL OF A NAZI COLLABORATOR [1946]

Created and imbued with authority by the United States, the Soviet Union, and the United Kingdom, the International Military Tribunal (IMT) tried twenty-two major war criminals between October 1945 and October 1946. An additional twelve high-ranking German officials were tried by American prosecutors working under the aegis of the IMT

Provided by Maurice Carasso, son of Eva and Pepo Carasso.

Karasso: This is the British spelling of Carasso.

from December 1946 to April 1949. An overwhelming proportion of the trials that resulted were of low-level officials. Only one Jewish collaborator was formally tried for his crimes at the behest of a Jewish community: Vital Hasson. A native of Thessaloniki and a tailor by trade, Hasson had served the Nazi authorities as they targeted Thessalonikian Jews for persecution and deportation and was known for his sadistic behavior, which included the rape of Jewish girls and women. One Jewish witness at Hasson's trial, which came before Greek courts in Athens, claimed that: "Hasson was more powerful than the Germans, [and] that the Germans stood at attention before him." Hasson, whose trial record notes that he smiled repeatedly throughout the proceedings, was found guilty of the charges against him. He was executed in Corfu in March 1948.

Karasso (witness for the prosecution): I am a victim. I was hiding in the house of a Greek friend, Anastassios Maretis, together with my entire family. This friend informed us about the deportations of the Jews and about the situation in general. Maretis was arrested on the first Sunday in June and was accused of hiding us. At this point, we were warned to disappear. We then thought of going to some village. Unfortunately, we did not have time to escape. Hasson came by car to the house where we were hiding, accompanied by two Germans in civilian clothes. They broke down the doors and arrested all of us—that is, myself, my father, my mother, my sister, and all the others. Hasson started to beat us, as well as the owner, Maretis. Maretis had been betrayed by a member of the "Security Battalion" (Greek collaborators) under Poulos and after being severely beaten, admitted that he was hiding us in his home. When they took us away, shoving, and kicking us, they put us in two cars and took us to the Baron Hirsch camp. Hasson was driving the car. During the ride, we complained to him about what he was doing and he replied that there was one way we could save ourselves: tell him where our gold was hidden. When we arrived at the Baron Hirsch camp, we were interrogated. They started to severely beat us, using a whip. The Germans did not beat us as much as Hasson did. They beat all of us. They took the gold that we had hidden in the heel[s] of our shoes. But they were not satisfied and continued to hit us to make us tell them where we had some gold bracelets. They even searched the women's genitals for gold. They did this to all of the women, to the little girls and my elderly mother, too. After this horrible scene, the women were taken to a barrack and the men thrown into a basement cell, where they were told that they would be shot. We had no contact with anyone in this cell for a whole day. As I learned from my wife while still in jail, Hasson proposed to her a scheme to free us. She and her sister should surrender to the Germans and to Hasson.

At this time, the judge turns to Hasson's wife, who is among the defendants, and says ironically, "Behold this guy!"

Witness: I warned my wife to keep away from Hasson and not to pay any attention to what he was saying. They should die rather than submit. Hasson made these proposals daily. Such orgies took place every day, for which Hasson and his organs were responsible. They would enter the camp and get any girl they liked and do with her anything they wanted. After being detained in the cell for three weeks, they took us out and we remained in the camp.

Judge: What else did Hasson do?

Witness: He went regularly to other towns together with others and would bring back Jews who had been hiding in various villages. There were some 165 of us in the camp and we were waiting for those who had been sent to labor camps in Thives and elsewhere in Thessaly, so that there would be a sufficient number to send a convoy to Poland. These workers returned to Thessaloniki nearly naked, hungry and in terrible condition. Their families that had already been deported to Poland had left some packages for them in the hands of acquaintances. When Hasson found out about these packages, he threatened the people who were holding them. He took the packages from them and sold them. On 7 and 8 August, once the required number of men had been reached, they put us into sealed cars and sent us to Birkenau. We were locked into the cars and bound with chains.

Judge: Did you see whether the Germans marked the place from where the people were sent for execution?

Witness: I had heard about that. It was done in our case. My wife had been afraid and anxious and very sad for about two months. She was inconsolable. I could not understand what was the matter with her. Finally, one day, as I insisted, she told me that Hasson had handed her over to the Germans, together with her sisters.

The witness then states that the Germans separated the men from the women when they arrived in Poland. Those who were not fit to work were put in cars or walked to their ultimate destiny.

Witness: We had the impression that nothing bad would happen to those who were being transported by car. Unfortunately, they were leading us, and those in the cars, to a swift death. We men who had been led away on foot for Birkenau were left naked one whole night and we were freezing. The next day, we found some Greeks and asked them about our parents who had been transported by car. They told us not to ask about them. Just look after yourselves, they said. Don't think about them. Try to save yourselves. Then they took us to the showers and gave us some rags to wear. We were terrorized in Birkenau. Many criminals from various countries and of different religions would savagely beat the inmates so as to exterminate the Jews, whom they did not allow to come into contact with older inmates. Some Jews who were electricians told us that the chimneys that we saw were the crematoria, where people enter and disappear. From that moment on, we lost all hope of salvation, because the crematoria were for us.

Judge: What kind of work did you do there?

Witness: We stayed in that camp for fifteen days, and then they sent some 500 Greek Jews to Warsaw to clean up the ghetto. In the interval between the first of September and January, my two brothers died of hunger and suffering. Meanwhile, of course, the other members of my family who had been transported by car had been thrown into the crematoria. Out of the nine members of my family, I was the only one to survive. As the resistance activities of the Poles had increased, the Germans transported us to Dachau, where we stayed for a few days in a labor camp. We had to carry enormous tree trunks, and when we complained, we were savagely beaten. Between four and five inmates died every evening from the torture and hard work.

Prosecutor: *Who appointed Hasson to the militia? The Germans?*

Witness: The Germans never made anyone enter the militia. Most of the militia members were volunteers, because it was said that they would get special treatment from the Germans as the privileged ones and be deported last. Most of the members who were deported to the camps not only came back safe and sound, but also brought back the children born in the camps. If Greeks had been members of the militia, surely the Jews' convoys would have been delayed and many Jews would have been saved, because in six months, many would have been able to join the Greek resistance in the mountains.

To a question from the judge, the witness states that Hasson did not have a job, but lived from his black market profits.

Judge: What do you know about Albala?

Witness: Just like Hasson, he was inhumane and had no feelings. He offered his services to the Germans like Hasson did...

The defense tries hard to question the witness in order to extract some statement favorable to its clients.

The witness gives the proper response to the defense's questions and stresses that all the defendants harmed their fellow Jews, and that Hasson bears the greatest responsibility.

When questioned by the defense about Hasson's father and sister, who was married to Sarfati, the witness states that he does not know anything specific, but wonders how Hasson's father and sister managed to survive and returned from the camps, when so many Jews, and especially the elderly, were sent to the crematoria.

Appendix B

A Moment of My Life in Auschwitz
by Eva Carasso

My name is Andreas Algava. The following, in her words, is an excerpt from an interview I conducted with my Aunt Eva Carasso on July 29, 1990. In this interview she talks about some of her experiences when she was a prisoner at the Auschwitz concentration camp during WWII. Eva met Pepo, Allegra's brother, in Auschwitz.

I wrote to him a letter. I don't remember what exactly I wrote in this letter but it was *verboten** to write a letter to speak with a man, you know.

Only he speak does he love me? Does he need me? Does I am his air? I am his oxygen. Love letters he send me. Yes.

My sister, she say, "What you do, Eva, you have a man here? You love this man; you write a letter like this; what is that? What you do?"

Did your sister get angry because she thought you were taking too much of a risk, too much of a chance by writing the letters?

———————

Verboten: Forbidden.

I think she was jealous. Because before Pepo, I care of her only. When after I know Pepo, I become to think very much of Pepo. And also, we find a place to speak together.

He whistled. And then each night when he whistled, I recognized his whistle. And I went to the fence and we spoke together.

And the two of you alone. Was it open? Could people see? The Germans, could they see you?

The Germans was out at that time. We careful very much. The people, everybody know that, and they know we love each other. And at that time I was without shoes and he gave me shoes.

So, always he come near to me. And we spoke together, always we spoke together.

How much time was this?

One year...

One year that you were meeting each other?

Yes...

What happened with the letter?

They catch him with the love letter and the Germans give Pepo ten beatings with a club.

They beat him very bad, he could not even walk. And me, they made me make the hole that they will kill me. Yes, for me. And everybody see me that I make the hole. (Ed. note: Her grave.)

My sister because she spoke very well in German, she worked in the house of the *Lagerführer*,* which is the biggest boss of all. He chose her to clean the house. She work at the house when that happened with Pepo and me and they want me to make my hole that they will shoot me. And I cry and everybody, all the people around me, they was crying very much. And I want to send a message to my sister that know what happened with us. And my sister, maybe can do something. You know?

Yes, she get the message and she crying and she don't know what to do, what to do. And the *Lagerführer* come inside in the room and see my sister was red, crying. And he say, "*Was ist los? Was hast du?** What's happening? Why you crying?" And my sister said, "How can I not crying? You put my sister to make her grave... to shoot her. But please..." and she did like this,* and the *Lagerführer*, she pulled on his knee, you see and hold on like this. "Please, if you will shoot my sister, please shoot me first, shoot me first. And after, her."

Lagerführer: The camp leader of Auschwitz.

Was ist los? Was hast du?: What's going on? What have you?

Did like this: Eva indicated her sister got on her knees to beg for Eva's life.

And this dog, I don't know how he change mind and he leave me...alive.

After God, that I live I can thank my sister.

THAT'S IT! I am alive!

Editor's note:

Eva is Eva Leichtman, and she became Eva Carasso after her marriage to Pepo Carasso, Allegra's brother. Pepo and Eva married three times during their travels from Auschwitz to Western Europe and then to Thessaloniki where they settled and raised a family. Maky (Mordechai) was the first Jewish child born in Thessaloniki of Auschwitz survivors. Their other two children are Maurice and Daisy. Maurice Carasso, the author's cousin, was an advisor for this book.

Appendix C

Yom HaShoah
Holocaust and Heroism
Remembrance Day

The following is a common service given in synagogues in remembrance of the approximately 6,000,000 Jews who died in the Holocaust because of the actions of Nazi Germany and its supporters, and in commemoration of the heroes of the Jewish resistance who fought against this evil. Yom HaShoah was started in 1953, and signed into law by the first Prime Minister of Israel, David Ben-Gurion. Holocaust and Heroism Remembrance Day is held on the 27th of Nisan (April/May), unless the 27th is next to the Jewish Sabbath, and if so, the date is shifted by a day.

**As we remember and pray,
Hope and believe,
Wait, and listen, and sing, and renew
May the God of justice and peace be present
with us.**

We light these six candles to honor the memory of the eleven million human beings, six million of them Jews, who died during the Holocaust. It's hard to wrap our heads around such a big number, but we are filled with sadness as we think about all that was lost, and all the pain that was felt. As we kindle the flames of memory, let us commit ourselves to responsibility for one another: to building a society that has no place for bigotry, no place for hatred, no tolerance for violence. Together, let us pray for the strength to fulfill this dream.

We light the first candle to remember those who died. Although we don't even know all of their names, and could not say them all aloud, we honor that each soul who died was an individual with a face, a name, a family, a life.

We remember, and we will never forget.

We light the second candle to remember those who fled to safety but were denied visas, or turned away at borders, and had to return to certain death.

We remember, and we will never forget.

We light the third candle to remember those who resisted. We remember the many who stood up to evil, who faced hardship, who fought for freedom and the right to live.

We remember, and we will never forget.

We light the fourth candle to remember all of the kind, generous, and brave people who helped rescue and protect others, especially people who are not Jewish who helped save Jews—we call them Righteous Among the Nations. We remember those people who did not ignore the suffering around them, who risk their own lives and safety to protect the innocent.

We remember, and we will never forget.

We light the fifth candle to remember the babies, children, the teenagers who died, who were killed before they were given a chance to shine.

We remember, and we will never forget.

We light the sixth candle as a message to ourselves—it is we who bear the responsibility to remember and to ensure that the world will remember, so that it will never happen again.

We remember, and we will never forget.

Prayer for Peace

May we see the day when war and bloodshed cease,
When a great peace will embrace the whole world.

Then nation will not threaten nation,
And humanity will not again know war.

For all who live on earth shall realize
We have not come into being to hate or to destroy.

We have come into being
To praise, to labor, and to love.

Compassionate God, bless the leaders of all nations
With the power of compassion.

Fulfill the promise conveyed in Torah:

I will bring peace to the land,
And you shall lie down, and no one shall terrify you.

I will rid the land of vicious beasts
And it shall not be ravaged by war.

Let love and justice flow like a mighty stream.

Let peace fill the earth as the waters filled the sea.

And let us say: *Amen.*

About For Passion Publishing Company

FOR-PASSION
PUBLISHING

For Passion Publishing Company serves authors with an important message to share so everyone can enjoy the feeling of accomplishment and fulfillment. Many people want to write a book...have a great story to tell...a great truth to reveal...yet so few do. For Passion Publishing will make your dream come true so others can make their dreams come true, too.

For more information:
www.ForPassionPublishing.com

Made in the USA
Middletown, DE
11 January 2022